BEST BIKE RIDES® SERIES

Best Bike Rides
Long Island

The Greatest Recreational Rides
in the Area

DAVID STREEVER

GUILFORD, CONNECTICUT

FALCONGUIDES®

An imprint of Globe Pequot
Falcon and FalconGuides are registered trademarks and Make Adventure Your Story is a
trademark of Rowman & Littlefield.

Distributed by NATIONAL BOOK NETWORK

Photos: David Streever
Maps: Melissa Baker and Alena Pearce © Rowman & Littlefield

British Library Cataloguing in Publication Information Available
Library of Congress Cataloging-in-Publication Data

Names: Streever, David, author.
Title: Best bike rides Long island : the greatest recreational rides in the
    area / David Streever.
Description: Guilford, Connecticut : FalconGuides, [2017] | Includes
    bibliographical references.
Identifiers: LCCN 2016054214 (print) | LCCN 2017003144 (ebook) | ISBN
    9781493007363 (pbk. : alk. paper) | ISBN 9781493025503 (e-book)
Subjects: LCSH: Cycling—New York (State)—Long Island—Guidebooks. | Bicycle
    trails—New York (State)—Long Island—Guidebooks. | Long Island
    (N.Y.)—Guidebooks.
Classification: LCC GV1045.5.N72 L666 2017 (print) | LCC GV1045.5.N72 (ebook)
    | DDC 796.609747/21—dc23
LC record available at https://lccn.loc.gov/2016054214

♾™ The paper used in this publication meets the minimum requirements of American
National Standard for Information Sciences—Permanence of Paper for Printed Library
Materials, ANSI/NISO Z39.48-1992.

Contents

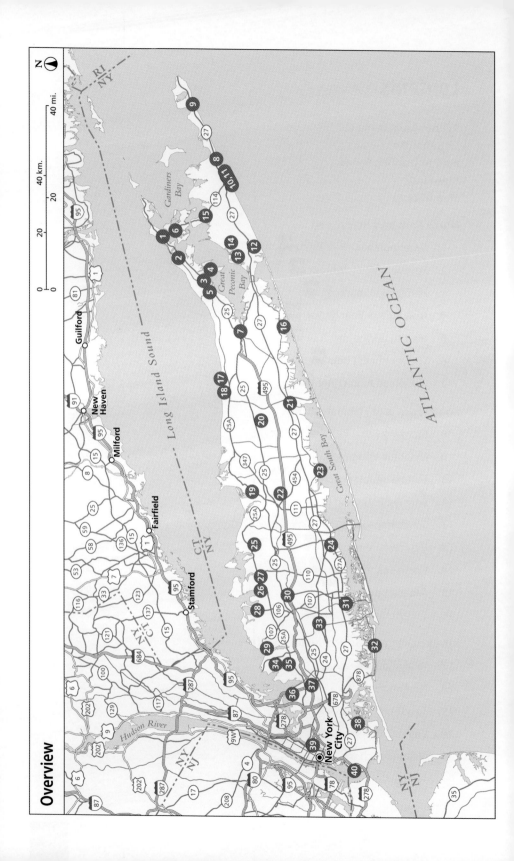

Overview

ATLANTIC OCEAN

Long Island Sound

Hudson River

Great Peconic Bay

Great South Bay

Gardiners Bay

New York City

Guilford

New Haven

Milford

Fairfield

Stamford

N

40 mi.

40 km.

Key to icons used in this edition:

 Road Bike   Mountain Bike   Hybrid

Acknowledgments

Although I grew up across the Sound in nearby Connecticut, Long Island was outside of my community and cycling network, and I am grateful to the many people I met who helped a stranger as he explored their island.

The research for this book involved repeated, lengthy stays on Long Island, in hotels, tents, and even in an RV, which my wife and I used as a home base while touring the North Fork over Thanksgiving. An incredible meal from Lombardi's Love Lane Market of Mattituck made us feel like we were home. I found help from good-natured, kind people wherever I went. The park rangers at Floyd Bennett Field helped with maps and routing. Friendly people in East Hampton opened their homes to me and showed me a more laid-back, relaxed Hampton's pace. A Sea Cliff resident dropped what she was doing to show me the Victorian homes of Sea Cliff. Everywhere I went, I found librarians who filled in the gaps on their towns and villages.

A couple I met, New York City commuters, invited me to a cookout at their home in Riverhead; others brought out floor-pumps and water when I flatted in front of their homes. Bike shop employees drew maps on paper illustrating specific routes. Servers introduced me to the vineyard owners and farmers at the restaurants I went to, and the extended work-families of diners helped me to find Internet access even in places without easy Wi-Fi. When I stayed in Hicksville, coming back after long, exhausting days on the road, the cooks at the restaurants downstairs, immigrants from countries all over the globe, sent me back to my room with extra servings.

Back home, in Richmond, my neighbor Michael helped with the house my wife and I had just bought, and a crew of painters made the 1908-home look brand-new, all while I typed the more than 60,000 words that make up this book. Friends from New Haven sent notes of encouragement, and praise for the just-released Connecticut book. Above all, I thank my wife, Hilary, for her unflagging support and love throughout this wild ride of back-to-back books.

Introduction

I was in some place called Long Island, and I walked here... Ding-donged if it ain't a Long Island.

—Tennessee Ernie Ford as "Cousin Ernie" on *I Love Lucy*

Contradictions and human ingenuity make Long Island what it is: Although both the longest and the largest island in America, Long Island is not legally an island. At least, this is what the Supreme Court decided in *United States v. Maine*, 469 U.S. 504 (1985), upholding state control over both Long Island and Block Island Sound. The unanimous decision found that without human efforts to widen the East River, the island would be a peninsula, a decision that clarified borders but changed little else.

The truth diminishes neither Long Island nor the legends that permeate it. The founding story of Smithtown is a fabricated myth conflating eponymous Richard Smythe with Dido, Queen of Carthage. No one really believes that Smythe determined the borders on a bull ride, but the story persists, taking physical form in a larger-than-life bull statue in the center of the town.

Developer William Reynolds built the island and city of Long Beach, partially with elephants, which he marched overland from his Coney Island amusement park to the former peninsula. He became mayor, wrote discriminatory laws around residency, and was indicted on graft and corruption charges, although the people of Long Beach loved him so much that they stopped the town clock until his release from prison.

This book explores the legends and contradictions in tandem with the roads and recreation of the area. The Hamptons may be for the rich and the famous, but they're also a vibrant community of farmers, laborers, and restaurant workers, who love their home and persist despite a rising cost of living. The beaches are popular and crowded, but they can also be secluded, solitary, and restorative. The roads can be car-centric and congested, but Long Island is full of hundreds of miles of quiet country roads, bike lanes, off-road greenways, and dedicated bike infrastructure. Counties and townships, residents and tourists, all work to make the roads more bike-friendly, either by converting shoulders to bike lanes, or by sharing the road and driving with courtesy.

Long Island is a beautiful, special place, containing some of the most important and diverse ecosystems on the East Coast, and the best way to experience it is by bike. For the novice or the expert, the roads of Long Island are full of opportunities and discoveries. Imagine rounding a corner and spotting an osprey perched an arm's length away, or following a twisty back-road to a little beach not listed on the map, where you can take off your shoes and listen to the waves. These experiences are unique to the cyclist, who wanders and explores in close contact with their environment.

Although I meticulously researched before visiting, I was still surprised by what I found, and some of my most memorable and enjoyable days on the bike were the days I went off-route or found something unexpected. In this small guide, I've tried my best to make Long Island manageable and predictable, safe and known, but I encourage you to explore and wander as you go. If a side road doesn't work out, you can always turn around and return to the mapped course.

Thank you for reading this book and letting me share my love of cycling with you. I hope I've provided the tools and resources to make your own journey as delightful as mine has been.

How to Use This Guide

This guide leads the reader on a journey across Long Island, starting in the east and heading west, from the North and South Forks, through Suffolk and Nassau County, and finally into the last two counties on Long Island, Queens and Kings, respectively, the New York City boroughs of Queens and Brooklyn.

Long Island is only 130 miles across and well served by the Long Island Rail Road. Directions to routes include not just automotive considerations but transit, too, with nearly every ride offering directions from train stations and from parking lots.

This book is written for Long Island residents, day-trippers, and vacationers. Restaurants and restrooms are listed at the end of each ride, to provide both planning assistance and peace of mind. Local events and attractions provide recreational, historical, and cultural interests for cyclists and non-cyclists alike.

These routes were designed with cyclists of all levels in mind, from the brand-new bike owner to the seasoned veteran. Distances vary from 2 to 35 miles, and most are around 20 miles. Many of the rides have connections to others, as noted in the descriptions, for anyone looking to extend their trip.

Long Island is quickly growing its cycling infrastructure, particularly in Suffolk County, where the shoulders of the major east-west roads already have or are in the process of converting to painted bike lanes. Cycling advocates and associations have lobbied and worked for these changes, and a vision of an even safer, more bike-friendly Long Island is being realized as I write this guide. By the time of its publication, many more miles of roads are expected to have bike lanes, thanks to the hard work of groups like the Nassau-Suffolk Bicycle Coalition and CLIMB. If you're looking for rides beyond the scope of this guide, consider reaching out to the groups working on Long Island, many of which are listed in the Bibliography section of this book.

GPS

This guide was prepared with mileage from a dedicated GPS unit, passed through a computer-mapping tool to correct and adjust calculations. Be aware of the limitations of whatever devices you decide to use, including battery power and accuracy, if you plan to follow mileage while riding these routes. Error-correcting phone apps can provide a high degree of accuracy for inexpensive phone-based GPS on roadways, but separate dedicated devices are slightly more accurate.

Cycling computers can also be used, but note that they work by measuring wheel rotations, and are subject to different variables than GPS units. Testing and calibrating is important for any device. Mileage is given to the tenth of the mile and rounded up when between units.

SAFETY

Biking carries inherent risks, and it is beyond the scope of this book to provide a comprehensive list of safety tips. Use the following general advice in conjunction with your own best judgment and always use caution.

Bike safety isn't always easy or intuitive. As a general guideline, stay on the road, riding with traffic; sidewalk riding or riding against traffic may feel safe, but often presents additional dangers. Adults ride bicycles too fast on most sidewalks, and the risk of collision at intersections and at driveways is very high for sidewalk riders. In many communities, it is illegal to ride on the sidewalk; if the sidewalk does provide a safe and legal option, defer to pedestrians and ride with care around them.

Most of the rides in this book follow open roads, alongside automobile traffic, and bicyclists are expected to follow the same rules and regulations. Stop at stop signs and red lights, signal your turns, and in general, be a courteous road user. Make eye contact with motorists and be aware that they may not see you, even if you are wearing reflective clothing and using lights, which are requirements in bad weather and the dark.

I encourage you to ride without any audio accompaniment. Your safety depends on having access to all of your senses, and wearing headphones will limit your ability to hear other riders, voices, and vehicles.

On Off-Road Trails and Singletrack

Look for signage explaining local rules before off-road rides. Hikers and horses always have priority; be aware of other road users and be prepared to stop for safety. Use a bell to alert other trail users before passing, and be courteous and polite in interactions. Stay to the right and pass on the left, and telegraph your actions to limit confusion.

Singletrack trails come with additional considerations. These are single-file trails that may also feature other users; dismount and let them take the entire trail to continue on their way. Follow the proper direction for trails (usually clockwise, except as indicated), and avoid "braiding" the trails by riding around obstacles. If you can't clear something, dismount and carry the bike without making grooves around the hazard. In general, stay off single-track in inclement conditions or after wet weather, and don't clear leaves off the route or make other changes.

Weather

Weather can vary dramatically. Always be aware of conditions and try to carry at least a snack, plenty of water, and a small phone (silenced) for emergencies. Wear sunblock, even in the colder months, as long periods of time on the bike will expose you to more sun than you may realize. Wear layers, especially when it is cold, to adjust to temperatures as they change and as you warm up or cool down.

Equipment

While helmets aren't required for adults, they should be worn on rides. On average, a cyclist crashes every 4,500 miles, and head injuries cause 75 percent of cycling-related deaths. While nearly every helmet meets the minimum safety requirements, the safest helmet will always be the one you wear; do not skimp on this purchase and make sure to buy a comfortable and well-fitting helmet that you will be happy wearing.

You should always have at minimum a front and rear LED light for visibility in case of weather changes or rides that go late. Keep lights charged. Always be prepared to deal with a flat or minor repair issue. Some of these rides take place in remote areas, and you may not be able to get a cab or assistance. Bring a patch kit (check it routinely to make sure it's still good), a spare inner tube, and a hand pump or CO_2 system. A good multi-tool will let you deal with other minor issues that could otherwise end your ride.

Some riders use mirrors, a good idea, but be aware of their limitations. Do not assume you are safe to pull into traffic without looking in all directions first. Mirrors have blind spots, and you will want to look first.

Even minor crashes can injure hands and lead to deep cuts between the fingers. For this reason, half-finger gloves are recommended; the tough material will shield your skin. Wicking clothes and padded shorts will make for more comfortable rides, and are less likely to become embedded in the skin if you do crash.

A GPS device is recommended to follow the mileage in this guide. Dedicated devices are increasingly affordable and let you measure your distance without draining the battery on a cell phone you might need for an emergency. Finally, consider buying a lock, especially for rides that involve leaving your bike while you eat lunch in a café or take a hike. Ask your local bike shop what they recommend.

Ride Finder

BEST ROAD RIDES

1. Greenport to Orient Point
6. Shelter Island Loop
7. Riverhead to Iron Pier
8. Montauk Point Ride
11. Springs: Parks and Beaches
14. North Sea to Noyac
16. Westhampton Beach
17. Wildwood
18. North Shore
19. The Three Villages
25. Kings Park Loop
27. Huntington to Oyster Bay
28. Oyster Bay Loop
34. Port Washington to Sea Cliff
35. Manhasset Bay Peninsulas Loop

BEST MTB

20. Cathedral Pines
22. Glacier 8 at Hidden Pond
37. Cunningham Park

SIGHTSEEING

2. Southold Vineyard Tour
3. Hamlets of Southold
5. Mattituck Vineyard Tour
9. Montauk Village
10. East Hampton Beaches
12. Southampton Beaches
13. Big Fresh Pond Loop
21. Mastic Beach
26. Two Harbors Ride
29. Glen Cove Parks
39. Brooklyn North to South

FAMILIES

9. Montauk Village (following the shorter version)
10. East Hampton Beaches
12. Southampton Beaches
24. Babylon to Lake Belmont
31. Jones Beach Bike Path

32. Long Beach Ride (boardwalk portion alone)
33. Eisenhower Park
36. Fort Totten
40. Shore Park Greenway

BACK AND OFF

4. New Suffolk Beach Loop
24. Babylon to Lake Belmont
30. Bethpage Bikeway
31. Jones Beach Bike Path

36. Fort Totten
38. Jamaica Bay
40. Shore Park Greenway

Map Legend

Symbol	Description	Symbol	Description
495	Interstate Highway	Airport	Airport
1	US Highway	Bridge	Bridge
25	State Highway	Building/Point of Interest	Building/Point of Interest
25	Featured State/Local Road	Dining	Dining
	Local Road	Lighthouse	Lighthouse
	Featured Bike Route	Marina	Marina
	Bike Route	17.1 Mileage Marker	Mileage Marker
	Trail	Museum	Museum
	Railroad	Parking	Parking
	Airfield/Runway	Restroom	Restroom
	State Line	School/College/University	School/College/University
	Small River or Creek	Small Park	Small Park
	Body of Water	Trailhead	Trailhead
	National Forest	Train Station	Train Station
	State Park/Forest/Wilderness/Preserve/Recreational Area	Visitor Center	Visitor Center

North Fork and Riverhead

The North Fork is a long peninsula extending east, bordered by Long Island Sound and the Peconic River and Gardiners Bay. The region is home to an ever-growing list of vineyards, and is highly accessible by ferry or train. Most of the North Fork is within the Town of Southold, a large township consisting of a number of villages and hamlets, most of which are visited in this section.

The rides in this section start with a trip from the charming maritime village of Greenport to the easternmost tip at Orient Point and then travel west, visiting vineyards, preserves, and quiet beaches on the Sound. The last two rides visit nearby settlements outside of the North Fork. The first is Shelter Island, a historic island community surrounded by the Shelter Island Bay and Gardiners Bay, then Riverhead, a charming waterfront town on the western border of the North Fork. Riverfront enjoyed a revival in the last decade following the construction of the Long Island Aquarium, a regional highlight, and is a picturesque little town with a peaceful river walk, upscale eateries, and locally owned shopping boutiques.

The North Fork is much smaller than its southern sibling, sometimes drawing negative comparisons, which locals take in stride. They refer to their quieter, country surroundings as "the Un-Hamptons" and take pride in the agricultural lifestyle that establishes this Fork as the heart of the Long Island wine industry.

Each summer, quiet roads see an influx of day-trippers and ferry-bound travelers passing through, headed to Connecticut casinos. This is still a lovely time to visit, but early spring and fall are probably ideal for cycling holidays when the water is chilly but the air is crisp and refreshing, and the roads are peaceful and easy to navigate.

The Long Island Rail Road's main line serves the area, with stations in Riverhead, Mattituck, Southold, and Greenport. Greenport has the North Ferry, providing service to Shelter Island, and the Cross Sound Ferry links Orient Point to New London, Connecticut. Both New York State Route 25 and County Route 48 provide automobile routes west–east for drivers.

Greenport to Orient Point

Greenport Village is truly the quintessential seaside village that could serve as the model for cute shoreline towns. This tourism destination was once a haven for bootleggers, speakeasies, and smugglers, but is more popular now with foodies and ferry riders. Greenport is part of the town of Southold, with neighboring East Marion and Orient, site of Orient Point. Formerly a single community, Oysterponds, Orient, and East Marion split in 1836. East Marion was named after Francis Marion, a Revolutionary general known for brutal guerilla fighting techniques, while Orient's name was chosen because it is the easternmost town on the North Fork. Orient is a historic village with few visitors, notable primarily because of Orient Point, where the Cross Sound Ferry operates.

Start: NY 114 by the Greenport Station of the Long Island Rail Road

Length: 20.0 miles

Riding time: 1.5–2 hours

Best bike: Road bike

Terrain and trail surface: Asphalt

Traffic and hazards: NY 25 can be busy with seasonal ferry riders. If traffic is particularly bad, consider using the outbound detour to return as well, increasing total mileage by 2.9 miles. NY 25 is a designated bikeway, featuring a wide, mostly car-free shoulder for comfortable cycling. A short stretch through downtown Greenport has on-street parking and can be very busy, albeit slow, and should be fairly safe for attentive riders.

Things to see: Long Island Sound, shingle-style homes and historical architecture, Orient Beach State Park, rare forest lands along the ocean.

Fees: None. Free parking is available by the train station.

Getting there: Transit users can come by land via the Long Island Rail Road to the Greenport Station where this ride begins or the North Ferry from Shelter Island. To ride the route in reverse, take the Cross Sound Ferry, from New London, Connecticut, to Orient Point. By car, take NY 25 to 4th Street in Greenport, and park behind the station, just after crossing Wiggins Street.

GPS: N41 05.996' / W72 21.796'

THE RIDE

This is one of the flattest pure road rides in this guide, with a maximum elevation of 33 feet. The combination of beautiful scenery, shoulders, and bike lanes makes it an ideal ride for even novice cyclists.

Start by the ferry queue, near the Railroad Museum of Long Island, and the East End Seaport Museum straight ahead, and turn left onto Wiggins Street (NY 114), then turn right onto Front Street (NY 25). This street is full of food options, from small bakeries and cafes to high-end tapas joints, and features a variety of architectural styles. The Greenport Theatre, just after the turn and on the right, is an art deco treasure with iconic signage. Shortly after passing the theatre, look right to catch sight of an antique carousel, housed in a modernist glass pavilion in the middle of the Mitchell Park & Marina.

The road continues past a second, more crowded, commercial block, before ending in a T-junction. Turn left onto Main Road to continue following NY 25 past retail boutiques on the left and markets and cafes to the right. Near the 1.0-mile mark, cross Washington Avenue and the shoulder widens for comfortable riding through a residential section with deeper setbacks and single-family homes.

Turn right at 1.3 miles onto North Road to continue following NY 25 east. Road speeds increase from 25 to 45 mph, but the shoulder increases in width. This area can be incredibly busy, especially on holiday weekends, but the shoulder should provide a safe buffer between cyclists and motorists.

Shortly after the turn, the route passes Stirling Cemetery, established in 1757, a historic burial site that uses bushes for natural fencing. After the cemetery, near the 2.3-mile mark, the road passes into East Marion, a historically significant location known to early English settlers as Oysterponds. During the Revolutionary War, settlers who had come from New Haven, Connecticut, were forced out by British soldiers under the leadership of Benedict Arnold, who would turn the region into a base to launch raids against Connecticut.

East Marion is a small, lightly populated hamlet. Scenery over the next mile-and-a-half or so includes shingle-style homes, a few restaurants, and shops of mostly local interest. The area also includes one of the highlights of

View from Causeway

the ride, a causeway at the 3.8-mile mark, passing between the Dam Pond and the Peconic River. The road twists along, passing by the Oysterponds Creek and marshes next, before arrival at the hamlet of Orient.

Follow the sign for Orient Hamlet, turning right at the 5.5-mile mark, onto Village Lane. On the left, note the grand obelisk memorializing the dead of the Civil War. Village Lane is a quiet street, largely bypassed by the majority of out-of-town drivers, who follow NY 25 to the Cross Sound Ferry to visit the casinos in Connecticut.

This narrow, tree-lined road passes through the heart of Orient, with a few stops of interest, including a farm store, a local market offering sandwiches, a coffee shop and bakery, and the Oysterponds Historical Society museum.

It curves to the left at the Orient Yacht Club, affording views of Orient Harbor on the right, before ending at the intersection with King Street, at the 6.0-mile mark.

The route continues along King Street for more than 0.5 mile, through a quiet residential neighborhood and large sections of open farmland and marshes. At the T-junction with Narrow River Road, turn left to continue on the route, past nearly 2 miles of marsh and open lands, all part of the Long Beach Bay State Tidal Wetlands. The preserves are open for bow hunters and hikers who have the appropriate state permit.

When Narrow River Road ends at North Road (NY 25), turn right to continue on the route. Speed limits and traffic volumes increase considerably on this 45 mph road, but the state has designated it a bikeway, leaving a comfortable shoulder. The road curves gracefully through a minimally developed

Causeway near Orient

stretch of the North Fork, continuing to follow the Tidal Wetlands on the right and farmland on the left, until reaching a picturesque historic cemetery and a "Road Ends 2,000 feet" sign just after it.

Continue along the route to the ferry, where there are restrooms and some views of the water, or turn right just before, at the Orient Beach State Park sign. The State Parkway provides a round-trip of 4.5 miles along the water for riders looking to increase their total mileage.

After a break, turn around and follow NY 25 west, bypassing the previous detour through Orient. Excepting a short stretch between the two outbound detour points, Narrow River Road and Village Lane, the return is across familiar territory for nearly 8 miles, until a left turn to continue on NY 25 onto Main Road.

In just under a mile, turn right onto Front Street to continue following NY 25, and then left onto Wiggins Street, after two blocks of storefronts and restaurants, to the finish.

MILES AND DIRECTIONS

0.0 Left onto Wiggins Street / NY 114.

0.1 Right onto Front Street / NY 25.

Greenport to Orient Point

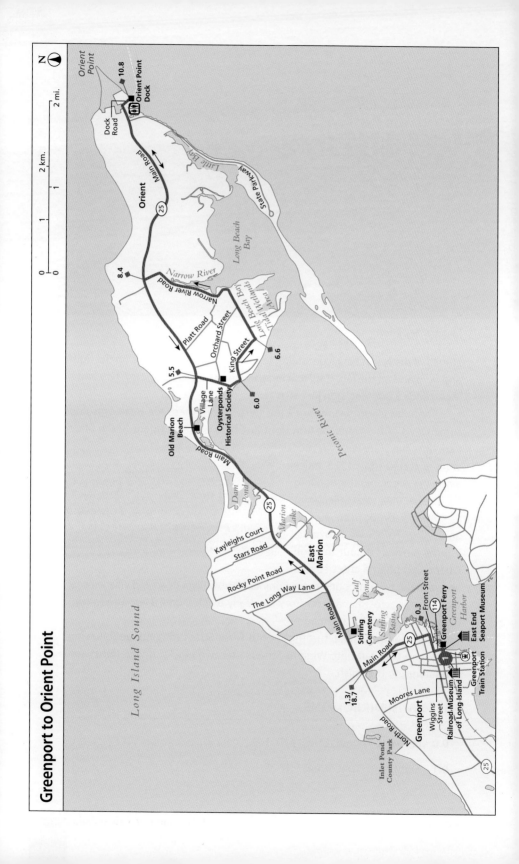

0.3	Left onto Main Road / NY 25.
1.3	Right onto Main Road / NY 25.
5.5	Right onto Village Lane.
6.0	Left onto King Street.
6.6	Left onto Narrow River Road.
8.4	Right onto North Road / NY 25.
10.6	Right onto Dock Road.
10.8	Turn around at Ferry Dock.
10.9	Left onto North Road / NY 25.
18.7	Left onto Main Road / NY 25.
19.6	Right onto Front Street / NY 25.
19.8	Left onto Wiggins Street / NY 114.
20.1	Arrive at Finish.

RIDE INFORMATION

Local Events/Attractions

Railroad Museum of Long Island: This museum showcases the history of trains in Long Island, at two separate locations in Riverhead and Greenport. Admission includes a ride on the miniature train from the 1964 World's Fair and a guided tour of each location. Visitors are encouraged to ride the Long Island Rail Road both ways, as the two museums are located at the stations in each town. The museum is open on weekends only. http://rmli.org.

East End Seaport Museum: This museum offers exhibits, special events, a working village blacksmith, and tours of a replica lighthouse built after the original Victorian-era structure. Open weekends, the museum operates on Friday between Labor Day and Halloween. eastendseaport.org.

Oysterponds Historical Society: The Historical Society operates a campus with nineteenth-century schoolhouses, historic residences, and other structures, in addition to a collection of over 70,000 artifacts. The founders, in 1944, were especially concerned with the disappearance of indigenous people, and they took care to preserve the documents, artifacts, and records that remained. oysterpondshistoricalsociety.org.

Cross Sound Ferry: This ferry offers daily service between New London, Connecticut, and Orient Point. longislandferry.com.

North Ferry: This small ferry runs daily service to and from Shelter Island. Tickets are purchased on board; only cash or checks are accepted. northferry.com.

Restaurants

Sterlington Deli: 3 Sterlington Commons, Greenport; (631) 477-8547; sterlingtondeli.net

By Aldo: 103-105 Front St., Greenport; (631) 477-6300; aldos.com

Little Creek Oyster Farm & Market: 37 Front St., Greenport; (631) 477-6992; littlecreekoysters.com

Lucharito's: 119 Main St., Greenport; (631) 477-6666; lucharitos.com

Bruce's Cheese Emporium and Cafe: 208 Main St., Greenport; (631) 477-0023; brucescheeseemp.com

D'latte Pastry Gelato Bar: 210 Main Rd., Greenport; (631) 477-6738

The Market: 44 Front St., Greenport; (631) 477-8803; themarketgreenport.com

Orient Country Store: 950 Village Ln., Orient; (631) 323-2580

Four & Twenty Blackbirds: 1010 Village Ln., Orient; (347) 940-6717; birdsblack.com

Restrooms

0.0: LIRR Station

10.6: Ticket office for Cross Sound Ferry

North Fork and Riverhead

Southold Vineyard Tour

Southold was known to the local Shinnecock tribes as Yennicott before English settlers arrived from the New Haven Colony in 1640. The region might have stayed part of Connecticut if not for the intervention of James, Duke of York, who demanded they be governed by the Province of New York. At the time, it was easier to travel to Long Island from Connecticut by ship than from New York over land, but James had a grudge against New Haven, which had harbored the infamous three regicide judges after they sentenced his father, Charles I of England, to death, in 1649. Regardless of political identity, little changed in Southold, where the settlers continued to cultivate their primary regional crop, potatoes, until switching to wine grapes in the late twentieth century.

Start: Southold Station of the Long Island Rail Road

Length: 10.3 miles

Riding time: 45–60 minutes

Best bike: Road bike or hybrid

Terrain and trail surface: Asphalt

Traffic and hazards: The left turn from CR 48 onto Old North Road can be dicey. A mile-long stretch of NY 25 exiting Southold has a wide shoulder, but cars are frequently parked there, and traffic speeds increase quickly as you leave town.

Things to see: Three popular vineyards, marshes, farmland, historic homes.

Fees: None. Free parking is widely available.

Getting there: Take NY 25 to Southold and then turn left onto Youngs Avenue to the train station. By train, take the Long Island Rail Road to the start of the ride at Southold Station.

GPS: N41 03.957' / W72 25.685'

2

THE RIDE

Long Island boasts more than fifty wine producers, with nearly as many vineyards, most of them on the North Fork. The first winery opened in 1973, and the region now sees more than a million visitors per year. This ride maps out three of the top vineyards in Southold, but many more are easily accessible off and on the route: Check the full list of vineyards in the Ride Information section below.

Starting at the Southold station on Traveler Street, the route immediately turns right, onto Youngs Avenue, past a town green and across NY 25. Youngs Avenue flows downhill over the next quarter-mile, curving left along the Town Creek and becoming Calves Neck Road.

Calves Neck Road winds around a residential neighborhood on the Harpers Point promontory, curving right, and becoming Hill Road. At the 1-mile mark, continue onto Hill Road West, then cross Wells Avenue onto Jernick Lane.

Jernick Lane ends in a T-junction with Oaklawn Avenue. Turn left and follow Oaklawn Avenue over scenic Jockey Creek on a small bridge, continuing through a quiet residential neighborhood until the 1.9-mile mark, then turn right onto Clearview Avenue.

When Clearview Avenue ends, turn left onto Gardiners Lane, then right onto Clearview Avenue West. At the T-junction with Main Bayview Avenue, turn left onto the slightly busier road. The route passes behind the Croteaux Vineyards property, then bears right at the fork onto Baywater Avenue. Turn right onto South Harbor Road, just before the 3-mile mark, and follow this quiet, narrow road up to Croteaux Vineyard.

Croteaux Vineyard is the only vineyard in the country that solely makes Rosé, of which they produce several varieties. They operate out of a historic farm, with a lovely tasting room in a vintage setting. After a stop at the vineyard, continue on South Harbor Road, until it ends in a T-junction with Main Road (NY 25).

Several vineyards are to the left, but this route turns right, past the Catapano Farms, and then right again onto Peanut Alley / Corwin Lane, after a picturesque little cemetery. Take the first left off this alley onto Main Bayview Road and then the immediate right onto Pine Neck Road. After a half-mile, turn left onto Oaklawn Avenue, back over Jockey Creek, until the road ends at Main Road (NY 25).

NY 25 can be busy, so use caution and take advantage of the wide shoulder if cars are not parked there. NY 25 heads back through Southold then through a short stretch of car-centric suburban businesses before opening up into a quieter section, just before the Old Fields Vineyard, on the right.

Scenic dock in Southold

This is the oldest continuously operated vineyard on Long Island, and the property has been family-owned and farmed since the early twentieth century. The Old Fields transitioned from potatoes to wine grapes in 1974 and produce an assortment of French-style wines, including Pinot Noir, Chardonnay, Merlot, Cabernet Franc, and Sauvignon Blanc.

After stopping there, carefully exit the Vineyard, turning left onto NY 25, then right onto Laurel Avenue. This is another quiet street without striping or painted lines. As the surroundings get woodsier, it ends in a T-junction with Long Creek Drive, where the route turns left and then left again onto Tuthill Road.

Take the first right off Tuthill Road onto Yennecott Drive, named for the Algonquian word for Southold. When the road ends, turn right onto Boisseau Avenue, which empties onto North Road (CR 48) just ahead.

> ### Bike Shops
>
> **Twin Forks Bicycles:** 121 East Main St., Riverhead; (631) 591-3082; twinforksbicycles.com
> **Country Time Cycle:** 6955 Main Rd., Mattituck; (631) 298-8700; ctcycle.com
> **Eagle's Neck Paddling Company:** (Rental/repair) 62300 Main Rd., Southold; (631)765-3502; eaglesneck.com

North Road is a faster and busier route, so exercise caution when making the left turn onto Old North Road in less than a half-mile. Just ahead is the entrance to One Woman Wines & Vineyard. The name is accurate; the majority of planting and work has been performed by one woman, Claudia Purita, who continues the traditions she learned growing up on her family's farm in Calabria, Italy. The 16-acre farm was hand-planted by Purita, who runs a tiny tasting room out of a charming red outbuilding that has picnic tables and beautiful views of the vineyard.

After this stop, turn right out of the driveway, and continue on Old North Road until it ends at Horton Lane. Turn left, riding past open farmlands, and cross CR 48 ahead and back into Southold. Turn left onto Traveler Street, immediately after crossing the train tracks, to finish this ride.

MILES AND DIRECTIONS

0.0   Start on Traveler Street and right onto Youngs Avenue.

0.3   Continue on Calves Neck Road.

0.8   Right onto Hill Road.

1.0   Continue on Hill Road West.

1.1   Cross Wells Avenue and continue onto Jernick Lane.

1.2   Left onto Oaklawn Avenue.

1.9   Right onto Clearview Avenue.

2.3   Left onto Gardiners Lane and right onto Clearview Avenue West.

2.4   Left onto Main Bayview Avenue.

2.8   Right onto Baywater Avenue.

2.9   Right onto South Harbor Road.

3.4   Right onto Main Road / NY 25.

3.8   Right onto Peanut Alley / Corwin Lane.

3.9   Left onto Main Bayview Road and right onto Pine Neck Road.

4.4   Left onto Oaklawn Avenue.

5.1   Right onto Main Road / NY 25.

6.4   Right onto The Old Field Vineyards driveway.

6.6   Left onto Main Road / NY 25 then right onto Laurel Avenue.

7.2   Left onto Long Creek Drive.

7.5   Left onto Tuthill Road.

7.6   Right onto Yennecott Drive.

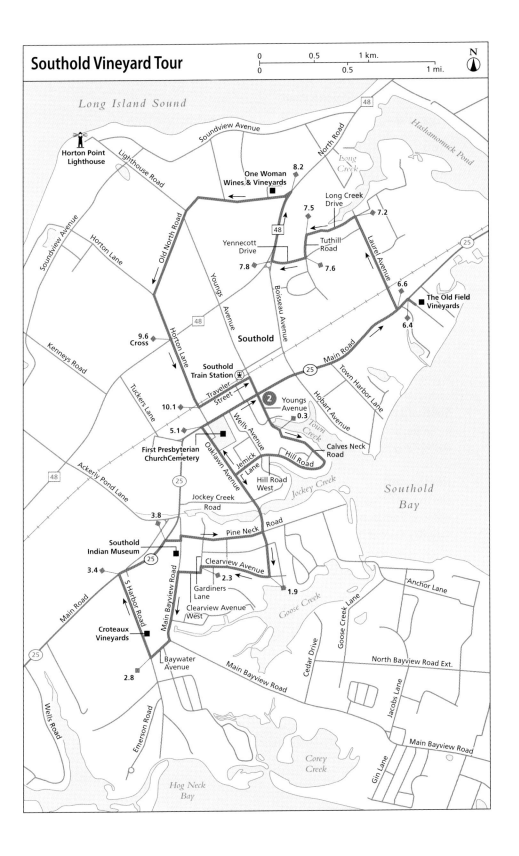

Southold Vineyard Tour

0   0.5   1 km.
0   0.5   1 mi.

N

Long Island Sound

Soundview Avenue

48

North Road

Hashamomuck Pond

Horton Point
Lighthouse

Lighthouse Road

One Woman
Wines & Vineyards

8.2

Long Creek
Drive

7.5

7.2

Long
Creek

Soundview Avenue

Horton Lane

Old North Road

48

Youngs Avenue

Yennecott
Drive

7.8

Tuthill
Road

7.6

Laurel Avenue

25

6.6

The Old Field
Vineyards

Kenneys Road

Horton Lane

48

9.6
Cross

Boiseau Avenue

Southold

Main Road

6.4

Town Harbor Lane

Tuckers Lane

Southold
Train Station

25

Traveler
Street

10.1

2

Youngs
Avenue

0.3

Hobart Avenue

Calves Neck
Road

5.1

Wells Avenue

Oaklawn Avenue

Jernick
Lane

Hill Road
West

Hill Road

Town
Creek

First Presbyterian
Church Cemetery

Ackerly Pond Lane

48

25

Jockey Creek
Road

Jockey Creek

Southold
Bay

3.8

Pine Neck   Road

Southold
Indian Museum

25

Clearview Avenue

Main Bayview Road

3.4

Gardiners
Lane

2.3

Clearview Avenue
West

1.9

Goose Creek

Anchor Lane

Goose Creek Lane

S Harbor Road

Croteaux
Vineyards

25

Baywater
Avenue

Main Bayview Road

North Bayview Road Ext.

Cedar Drive

Main Road

2.8

Emerson Road

Wells Road

Hog Neck
Bay

Corey
Creek

Gin Lane

Jacobs Lane

Main Bayview Road

7.8 Right onto Boisseau Avenue to North Road / CR 48.

8.2 Left onto Old North Road.

9.4 Left onto Horton Lane.

10.1 Left onto Traveler Street.

10.3 Arrive at finish.

RIDE INFORMATION

Local Events/Attractions

Horton Point Lighthouse and Nautical Museum: Commissioned in 1790 by President George Washington, this lighthouse was finally built in 1857, and automated in 1933. For a nominal fee, visitors can tour the lighthouse and visit the museum, operated by the Southold Historical Society.

Southold Indian Museum: This New York State Archaeological Association property hosts the largest collection of Algonquin ceramic pottery in existence, as well as an extensive collection of hunting, fishing, farming, building, and cooking tools. Open Sunday afternoon year-round, the museum also opens on Saturday each summer.

Southold Historical Society: The society offers tours of their main complex, including an eighteenth-century home, a working smithy, printing press, and barns. They hold special events year-round.

Restaurants

North Fork Roasting Company: 55795 Main Rd., Southold; (631) 876-5450; noforoastingco.com
Country Corner Cafe: 55765 Main Rd., Southold; (631) 765-6766; countrycornersouthold.com
Wayside Market: 55575 Main Rd., Southold; (631) 765-3575
Grateful Deli: 55700 Main Rd., Southold; (631) 765-6408; gratefuldeliny.com
The Blue Duck Bakery Cafe: 56275 Main Rd., Southold; (631) 629-4123; blueduckbakerycafe.com

Vineyards

For more wineries and vineyards, see liwines.com, the official website of the Long Island Wine Region.
Croteaux Vineyards: 1450 S Harbor Rd., Southold; (631) 765-6099; croteaux.com
The Old Field Vineyards: 59600 Main Rd., Southold; (631) 765-0004; theoldfield.com

One Woman Wines & Vineyards: 5195 Old North Rd., Southold; (631) 765-1200; onewomanwines.com

Southold Farm + Cellar: 860 Old North Rd., Southold; (631) 353-0343; southoldfarmandcellar.com

Mattebella Vineyards: 46005 Main Rd., Southold; (631) 655-9554; mattebellavineyards.com

Duck Walk Vineyards North: 44535 Main Rd., Southold; (631) 765-3500; duckwalk.com

Corey Creek Vineyards: 45470 Main Rd., Southold; (631) 765-4168; bedellcellars .com/corey-creek-tr

Sparkling Pointe: 39750 County Rd. 48, Southold; (631) 765-0200; sparklingpointe.com

Restrooms
0.0: Southold Train Station

Hamlets of Southold

The little hamlets of Cutchogue and Peconic are full of vineyards and wineries. The area is also rich in history and natural beauty, featured prominently on the roads this route covers. Beside the Downs Farm Preserve at the start, the ride also passes the Goldsmith Inlet, a 35-acre park on Long Island Sound surrounded by old-growth forests.

Start: Downs Farm Preserve / Fort Corchaug at 23800 Main Rd. (NY 25), Cutchogue

Length: 16.3 miles

Riding time: 60–75 minutes

Best bike: Road bike

Terrain and trail surface: Asphalt

Traffic and hazards: NY 25 can be busy but features a wide shoulder and is popular with local cyclists.

Things to see: A number of vineyards and wineries, historic sites, and a long stretch of road through forests and beaches.

Fees: None. Parking at the preserve is free.

Getting there: From NY 25, turn right onto the little gravel driveway for Downs Farm Preserve, just a few miles out of Mattituck. The route passes very near the Southold train station. To ride the route from the station, follow Traveler Street to Horton Lane, and turn right to ride the route in reverse.

GPS: N41 00.194' / W72 29.861'

THE RIDE

This ride starts at the Downs Farm Preserve, a quiet natural spot just outside of nearby Mattituck. Following NY 25, it passes through Cutchogue and Peconic, past a number of vineyards and wineries, then turns just before downtown Southold to explore some of the quieter back roads and public beaches in Peconic. Food options are limited, but many of the vineyards serve meat and cheese boards and other rustic food offerings for al fresco dining.

Exiting the gravel driveway, turn right onto Main Road (NY 25), the fast but wide-shouldered road that covers the entire North Fork region. On the left, you'll pass the Cutchogue location for Macari Winery, a family-owned winery dating back to an operation started in the 1930s in a basement in Queens. The family farms with an eye to conservation and biodiversity; their property is also an excellent spot for birding.

Until reaching the center of Cutchogue, the route continues through a largely suburban area bordered by attractive white fences over the next three-quarters of a mile. Traffic speeds slow down and the shoulder opens for parking along a short commercial stretch composed primarily of realtors, hair care, and professional services, in addition to the Cutchogue Diner and an ice cream parlor.

The shoulder opens again after the center. Near the 1.7-mile mark, note the historic Southold burying grounds on the right, which was probably used by the founders of Southold, the oldest English township in the state of New York.

Pugliese Vineyards, Bedell Cellars, Pindar Vineyards, Lenz Winery, and Raphael Vineyard are just ahead along a half-mile stretch beginning just before Bridge Lane. The first, Pugliese, is known for sparkling wines. The second, Bedell, makes wines that were selected for the 2013 US Presidential Inauguration. The next winery, Pindar, is wind-powered, with impressive turbines rising out of the 500-acre fields. Lenz Winery sees France as their competitor and enters their small-batch wines in blind taste competitions against distinguished French wines. Raphael Vineyard, just ahead on the right, operates a tasting room in a beautiful Mediterranean-style building inspired by Italian monasteries.

In another half-mile, NY 25 passes the Peconic taproom of Greenport Harbor Brewing. Turn left onto Peconic Lane, a quieter, narrow road that passes Sannino Bella Vita Vineyards on the way into the tiny town center of Peconic.

After crossing railroad tracks into Peconic, note the Winemakers Studio, a co-op tasting room and retail operation, on your left. This town center is tiny and ends where Peconic Lane crosses CR 48 onto quiet, narrow Mill Road.

At the fork, bear left to stay on Mill Road, curving around the Goldsmith Inlet to the right. At the end of the road is the Goldsmith Inlet beach, a quiet, sandy beach on Long Island Sound, just after the Peconic Sound Shores property.

When ready, turn around and proceed back to the fork, then left onto Soundview Avenue, through a heavily forested neighborhood with few homes. Near the end of this stretch of the route, the road passes the Peconic Dunes County Park, now a 4-H Camp. At the four-way intersection ahead, turn left onto Kenneys Road, away from the woods and back toward the Sound. The route follows Kenneys Road up to Kenneys Beach, where it turns right onto North Sea Drive, a sunny beachfront road through a neighborhood of seasonal cottages and small homes.

After a half-mile, the road opens up into a large parking area at McCabe's Town Park, and the route continues through, onto Hortons Lane, before turning left back onto Soundview Avenue at the 8.1-mile mark.

Soundview Avenue continues through another forested neighborhood, with a lovely view of Hummels Pond just before the left turn onto Lighthouse Road. Follow Lighthouse Road to Horton Point Lighthouse, a historical society site that offers tours of a working lighthouse, then turn around, following Lighthouse Road to its end in a T-junction with Old North Road.

Quiet pond on back road

North Fork and Riverhead

Turn right onto Old North Road, another unpainted, quiet side street, and ride for nearly a half-mile until the route turns left onto Hortons Lane when Old North Road ends.

Hortons Lane crosses CR 48, becoming Horton Lane, and ends in downtown Southold, just after Traveler Street, which connects to the train station. Southold has a number of food options, accessible by turning left at the historic cemetery onto NY 25. If interested, refer to the Southold Vinery Tour in chapter 2, for a listing of Southold restaurants.

To continue on this route, turn right onto NY 25. Bear left at the fork ahead to stay on NY 25 through a slightly dicey intersection. After a quarter-mile of riding, you pass another small historic cemetery on the right, and then find another cluster of vineyards just ahead, in order: Corey Creek Vineyards, Mattebella Vineyards, Duck Walk Vineyards, and Osprey's Dominion Vineyards. All produce a wide variety of wines, in bucolic, natural settings.

> ## Bike Shops
>
> **Twin Forks Bicycles:** 121 East Main St., Riverhead; (631) 591-3082; twinforksbicycles.com
> **Country Time Cycle:** 6955 Main Rd., Mattituck; (631) 298-8700; ctcycle.com
> **Eagle's Neck Paddling Company:** (Rental/repair) 62300 Main Rd., Southold; (631)765-3502; eaglesneck.com

This entire segment from Horton Lane to the finish is roughly 5.5 miles, most of it in a wide shoulder and over familiar territory from the outbound route, passing the same vineyards and wineries from before. The ride ends around the 16.3-mile mark, back at Downs Farm Preserve in Cutchogue.

MILES AND DIRECTIONS

0.0 Start at Downs Farm Preserve and turn right onto Main Road / NY 25.

3.5 Left onto Peconic Lane.

4.1 Cross CR 48 and continue on Mill Road.

4.9 Turn around.

5.4 Left onto Soundview Avenue.

7.2 Left onto Kenney Road.

7.4 Right onto North Sea Drive.

7.8 Continue on Hortons Lane.

8.1 Left onto Soundview Avenue.

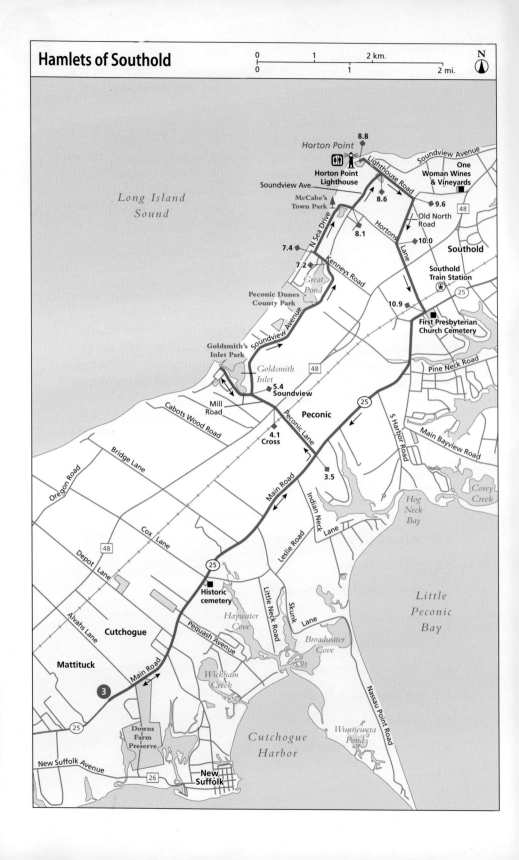

Hamlets of Southold

0   1   2 km.

0   1   2 mi.

N

Long Island Sound

Horton Point

8.8

Horton Point Lighthouse

Soundview Ave.

Lighthouse Road

Soundview Avenue

One Woman Wines & Vineyards

8.6

9.6

48

McCabe's Town Park

Old North Road

Southold

N Sea Drive

8.1

Hortons Lane

10.0

7.4

Kenneys Road

Southold Train Station

7.2

Great Pond

25

Peconic Dunes County Park

10.9

Soundview Avenue

First Presbyterian Church Cemetery

Goldsmith's Inlet Park

Goldsmith Inlet

48

Pine Neck Road

5.4 Soundview

Mill Road

Peconic Lane

Peconic

Cabots Wood Road

25

S Harbor Road

Main Bayview Road

4.1 Cross

Corey Creek

Bridge Lane

Hog Neck Bay

Main Road

3.5

Oregon Road

Indian Neck Lane

Cox Lane

Leslie Road

Little Peconic Bay

48

Depot Lane

25

Historic cemetery

Little Neck Road

Skunk Lane

Alvahs Lane

Haywater Cove

Cutchogue

Pequash Avenue

Broadwater Cove

Mattituck

Main Road

Wickham Creek

3

25

Nassau Point Road

Downs Farm Preserve

Cutchogue Harbor

Winneweta Pond

New Suffolk Avenue

26

New Suffolk

8.6 Left onto Lighthouse Road.

8.8 Turn around.

9.6 Right onto Old North Road.

10.0 Left onto Hortons Lane.

10.4 Cross CR 48.

10.9 Right onto Main Road / NY 25.

16.3 Arrive at finish.

RIDE INFORMATION

Local Events/Attractions

Downs Farm Preserve: This 51-acre nature preserve includes the historical site of Fort Corchaug, a log cabin fortification built by the local Corchaug tribe to fight off raids from the Narragansetts of Connecticut. The archaeological site is one of the few such sites undisturbed in the Northeast. The preserve has a tranquil mile-long hiking trail with excellent birding and a picturesque creek with waterfowl.

Peconic Dunes County Park: Now a 4-H Camp, of interest mostly for the natural land it has preserved on a long stretch of this route.

McCabes Town Park: This town beach is a popular spot to watch stunning sunsets on the Long Island Sound.

Horton Point Lighthouse and Nautical Museum: Commissioned in 1790 by President George Washington, this lighthouse was finally built in 1857 and automated in 1933. Visitors can tour the lighthouse and visit the museum, operated by the Southold Historical Society, for a nominal fee.

Southold Indian Museum: This New York State Archaeological Association property hosts the largest collection of Algonquin ceramic pottery in existence as well as an extensive collection of hunting, fishing, farming, building, and cooking tools. Open Sunday afternoon year-round, the museum also opens on Saturday in summer.

Restaurants

The Cutchogue Diner: 27800 Main Rd., Cutchogue; (631) 734-7016; cutchoguediner.com

A Taste of the North Fork: (Gourmet store) 2885 Peconic Ln., Peconic; (631) 765-8760; atasteofthenorthfork.com

Vineyards and Breweries

For more wineries and vineyards, see liwines.com, the official website of the Long Island Wine Region.

Macari Winery: 24385 Main Rd., Cutchogue; (631) 734-7070; macariwines.com

Pugliese Vineyards: 34515 Main Rd., Cutchogue; (631) 734-4057; pugliesevineyards.com

Bedell Cellars: 36225 Main Rd., Cutchogue; (631) 734-7537; bedellcellars.com

Pindar Vineyards: 37645 Main Rd., Peconic; (631) 734-6200; pindar.net

Lenz Winery: 38355 Main Rd., Peconic; (631) 734-6010; lenzwine.com

Raphael Vineyards: 39390 Main Rd., Peconic; (631) 765-1100; raphaelwine.com

Osprey's Dominion Vineyards: 44075 Main Rd., Peconic; (631) 765-6188; ospreysdominion.com

Duck Walk Vineyards North: 44535 Main Rd., Southold; (631) 765-3500; duckwalk.com

Corey Creek Vineyards: 45470 Main Rd., Southold; (631) 765-4168; bedellcellars.com/corey-creek-tr

Mattebella Vineyards: 46005 Main Rd., Southold; (631) 655-9554; mattebellavineyards.com

Sannino Bella Vita Vineyard: 1375 Peconic Ln., Peconic; (631) 734-8282; sanninovineyard.com

Winemakers Studio: 2885 Peconic Ln., Peconic; (774) 641-7488; winemaker-studio.com

Greenport Harbor Brewing: 42155 Main Rd., Peconic; (631) 477-1100; greenportharborbrewing.com

Restrooms

0.0: Downs Farm Preserve
7.8: McCabe's Town Park
8.8: Horton Point

New Suffolk Beach Loop

New Suffolk is a charming waterfront community located in the larger Town of Southold. The hamlet, which housed the first submarine base in the country, is almost entirely contained in a tiny grid of three blocks by four blocks. New Suffolk only has a few hundred residents living in a 0.62-square mile area, and the smallest school district in New York, serving less than a dozen children.

New Suffolk doesn't have the restaurants or tourist districts of larger towns on the North Fork, but it does have long stretches of waterfront and easy access via quiet back roads to nearby parks and beaches. There are two eateries in New Suffolk: Legends, a split establishment with a casual sports bar and a more upscale dining room, and Case's Place, a seafood restaurant with low-key al fresco dining and a more formal indoor dining room. This ride passes a number of vineyards and farm markets, some of which are featured in the next ride, the Mattituck Vineyard Loop (Rte. 5).

Start: Downs Farm Preserve / Fort Corchaug at 23800 Main Rd. (NY 25), Cutchogue

Length: 13.8 miles

Riding time: About 1 hour

Best bike: Road bike

Terrain and trail surface: Asphalt

Traffic and hazards: NY 25 can be busy, especially on summer weekends, but features a wide shoulder, popular with local cyclists. This route minimizes time spent on NY 25, featuring the quieter, low-key side roads of the area.

Things to see: The beach in New Suffolk, a long ride on Oregon Road through forestlands, charming creeks and wetlands, and Bailie's Beach Park in Mattituck.

Fees: None. Free parking is available throughout New Suffolk.

Getting there: Take NY 25 through Mattituck to Cutchogue and turn right onto New Suffolk Road into the center of New Suffolk. Transit users will take the Long Island Rail Road to Mattituck, then turn right onto Love Lane, and continue westbound for a block on NY 25 to New Suffolk Avenue. Turn left onto New Suffolk Avenue following the road into New Suffolk, to the start of the ride at 1st and Jackson.

GPS: N40 59.447' / W72 28.298'

THE RIDE

It is hard to travel around the North Fork without using NY 25 or CR 48, which can be intimidating for less experienced cyclists. This ride avoids both as much as is practical, and explores nearly 14 miles of quiet back roads, visiting two beaches and several scenic spots, with very little elevation gain. This would be the perfect ride for someone new to road cycling, or someone looking for a quiet vacation ride on a hybrid bike.

Starting at the intersection of 1st and Jackson, take the first left onto Main Street, a narrow little neighborhood road. At the four-way stop, continue

Marsh view from Grathwohl Road

straight onto New Suffolk Avenue for the next third of a mile, and then turn right onto Grathwohl Road.

This is an unpainted road with minimal traffic. Halfway along, a tranquil view of West Creek opens on the left. Continue until Grathwohl ends at New Suffolk Avenue, and carefully turn left, following the road through open farmland on either side.

New Suffolk Avenue ends in downtown Cutchogue, directly across from a craft store and art gallery. Turn right onto NY 25 to continue following the route for just under a mile. After passing the Southold burying grounds, turn left onto Cox Lane, a quiet residential street running through local vineyards. Cross CR 48 at the 4.0-mile mark, continuing on Cox Lane, until the long road ends at Oregon Road.

Oregon Road is one of the most scenic and relaxing in the area, and it is featured on both this ride and the next one, the Mattick Vineyard Loop. The next 2.3 miles of road pass through farmland and vineyards on this narrow country road.

Bear right onto East Mill Road at the end of Oregon Road, near the 7.0-mile mark, for another 0.3 mile of quiet, bucolic riding. This section of road may not be well maintained, so watch for cracks and potholes. The route turns right onto Reeve Road, a slightly busier road with a center stripe, for a half-mile, until a left turn onto Bailie Beach Road.

The narrow and windy Bailie Beach Road heads downhill quickly to a sandy beach. Bailie Beach has excellent views of Long Island Sound and extensive dunes used by nesting birds. Pay attention to signs and use caution if exploring. To the left is a tidal wetland with excellent birding, particularly shorebirds, red-winged blackbirds, and many other small passerines.

Bike Shops

Twin Forks Bicycles: 121 East Main St., Riverhead; (631) 591-3082; twinforksbicycles.com
Country Time Cycle: 6955 Main Rd., Mattituck; (631) 298-8700; ctcycle.com

After visiting the beach, turn around, climbing the short and steep hill you rode down on, to retrace the route along Bailie Beach Road back to Reeve Road. Turn right onto Reeve, then left onto East Mill Road, bearing left to continue on East Mill Road until it ends at a stop sign before Mill Lane.

Turn right onto Mill Lane, another long, quiet road through wine country. Mill Lane crosses CR 48 and the train tracks at the 10.3-mile mark, then continues on, ending in a T-junction with NY 25.

Carefully turn left onto NY 25, watching for oncoming traffic, and stay in the wide shoulder over the next 0.8 mile of busier road. NY 25 is busier than the rest of the roads on this route, but this particular stretch is scenic, passing through the vineyards of Osprey's Dominion.

At the 11.4-mile mark, turn right onto Locust Avenue, over nearly a quarter-mile of additional farmland. Being mindful again of oncoming traffic, turn left onto New Suffolk Avenue, which has no stop at this intersection.

The next 1.5 miles are especially scenic, crossing three bridges over a small creek, an inlet, and the West Creek, with views of farmland, vineyards, and the Peconic River on the right. As New Suffolk Avenue reaches the village center, turn right onto 5th Street, then left onto Jackson Street, ending the ride as the Peconic River comes into view where Jackson intersects with 1st St.

The New Suffolk Beach is on your right, and Legends and Case's Place to the left, for post-ride food and relaxation.

MILES AND DIRECTIONS

0.0   Start on 1st St. and left onto Main Street.

0.2   Continue on New Suffolk Avenue.

0.5   Right onto Grathwohl Road.

1.3   Left onto New Suffolk Road.

2.0   Right onto Main Street / NY 25.

2.9   Left onto Cox Lane.

4.0   Cross CR 48.

4.7   Left onto Oregon Road.

7.0   Continue on East Mill Road.

7.3   Right onto Reeve Road.

7.8   Left onto Bailie Beach Road.

8.2   Turn around.

8.5   Right onto Reeve Road.

9.0   Left onto East Mill Road.

9.4   Right onto Mill Lane.

10.6   Left onto Main Street / NY 25.

11.4   Right onto Locust Avenue.

11.8   Left onto New Suffolk Avenue.

13.6   Right onto 5th St. then left onto Jackson Street.

13.8   Left onto 1st St. and arrive at finish.

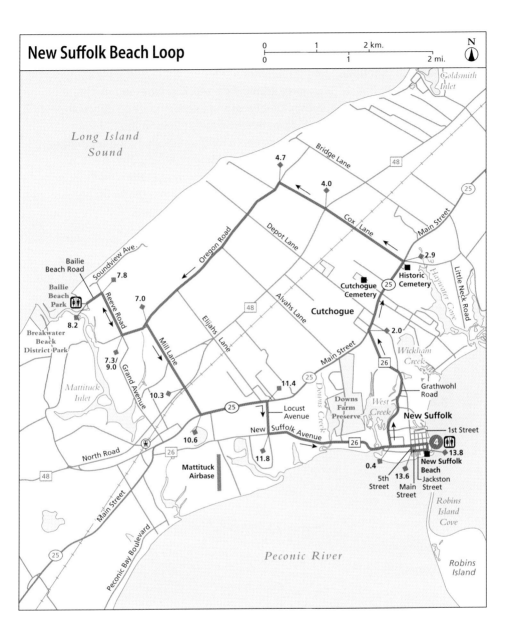

New Suffolk Beach Loop

0   1   2 km.

0   1   2 mi.

N

Goldsmith Inlet

Long Island Sound

Bridge Lane

48

4.7

4.0

25

Depot Lane

Cox Lane

Main Street

Oregon Road

2.9

Bailie Beach Road

Soundview Ave.

7.8

Historic Cemetery

Cutchogue Cemetery

25

Little Neck Road

Hawater Cove

Bailie Beach Park

7.0

Reeve Road

Alvahs Lane

48

Cutchogue

8.2

Elijahs Lane

Mill Lane

2.0

Breakwater Beach District Park

7.3/ 9.0

Wickham Creek

Mattituck Inlet

Grand Avenue

10.3

Main Street

26

Grathwohl Road

11.4

25

Downs Creek

West Creek

New Suffolk

Locust Avenue

Downs Farm Preserve

10.6

New Suffolk Avenue

1st Street

North Road

26

26

4

13.8

48

Mattituck Airbase

11.8

0.4

New Suffolk Beach

Peconic Bay Boulevard

5th Street

13.6

Main Street

Jackston Street

25

Peconic River

Robins Island Cove

Robins Island

RIDE INFORMATION

Local Events/Attractions

Downs Farm Preserve: This 51-acre nature preserve includes the historical site of Fort Corchaug, a log cabin fortification built by the local Corchaug tribe to fight off raids from the Narragansetts of Connecticut. The archaeological site is one of the few such sites undisturbed in the Northeast. The preserve has a tranquil mile-long hiking trail with excellent birding and a picturesque creek with waterfowl.

New Suffolk Beach: This quiet, scenic little beach in New Suffolk charges non-residents for daily parking. Lifeguards and attendants are on duty daily.

Bailie's Beach Park: Low-key town beach on Long Island Sound.

New Suffolk Beach: Peconic Harbor beach for New Suffolk, on the south side of the North Fork.

New Suffolk Waterfront Fund: This association manages the waterfront of New Suffolk. They host events for locals and visitors alike, to highlight the historic character and charm of the hamlet. newsuffolkwaterfront.org.

Restaurants

Case's Place: 650 1st St., New Suffolk; (631) 734-8686;

Legends: 835 1st St., New Suffolk; (631) 734-5123; legends-restaurant.com

The Cutchogue Diner: 27800 Main Rd., Cutchogue; (631) 734-7016; cutchoguediner.com

Scoops: 28080 Main Rd., Cutchogue; (631) 734-6331

Restrooms

0.0: New Suffolk Beach

8.2: Bailie's Beach

Mattituck Vineyard Tour

Mattituck is another picturesque hamlet in the Town of Southold, founded on land purchased by a governor of New Haven, Connecticut. The name Mattituck was probably derived from an Algonquian place name, but experts disagree if it meant "a place without wood" or the more prosaic "Great Creek." Both were descriptive of the heavilyfarmed region, which is still an agricultural community centered on Mattituck Inlet, a great creek popular for nature-watching and recreational uses. Despite the beauty of the Inlet, most scholars agree with the nineteenth-century linguist, James H. Trumbull, that the area was probably named for its deforested state. Like the rest of Southold, the former potato fields are now used for wine grapes, making the region a popular tourist destination. Included among the three wineries on this route is the first commercial operation on Long Island, open since 1973.

Start: The Mattituck station of the Long Island Rail Road, on Pike Street by Love Lane.

Length: 10.2 miles

Riding time: About 1 hour

Best bike: Road bike or hybrid

Terrain and trail surface: Asphalt

Traffic and hazards: North Road (CR 48) is a busy road popular with tourists and visitors. The shoulder is wide, but there are several intersections on the return leg where the shoulder is replaced with a turning lane.

Things to see: Three popular vineyards in Mattituck and Cutchogue, a long stretch of beautiful road through farmland and forest, historic barns and farm buildings.

Fees: None. Parking is free at the train station.

5

THE RIDE

Similar to the Southold Vinery Tour, this ride visits several wineries in the area, following the entire length of Oregon Avenue, one of the best cycling roads in Southold. The return route along North Road (CR 48) can be a little busier and potentially intimidating for novice cyclists, but CR 48 has a wide shoulder, and shouldn't be too challenging. If it makes you nervous, it's easy to avoid it, with a slight detour. When the ride reaches the end of Oregon Avenue, simply turn around, and then turn left onto Alvahs Lane to visit the third and final stop at Castello di Borghese Vineyard, just across CR 48. After the stop, turn around and retrace your route back to Oregon Avenue, then turn left, and follow the outbound route back to the start. This adds less than a mile of additional riding.

This route is as flat as most rides in the North Fork, with a max elevation gain of 60 feet and a total gain of 220 feet over the 10.2-mile route.

Starting at the train station on Pike Street in Mattituck, cross Love Lane, and turn left at the next intersection onto Wickham Avenue, passing a war memorial on the right. Wickham Avenue is a low-volume 35-mph neighborhood road without shoulders, comfortable to ride along. Use caution with the two crossings early in the ride, first over the train tracks and the second over the potentially busy CR 48.

The right turn to continue on Wickham is easy to miss. Bear right at a fork at the half-mile mark, onto a quieter, smaller side street. If you reach the scenic little Grand Avenue Bridge, you've just overshot the turn.

Wickham Road continues through an even quieter little neighborhood, bordered by trees and open fields. Turn left when it reaches Mill Lane, territory previously visited in the New Suffolk Beach Loop, for more than a half-mile of quiet country road.

Mill Lane ends at the intersection with Oregon Avenue, at the 1.8-mile mark. Turn right onto Oregon Avenue to Shinn Estate Vineyards, just ahead on the right. This family-owned vineyard makes wine from grapes grown on the property, which houses a historic farmhouse inn, a bar, and an outdoor patio with spectacular views of the hundreds of acres of preserved farmlands. Shinn Estates also distills brandies and grappa, available for sale on location.

After a stop, continue on Oregon Avenue, over nearly 3 miles of farm country before the next stop, at Lieb Cellars Tasting Room. This is a major vineyard operation with the largest plot of Pinot Blanc in the States, and an extensive portfolio of sparkling and still wines. Tastings are held in a converted barn on the scenic property.

Continue on Oregon Avenue, then turn right onto Bridge Lane. This is another quiet road with farmland views on the left, shaded by tree-filled yards on the right.

When the road reaches North Road (CR 48), bear right at the fork then turn right, into a wide shoulder along the fast main route. Use extra caution when crossing side streets, as the shoulder frequently converts into a turning lane a few yards before the intersection. Outside of a short strip-mall after Cox Lane, most of CR 48 is quite scenic, despite the traffic.

The final vineyard is also the first vineyard on Long Island. Just less than 2 miles from the turn onto CR 48, Castello di Borghese Vineyard and Winery will be on the left, on the other side of CR 48. Carefully turn left, onto Alvahs Lane, to the vineyard.

When ready, carefully use Alvahs Lane to re-cross CR 48, and turn left to continue for another three-quarters of a mile. Bear right onto North Road, a tiny strip of connecting asphalt, and then continue onto Wickham Avenue, retracing the outbound loop from earlier. Turn left to continue on Wickham in just over a mile, then turn right onto Pike Street, finishing at the train station ahead.

Bike Shops

Twin Forks Bicycles: 121 East Main St., Riverhead; (631) 591-3082; twinforksbicycles.com
Country Time Cycle: 6955 Main Rd., Mattituck; (631) 298-8700; ctcycle.com

MILES AND DIRECTIONS

0.0 Start on Pike Street.

0.2 Left onto Wickham Avenue.

0.3 Cross CR 48.

0.5 Right onto Wickham Avenue.

1.2 Left onto Mill Lane.

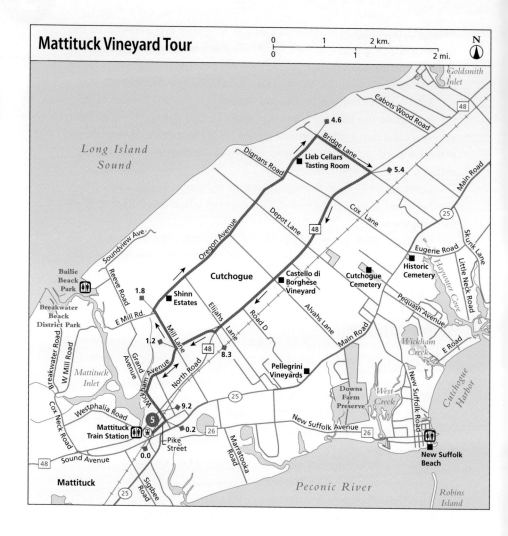

Mattituck Vineyard Tour

1.8 Right onto Oregon Avenue.

4.6 Right onto Bridge Lane.

5.4 Right onto North Road / CR 48.

8.3 Bear right onto North Road.

8.6 Continue on Wickham Avenue.

9.6 Left onto Wickham Avenue.

10.0 Right onto Pike Street.

10.2 Arrive at finish.

Castello di Borghese Vineyard

The first commercial winery on Long Island was opened on this property, in 1973, as Hargrave Vineyards. Louisa Hargrave and her then husband, Alex, grew grapes in a former potato field, against the advice of friends, family, and their accountant. Their story is recounted in Louisa's memoir, *The Vineyard,* now out of print but available second hand from online retailers.

The Hargraves sold the property in 1999 to Prince Marco and Princess Ann Marie Borghese, a low-key couple from Philadelphia who just happened to be Italian royalty. The two renamed it Castello di Borghese, maintaining the original vineyards and grape varietals, until Marco died in a car accident in 2014, shortly after Ann passed from cancer. The two were pillars of their North Fork community, remembered fondly as easy-going neighbors and friends.

The winery is operated today by their three children, Fernando, Giovanni, and Allegra, who continue to produce the wide variety of red, white, and blush wines that the vineyard is famous for.

RIDE INFORMATION

Local Events/Attractions

Mattituck Strawberry Festival: This yearly festival is timed to occur over Father's Day Weekend. Local strawberries are the primary focus, in desserts and on their own. For more information and tickets, visit the website: mattituckstrawberryfestival.org.

Downs Farm Preserve: This 51-acre nature preserve includes the historical site of Fort Corchaug, a log cabin fortification built by the local Corchaug tribe to fight off raids from the Narragansetts of Connecticut. The archaeological site is one of the few such sites undisturbed in the Northeast. The preserve has a tranquil mile-long hiking trail with excellent birding and a picturesque creek with waterfowl.

New Suffolk Beach: This quiet, scenic little beach in New Suffolk charges non-residents for daily parking. Lifeguards and attendants are on duty.

Bailie's Beach Park: Low-key town beach on Long Island Sound.

New Suffolk Beach: Peconic Harbor beach for New Suffolk, on the south side of the North Fork.

Restaurants

Shinn Estate Vineyards and Farmhouse: 2000 Oregon Rd., Mattituck; (631) 804-0367; shinnestatevineyards.com

Lieb Cellars Tasting Room: 13050 Oregon Rd., Cutchogue; (631) 734-1100; liebcellars.com

Castello di Borghese Vineyard and Winery: 17150 North Rd., Cutchogue, NY; (631) 734-5111; castellodiborghese.com

Lombardi's Love Lane Market: 170 Love Ln., Mattituck; (631) 298-9500; lombardislovelanemarket.com

Village Cheese Shop: 105 Love Ln., Mattituck; (631) 298-8556; thevillagecheeseshop.com

Love Lane Coffee: 240 Love Ln., Mattituck; (631) 298-8989; lovelanekitchen.com

Goodfood: 535 A Pike St., Mattituck; (631) 298-7599; gfperiod.com

Restrooms

1.8: Shinn Estate Vineyards and Farmhouse
4.6: Lieb Cellars Tasting Room
7.5: Castello di Borghese Vineyards

Shelter Island Loop

Shelter Island is rich in history and natural beauty, only a short ferry ride from the North and South Forks. The island was settled nearly 4,000 years ago by Algonquian-speaking people, erroneously called the Manhanset, who were largely assimilated by European settlers. The island is a popular tourism spot, but one-third of the land is set aside as nature preserve, protecting it from overdevelopment.

Start: North Ferry Terminal on Shelter Island

Length: 26.0 miles

Riding time: About 2 hours

Best bike: Road bike

Terrain and trail surface: Asphalt

Traffic and hazards: Traffic tends to be slower on Shelter Island, especially when busy. Drivers are used to seeing cyclists on these popular riding roads.

Things to see: Kousa dogwoods are planted all over the island, especially on NY 114, and flower in the summer. In the fall, the trees produce red fruit, and the leaves turn a brilliant purple. Ram Island provides many picturesque views, especially along the causeways, as does Shore Road near the end of the ride.

Fees: The ferry charges a small fee for bicyclists, payable by cash or check only.

Getting there: Take NY 25 to Greenport and turn right onto NY 114 to the North Ferry terminal just ahead. By train, take the Long Island Rail Road to the Greenport station; the ferry terminal is within sight from the train platform.

GPS: N41 05.218' / W72 21.482'

THE RIDE

This ride shakes things up after the flat farmland riding throughout the North Fork. Maximum elevation gain is still low, only 85 feet, but the steep and short climbs bring the total elevation gain to over 1,200 feet. Riders who struggle on hills may wish to cut the ride short, riding from the North Ferry terminal to Ram Island or Shore Road and Crescent Beach.

The route begins at the North Ferry terminal on Summerfield Place. Climb the short hill into the historic neighborhood of Shelter Island Heights and bear right onto Grand Avenue (NY 114). This is a narrow little one-way road, winding uphill through open yards and past several historic homes in a variety of architectural styles, from the artsy folk styles of the eighteenth century to the elaborate colonial revival buildings of the end of the nineteenth century.

After the hill, the road opens for two-way traffic. Bear left to stay on Grand Avenue, past the distinctive historic building housing the Chequit, an upscale bed and breakfast. The next block passes restaurants and cafes along the main commercial strip on the island before the route turns left, down Chase Avenue. Descend to the bridge and cross onto Bridge Street, through a small maritime district of shops and a marina. As the road curves right, the route turns left, onto Winthrop Road.

This quiet neighborhood street winds past a number of homes before crossing a small bridge, with views of Gardiners Creek to the right and Dering Harbor on the left. Note the historical marker for Shelter Island, honoring the first European settler, Nathaniel Sylvester, as the road curves left, following the coast.

Winthrop Road heads slightly uphill and plateaus with an open view on the left of Dering Harbor, a very pretty protected spot full of sailing boats. Bear right, onto Locust Road, past a picturesque pond on the right. Dering Harbor is both the body of water and the village these roads head through; the total population was at a low of 11 in 2010, making it the least populated village in New York.

Locust Road ends at a grassy triangle. Bear right then turn right onto Manhanset Road, and then bear right again to stay on Manhanset. After 0.3 mile of manicured lawn and rustic farm-style fences, bear left onto Dinah Rock Road, through the Gardiner's Bay Country Club property. After a short stretch through the golf course, bear left to stay on Dinah Rock Road, uphill, into a shaded, tree-filled neighborhood. Turn left to continue on Dinah Rock Road at the first intersection over a series of little rolling hills.

The homes are a mix of contemporary and traditional shingle-style architecture, built mostly on the water, along the left. The route turns left onto

Hiberry Lane, then right onto Point Lane. Point Lane curves around Hay Beach Point, ending in a T-junction with Gardiners Bay Drive. Turn left onto the drive and head downhill on this quiet, shaded road.

Turn left onto Ram Island Drive, at the 4.4-mile mark, for a long scenic stretch of road. The route cruises along a flat causeway with beautiful views in both directions, then into a hilly little neighborhood, before bearing left to continue on Ram Island Drive, back onto another gorgeous causeway, longer than the last and more open.

After the causeway, follow Ram Island Drive up the next hill, past the Ram's Head Inn, and stay left to continue onto North Ram Island Drive. The route follows the road as it curves around the island, then turns right onto South Ram Island Drive, before a private beach. Turn left at the Ram's Head Inn, retracing the outbound route along Ram Island Drive.

Ram Island Drive turns left at the 10.0-mile mark, with Gardiners Bay Drive on the right. After more scenic harbor views, turn left onto North Cartwright Road. Near the 12.2-mile mark, enter a traffic circle, and take the second exit onto South Ferry Road (NY 114). NY 114 continues along a sometimes-busy road to the South Ferry terminal, on a spit of land jutting out into the Peconic River with picturesque views. After a stop, turn around,

View from the causeway

and head three-quarters of a mile back on NY 114 to a left turn onto South Midway Road.

This quiet little road winds around through densely forested areas and past tall privet fences until it swings right, with a view of Dickerson Creek on the left, and enters a small neighborhood. The route takes the second left to stay on South Midway Road, through another marshy area past several shingle-style homes. South Midway follows the water on the left, and then heads out, slightly uphill, to a four-way intersection with Smith Street.

Turn left onto Smith for a half-mile, and then right onto Menantic Road for another mile of woodsy neighborhood riding. At West Neck Road, turn left, for a short, steep hill along the Shelter Island Town recreation area.

Turn left again, before the wayfinding signs, to stay on West Neck Road. The route will pass the West Neck Bay ahead, a lovely sheltered spot full of small boats and docks, and continue, bearing right at a yield sign, to a four-way intersection with Brander Parkway.

Turn left onto Brander Parkway, a faster road through a mix of open land and small homes, until the fork. Bear left onto North Brander Parkway, past the grassy triangle, for a third of a mile, until the route curves right onto East Brander Parkway.

Quiet spot near Shore Road

The parkway curves around to the right and becomes Peconic Avenue, a similar tree-lined street with some lovely water views on the left. At the stop sign, turn left to stay on Peconic Avenue, which dead ends at a scenic view of marshy Crab Creek ahead. Turn right just before the dead end onto Lilliput Lane, then left onto Brander Parkway. Pass West Neck Avenue, on the right, and continue on Nostrand Parkway, a very exclusive street with incredible mansions, primarily along the left.

Nostrand Parkway ends in a T-junction with Rocky Point Avenue. Turn right, following the sign for Quinipet Camp, and then bear left onto Shore Road for a nearly mile-long ride along Crescent Beach past old resorts and vacation properties.

After the beach, bear right up the big hill, following Shore Road back to West Neck Road. Continue, keeping the golf course and recreation area on the left, to the intersection of West Neck and New York Avenue, and then turn left onto New York Avenue.

> ### Bike Shops
> **Piccozzi's Bike Shop:** 177 North Ferry Rd., Shelter Island Heights; (631) 749-0045; jwpiccozzi.com

Follow New York Avenue back into Shelter Island Heights, bearing right at a fork onto Grand Avenue, and into familiar territory from the start of this ride. Turn right onto Chase Avenue again, but then turn left before the bridge onto Cedar Avenue and bear right, following the water and signage, back to the ferry terminal.

MILES AND DIRECTIONS

0.0 Start at North Ferry then right onto Grand Avenue.

0.3 Left onto Chase Avenue.

0.4 Continue on North Ferry Road / NY 114.

0.6 Left onto Winthrop Road.

1.4 Right onto Locust Road.

1.8 Right onto Manhanset Road.

2.1 Left onto Dinah Rock Road.

2.9 Left onto Highberry Lane.

3.0 Right onto Point Lane.

Shelter Island Loop

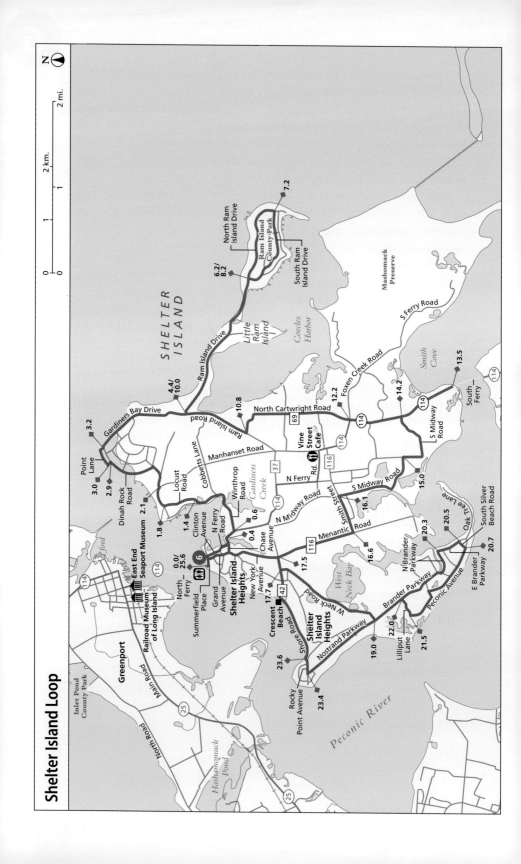

3.2 Right onto Gardiners Bay Drive.

4.4 Left onto Ram Island Drive.

6.2 Continue on North Ram Island Drive.

7.0 Right onto Ram Island Drive.

7.2 Right onto South Ram Island Drive.

8.2 Left onto Ram Island Drive.

10.0 Left onto Ram Island Road.

10.8 Left onto North Cartwright Road.

12.2 Enter traffic circle, take second exit onto South Ferry Road.

13.5 Turn around.

14.2 Left onto South Midway Road.

16.1 Left onto Smith Street.

16.6 Right onto Menantic Road.

17.5 Left onto West Neck Road.

17.7 Left to continue on West Neck Road.

19.0 Left onto Brander Parkway.

20.0 Bear left onto North Brander Parkway.

20.3 Right onto East Brander Parkway.

20.5 Right onto South Silver Beach Road.

20.7 Right onto Peconic Avenue.

21.3 Left to continue on Peconic Avenue.

21.8 Right onto Lilliput Lane.

22.0 Left onto Brander Parkway.

22.4 Continue on Nostrand Parkway.

23.4 Right onto Rocky Point Avenue.

23.6 Left onto Shore Road.

24.9 Left onto New York Avenue.

25.4 Continue on Grand Avenue.

25.5 Right onto Chase Avenue.

25.6 Left onto Cedar Avenue / NY 114.

25.9 Left onto Summerfield Place / NY 114.

26.0 Arrive at finish.

RIDE INFORMATION

Local Events/Attractions

Shelter Island Chamber of Commerce: The chamber maintains an active web presence to assist residents and visitors. Their site lists the town beaches: Crescent Beach, Wades Beach, Menhaden Lane Beach, Shell Beach, and Fresh Pond. Crescent and Wades have comfort stations and lifeguards. Details and maps are available on the Shelter Island Chamber site: shelterislandchamber .org/beaches.

They also maintain an exhaustive calendar of events, festivals, fairs, and concerts: shelterislandchamber.org/community-calendar.

Restaurants

Stars Cafe: 17 Grand Ave., Shelter Island; (631) 749-5345
Marie Eiffel Market: 184 North Ferry Rd., Shelter Island; (631) 749-0003; marieeiffelmarket.com
Eagle Deli: 25 West Neck Rd., Shelter Island; (631) 749-5363
Vine Street Cafe: 41 South Ferry Rd., Shelter Island; (631) 749-3210; vinestreetcafe.com
Shelter Island Heights Pharmacy: 19 Grand Ave., Shelter Island; (631) 749-0445
Tuck Shop Ice Cream: 75 North Menantic Rd., Shelter Island; (631) 749-1548
Shelter Island Craft Brewery: 55 North Ferry Rd., Shelter Island; (631) 749-5977; shelterislandcraftbrewery.com

Restrooms

0.0: North Ferry Terminal
13.5: South Ferry Terminal
24.0: Crescent Beach

Riverhead to Iron Pier

Riverhead is on the edge of the North Fork, at the head of the Peconic River. Similar in many respects to neighboring Southold, this town contains a number of hamlets and villages, with a healthy wine industry. The downtown is a lively commercial district, home to locally owned retail, an eclectic restaurant scene, and the Long Island Aquarium, a regional highlight.

Start: Peconic Riverfront Park on Heidi Behr Way

Length: 19.2 miles

Riding time: About 1 hour 30 minutes

Best bike: Road bike

Terrain and trail surface: Asphalt

Traffic and hazards: Cross River Drive is essentially a highway: Many riders may want to skip this short section by continuing on Main Road (NY 25) and turning right onto Hubbard Avenue, which rejoins the mapped route. Use caution on the short stretches of NY 25 and CR 48, especially when turning left across NY 25 onto Manor Lane and when turning left across CR 48 onto Doctors Path. The rest of the roads covered are slower-speed, local, and very peaceful.

Things to see: The Long Island Aquarium, Iron Pier Beach, Jamesport, Indian Island County Park, South Jamesport Beach, wineries, and vineyards.

Fees: None. There is a municipal lot and many other options for free parking.

Getting there: Take NY 25 to Riverhead, and turn right on Peconic Avenue, then immediately left onto Heidi Behr Way, following signs for municipal parking.

Transit users disembark at the Riverhead station, turn right from Railroad Avenue onto Griffing Avenue, then left onto NY 25. Take the first right onto Peconic Avenue, then left onto Heidi Behr Way as above.

GPS: N40 54.985' / W72 39.589'

THE RIDE

This ride starts in downtown Riverhead, along the Peconic Riverfront Park, and passes near the South Jamesport Beach on a bucolic route to Iron Pier Beach in the north. Both beaches are beautiful, but Iron Pier Beach, surrounded by beautiful farmland full of historic buildings, is usually considered the top destination. You can evaluate both beaches for yourself with a quick 1.6-mile detour, noted in the narrative below. The route is light on hills and should not be particularly challenging.

Starting on Heidi Behr Way, follow the road to McDermott Avenue, keeping the waterfront walking trail on your right. Turn left onto McDermott, then right onto Main Road, following the sign for bike NY 25. Downtown can be dense with traffic and parked cars: Use caution, and watch the door zone until the shoulder widens past the Long Island Aquarium.

Before the train tracks, turn right onto Riverside Drive into a quiet neighborhood through the heavily forested Peconic Estuary. After the Riverhead Golf Course the route reaches Cross River Drive, essentially a highway—four lanes, separated by a median, with traffic operating at 55 mph. The shoulder is large, and should be comfortable for the 0.4-mile stretch on Cross River,

Iron Pier Beach

but anyone with reservations should bypass this stretch, following the detour detailed in "traffic and hazards" above.

Following the route, bear right at the first turn to Indian Island County Park onto Indian Point Road, then turn right into the park. Turn left at the 2.1-mile mark to stay on Indian Point Road, possibly unmarked here, following signage for the park offices and restrooms. Follow the little road through an opening for walkers and cyclists, over the railroad track, then right onto Hubbard Avenue.

Hubbard Avenue is a long, straight stretch of road, bordered by railroad property and woods. Turn right at the first intersection, toward and then over the railroad tracks, onto Meeting House Creek Road. The road crosses a little bridge next to Meeting House Creek Park then curves right behind the marina.

At the dead end sign ahead, turn left onto Peconic Bay Boulevard, one of the most scenic roads in the area. The route follows 2.4 miles of Peconic Bay Boulevard winding through open farmland and past picturesque bay views, all on a wide road with minimal traffic.

At the four-way intersection with South Jamesport Avenue, the route turns left. To take a quick detour to South Jamesport Beach, follow Peconic

Farmland in Riverhead

Bay Boulevard to Town Beach Drive, a half-mile ahead and turn right to the beach. Round-trip detour adds 1.6 miles.

The mapped route turns left up South Jamesport Avenue, a tiny little village center with bakeries, boutiques, and delis. Turn right onto Main Road, then left onto Manor Lane, just after the oldest building on the East End, the Jamesport Meeting House.

Manor Lane heads gently uphill through 2.4 miles of farms and vineyards, ending in a T-junction at a usually quiet section of Sound Avenue (CR 48). Carefully turn left, then right onto Pier Avenue, until the road ends at Iron Pier Beach, a well-developed town beach with bike racks, seasonal snack sales, and restrooms.

After visiting the beach, turn around and take the first right onto Sound Shore Road, a mostly residential street with stretches of open field and forest. Turn left onto Pennys Road at the 12.5-mile mark, a quiet country road, ending in a T-junction with Sound Avenue.

The road is 45 mph here but quite scenic, passing a number of farm stands and open markets. Just before the 15-mile mark, where the shoulder narrows, prepare to turn left onto Doctors Path, being mindful of the faster traffic around you.

Bike Shops

Twin Forks Bicycles: 121 East Main St., Riverhead; (631) 591-3082; twinforksbicycles.com
Country Time Cycle: 6955 Main Rd., Mattituck; (631) 298-8700; ctcycle.com

Doctors Path is scenic but still fast. Be attentive, especially at the crossing with Northville Turnpike, and then again approaching East Main Street (NY 25). Follow East Main Street back into downtown Riverhead, then turn left onto McDermott Avenue to Heidi Behr Way to arrive at the finish.

MILES AND DIRECTIONS

0.0 Start on Heidi Behr Way then left onto McDermott Avenue.

0.2 Right onto East Main Street / NY 25.

0.5 Right onto Riverside Drive.

1.5 Left onto Cross River Drive.

1.9 Slight right toward Indian Island County Park.

2.0 Right onto Indian Point Road.

2.1 Left to stay on Indian Point Road toward park offices and restrooms.

2.5 Right onto Hubbard Avenue.

3.3 Slight right onto Meeting House Creek Road.

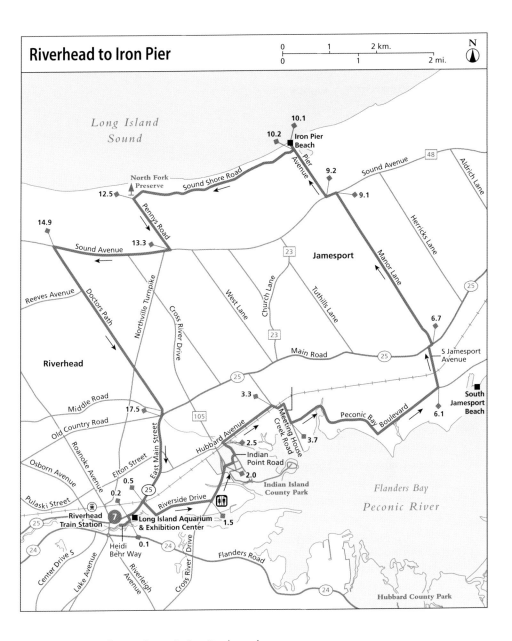

Riverhead to Iron Pier

3.7 Left onto Peconic Bay Boulevard.

6.1 Left onto South Jamesport Avenue unless following detour (below).

   Optional Detour: Cross South Jamesport to continue on Peconic Bay Boulevard, then right onto Town Beach Road at 6.6, to visit South Jamesport Beach. Round-trip detour adds 1.6 miles to following mileage points.

6.7   Cross Main Road / NY 25 and left onto Manor Lane.

9.1   Left onto Sound Avenue / CR 48.

9.2   Right onto Pier Avenue.

10.1   Turn around.

10.2   Right onto Sound Shore Road.

12.5   Left onto Pennys Road.

13.3   Right onto Sound Avenue / CR 48.

14.9   Left onto Doctors Path.

17.5   Cross and continue onto East Main Street / NY 25.

19.0   Left onto McDermott Avenue then right onto Heidi Behr Way.

19.2   Arrive at finish.

RIDE INFORMATION

Local Events/Attractions

Long Island Aquarium: This innovative aquarium is full of family-friendly exhibits, especially appealing to children, in large, well-designed habitats. The Aquarium also operates a large scientific program and a rescue and rehabilitation center for dolphins, sea turtles, and other marine animals. The centerpiece is a 120,000-gallon shark tank. Longislandaquarium.com.

Railroad Museum of Long Island: This museum showcases the history of trains in Long Island, at two separate locations in Riverhead and Greenport. Admission includes a ride on the miniature World's Fair Train and a guided tour of each location. Visitors are encouraged to ride the Long Island Rail Road both ways, as the two museums are located at the stations in each town. The museum is open on weekends only. rmli.org.

Riverhead Beaches: Riverhead operates four beaches, all with restrooms and other amenities: Reeves Beach, South Jamesport Beach, Iron Pier Beach, and Wading River Beach. riverheadrecreation.net/beaches.html.

Riverhead Farmers' Market: Open every Saturday from mid-November to the end of April, downtown Riverhead hosts an indoor market for farmers and artisans to sell crafts, produce, and prepared food.

Suffolk County Historical Society: This historical society was founded just after the Civil War and built the current structure in 1930. They operate a museum and gift shop with special exhibits, tours, and an extensive permanent collection. suffolkcountyhistoricalsociety.org.

Jamesport Meeting House: Built as a church in 1731, the oldest building on the East end of Long Island is now a not-for-profit event venue, hosting Broadway shows, classical concerts, Shakespearean works, lectures, and a local spelling bee. jamesportmeetinghouse.org.

Restaurants
Goldbergs Bagels: 130 East Main St., Riverhead; (631) 740-9131; theoriginalgoldbergsbagels.com
Village of Riverhead Delicatessen: 318 East Main St., Riverhead; (631) 369-7302
Blue Duck Bakery Cafe: 309 East Main St., Riverhead; (631) 591-2710; blueduckbakerycafe.com
Farm Country Kitchen: 513 West Main St., Riverhead; (631) 369-6311; farmcountrykitchen.net
Junda's Pastry Crust & Crumbs: 1612 Main Rd., Jamesport; (631) 722-4999; jundaspastry.com

Restrooms
0.0: Municipal lot
2.1: Indian Island County Park
10.1: Iron Pier Beach

South Fork and the Hamptons

The South Fork is known for being a glitzy, glamorous location, made popular by the rich and famous who live in magnificent estates throughout the Hamptons. It's also home to the working class, who staff the boutiques, restaurants, and attractions throughout the area, and a newly arrived middle-class of commuters who still work in even more expensive New York City.

This section explores the length of the Hamptons, including the easternmost portion at Montauk Point; the beaches and more modest villages of East Hampton; historic Sag Harbor; the rural communities of North Sea and Noyac; the most beautiful beaches in Southampton; and, lastly, the communities of Westhampton Beach and West Hampton Dunes, along the western border.

Highlights of the area include the first lighthouse in the United States, commissioned by President George Washington at Montauk Point, a stunning causeway along Noyac Bay, dozens of beautiful Atlantic Ocean beaches, and pristine nature preserves, all freely accessible via bicycle. Historically, the area was the site of the first English settlement in New York, a major whaling center, and the site where the US Navy took the *Amistad*, the ship commandeered by the enslaved men and women who'd been transported on it as if they were cargo.

Most visitors arrive via the Montauk Highway, New York State Route 27, although the Long Island Rail Road's Montauk Line provides service to Hampton Bays, Southampton, Bridgehampton, East Hampton, Amagansett, and Montauk. The train operates on only one line, making the service slow and unpopular. Many visitors prefer the Hampton Jitney bus line, which accepts bicycles with an additional fee. Ferry access is offered to Montauk, albeit irregularly, from New London, CT, Block Island, RI, and Martha's Vineyard, MA. The South Ferry makes regular runs to and from Shelter Island.

Montauk Point Ride

Montauk Point is an 862-acre park on the easternmost tip of Long Island, containing the oldest lighthouse in New York and spectacular views of the Atlantic Ocean where it meets Block Island Sound. The location is a popular tourist attraction, with walking trails, a rocky ocean beach, and a monument to the Amistad, *the Spanish slave-trade schooner, and its final crew of fifty-three people from Sierra Leone.*

Start: Amagansett station of the Long Island Rail Road in the hamlet of Amagansett

Length: 33.6 miles

Riding time: About 2 hours 45 minutes

Best bike: Road bike

Terrain and trail surface: Asphalt

Traffic and hazards: Much of this ride takes place on Montauk Highway (NY 27), which can be quite busy with tourists. Most of the road has a wide shoulder and should feel comfortable, but use caution when crossing NY 27 in downtown Amagansett and exiting Napeague Meadow Road onto NY 27 later in the ride.

Things to see: Montauk Point, scenic vistas of the Atlantic Ocean, the Art Barge near Napeague, and beautiful marshland between Amagansett and Napeague.

Fees: None. The train station offers free parking, as does the nearby municipal lot behind the library and town hall.

Getting there: Follow the Southern State Parkway toward Eastern Long Island, and take exit 40 for Robert Moses Causeway South toward Oceans Beaches. Take exit RM1E to NY 27E/Montauk. Follow NY 27E through Amagansett; the train station is on the left.

Transit users can take the Long Island Rail Road to the Amagansett station, where the ride starts.

GPS: N40 58.783' / W72 07.904'

THE RIDE

This sometime hilly ride covers 16.5 miles from Amagansett to Montauk Point, with a number of food stops and points-of-interest along the route. Amagansett and Montauk are both hamlets of the town of East Hampton. Both are popular tourist destinations, but Montauk in particular is full of hotels, restaurants, and amenities for visitors.

The route starts just outside of Amagansett at the Long Island Rail Road station. Exit onto Main Road (NY 27), headed west, and turn left, carefully crossing NY 27 onto Atlantic Avenue. This village road passes along a historic cemetery and through a small residential neighborhood, bordered by privet bushes, street trees, and white slat fences.

The route turns left at the intersection with Bluff Road, just before the Atlantic Avenue Beach, part of the next route (East Hampton Beach Cruise, Rte. 9). Follow Bluff Road to NY 27, then carefully cross, mindful of oncoming traffic, onto Cranberry Hole Road.

After a small bridge over the railroad tracks, bear right to stay on Cranberry Hole Road, through a long, mostly uninhabited stretch of woods and marshlands. At the 4.0-mile mark, turn right onto Napeague Meadow Road, another long, quiet road through the wilds.

Near the end, note The Art Barge on the left, a gallery and studio space founded by Victor D'Amico, the founding Director of the Education Department at the Museum of Modern Art.

Just ahead, the road curves to the right and ends in a T-junction with NY 27. Carefully turn left and ride the wide shoulder along this sometimes fast and busy highway, bordered by wetlands and summer resort properties.

At the 6.9-mile mark, where the road forks, bear right onto the Old Montauk Highway. This slower road runs parallel to the main highway and affords numerous vistas of the Atlantic Ocean on the right. One of the longest stretches of unobstructed views occurs near the end of the road, approaching the intersection with NY 27 in Montauk. Bear right onto NY 27 and head downhill into the commercial strip, which has a number of food stops and retail offerings. The shoulder has parking; use caution navigating the next mile or so.

The road heads into a sometimes-steep section of rolling hills over the next several miles. The last steep climb comes just after Deep Hollow Ranch, the oldest ranch in the United States, and ends with a scenic overlook in 1,000 feet.

The route heads downhill to flat after the overlook, and then bears right into Montauk Point Park. Just past a turn for Camp Hero State Park, the lighthouse should come into view, up NY 27 and on the right. Continue following NY 27 through the park, with possible stops at the lighthouse or the concession area and pavilion, until the loop exits the park back onto NY 27.

Montauk Point Lighthouse

NY 27 covers familiar territory back to downtown Montauk. Stay on NY 27 this time, skipping the bypass on Old Montauk Highway to avoid having to make a dangerous turn across NY 27. At the 28.8-mile mark, turn right onto Napeague Meadow Road, to a left turn onto Cranberry Hole Road.

Follow Cranberry Hole Road for 2.6 miles, turning left at the end onto NY 27, and follow NY 27 back into Amagansett, ending at the train station.

Bike Shops

The Amagansett Beach & Bicycle Company: 1 Cross Hwy., Amagansett; (631) 267-6325; amagansettbeachco.com
Montauk Bike Shop: 725 Montauk Hwy., Montauk; (631) 668-8975; montaukbikeshop.com
Bermuda Bikes Plus: 36 Gingerbread Ln., East Hampton; (631) 324-6688; bermudabikes.com
Khanh Sports: 60 Park Place, East Hampton; (631) 324-0703; khanhsports.com

MILES AND DIRECTIONS

0.0 Start at Amagansett Train Station.

0.1 Left onto Atlantic Avenue.

0.6 Left onto Bluff Avenue.

1.4 Cross Montauk Highway / NY 27 onto Cranberry Hole Road.

4.0 Right onto Napeague Meadow Road.

Montauk Point Ride

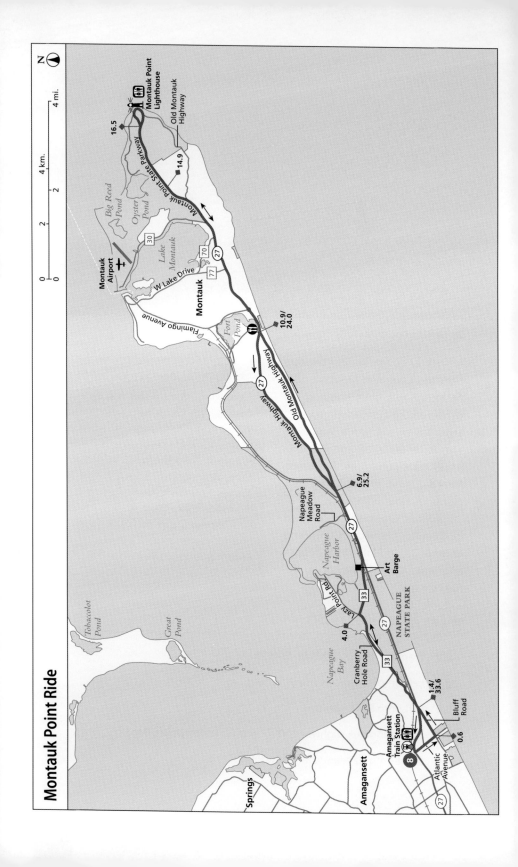

Montauk Point Lighthouse

Old Montauk Highway

16.5

14.9

Montauk Point State Parkway

Big Reed Pond

Oyster Pond

30

Lake Montauk

W Lake Drive

77

70

27

Montauk Airport

Montauk

Flamingo Avenue

Fort Pond

10.9/24.0

Old Montauk Highway

27

Montauk Highway

6.9/25.2

27

Napeague Meadow Road

Napeague Harbor

Art Barge

33

NAPEAGUE STATE PARK

Tobaccolot Pond

Great Pond

Napeague Bay

Lazy Point Road

4.0

Cranberry Hole Road

33

Springs

Amagansett

Amagansett Train Station

8

Atlantic Avenue

27

1.4/33.6

Bluff Road

0.6

N

0   2   4 km.

0   2   4 mi.

5.2 Left onto Montauk Point State Parkway / NY 27.

6.9 Slight right onto Old Montauk Highway.

10.9 Right onto Montauk Highway / NY 27.

16.5 Slight right on park loop.

17.4 Right to stay on Montauk Highway / NY 27.

23.0 Continue on Montauk Highway / NY 27.

28.8 Right onto Napeague Meadow Road.

30.1 Left onto Cranberry Hole Road.

32.7 Right onto Montauk Highway / NY 27.

33.6 Arrive at finish.

RIDE INFORMATION

Local Events/Attractions

Victor D'Amico Institute of Art and The Art Barge: In 1955, in the middle of a long career at the Museum of Modern Art, Victor D'Amico started a summer series of painting classes in distant East Hampton, Long Island. Five years later, he had acquired and anchored a retired Navy Barge in Napeague Harbor where he continued to teach until his death in 1987. The studio and gallery are open from June through the end of September each year. Theartbarge.org.

Montauk Point State Park: This site on the eastern tip of Long Island houses the oldest and first lighthouse in New York, commissioned by President George Washington in 1792. Hiking, fishing, surfing, and picnicking make the park a popular tourist destination.

Montauk County Park: Beach access, hiking, biking, and horseback riding are all permitted at this park, formerly known as the Theodore Roosevelt County Park. Historically, this site was an American headquarters during the Spanish-American War, and served as a quarantine for ill yet victorious soldiers, including Roosevelt and his Rough Riders. This route passes one of the entrances to the park, a half-mile along NY 27, after Montauk village and passing East Lake Drive on the left.

Montauk Sprint Triathlon & Relay: This national championship qualifying triathlon is a fundraiser for Montauk Lighthouse. Held at the end of July for more than 20 years, registration and details are provided on the Montauk Lighthouse site, at montauklighthouse.com.

Camp Hero State Park: This 415-acre park on the border of Montauk Point park includes miles of trails for hiking, biking, and horseback riding. Swimming is not permitted due to safety concerns, but the beach is considered one of the best in the world for surf fishing.

East Hampton Town Marine Museum: Just off the route, on Bluff Avenue, this East Hampton Historical Society property uses three floors of exhibits to tell the story of Long Island's East End community through photographs, artifacts, and displays. The museum is open from the end of April through Columbus Day weekend. A complete list of East Hampton Historical Society properties is available on its website, easthamptonhistory.org.

Deep Hollow Ranch: Operated continuously since its founding in 1658, this site claims to be the oldest cattle ranch in America. The location hosts educational tours and horseback rides. deephollowranch.com.

Restaurants

Mary's Marvelous: 207 Main St., Amagansett; (631) 267-8796; marysmarvelous.com

Jack's Stir Brew Coffee: 146 Montauk Hwy., Amagansett; (631) 267-5555; jacksstirbrew.com

Lobster Roll Restaurant: 1980 Montauk Hwy., Amagansett; (631) 267-3740; lobsterroll.com

Clam Bar at Napeague: 2025 Montauk Hwy., Amagansett; (631) 267-6348; clambarhamptons.com

SagTown Coffee Montauk: 19 South Elmwood Ave., Montauk; (631) 668-8021; sagtown.com

Goldberg's Famous Bagels (Napeague): 2101 Montauk Hwy., Amagansett; (631) 267-5552; goldbergsmontauk.com

Goldberg's Famous Bagels (Montauk): 28 South Etna Ave., Montauk; (631) 238-5976; goldbergsmontauk.com

Naturally Good Foods & Cafe: 779 Montauk Hwy., Montauk; (631) 668-9030; naturallygoodfoodsandcafe.com

La Fondita: 74 Montauk Hwy., Amagansett; (631) 267-8800; lafondita.net

Brent's General Store: 8 Montauk Hwy., East Hampton; (631) 267-3113; brentsgeneralstore.com

Herb's Market: 778 Montauk Hwy., Montauk; (631)668-2335; herbsmontaukmarket.com

Restrooms

17.0: Montauk Point State Park

Montauk Village

The first Europeans in Montauk were cattle farmers from nearby East Hampton, who pastured their animals here. Today, the area is a tourist destination full of historical sites and beautiful beaches.

Start: Municipal parking lot in Montauk at the intersection of Euclid Avenue and Edison Street.

Length: 15.8 miles

Riding time: About 1 hour 15 minutes

Best bike: Road bike, although a shorter version detailed below, would be ideal for a hybrid ride.

Terrain and trail surface: Asphalt

Traffic and hazards: Use caution when crossing the angled train tracks on Industrial Avenue. Flamingo Avenue is a busy road, but it has a wide shoulder. Exercise caution when turning left from West Lake Drive onto NY 27: Oncoming traffic is fast and has no stop.

Things to see: Montauk beaches and historical sites.

Fees: None. Parking is free in the Montauk municipal lot.

Getting there: Follow the Southern State Parkway toward Eastern Long Island and take exit 40 for Robert Moses Causeway South toward Oceans Beaches. Take exit RM1E to NY 27E/Montauk. Follow NY 27E to Montauk. Turn left onto Edison Street to the lot at the intersection with Euclid Avenue.

Transit users can take the Long Island Rail Road to the Montauk station, and either start the ride here, adjusting mileage points by +2.5 miles, or where the ride starts. Turn right onto Flamingo Avenue to Edgemere Street, around the east side of Fort Pond, and turn left onto Euclid Avenue. The ride start is at the municipal lot ahead, at the intersection with Edison Street.

GPS: N41 01.951' / W71 56.864'

THE RIDE

This route showcases the beaches, parks, historical attractions, and commercial districts of Montauk village over a fairly flat 15.8 miles. This route starts in downtown Montauk and circles around Fort Pond before heading northeast to Montauk Harbor. From Montauk Harbor, it follows the western shore of Lake Montauk south and then north, up the eastern shore, to Gin Beach.

Riders looking for a short, easy hybrid route could simply cut off the East Lake Drive portion by skipping Old West Lake Drive. For this shorter route, follow West Lake Drive directly to NY 27 and then turn right, continuing along the mapped route, for an 8.3-mile ride. The full or shortened loop can also be added to Amagansett to Montauk Point (Rte. 8) for a 40-mile plus ride.

To start the ride, exit right onto South Edison Street to Main Road (NY 27) and turn right through bustling downtown Montauk. After an open stretch on the south shore of Fort Pond, turn right onto South Delrey Road, then right onto Second House Road.

The road follows a quiet section along Fort Pond, curves away to the left, then back, following the contour of the pond around on a right-hand turn over Midland Drive to Industrial Road. After the angled railroad tracks, the route crosses a small causeway through the pond, then turns left onto

Water view from road shoulder

Edgemere Street. Stay left to continue onto Flamingo Avenue, a wide-shouldered road, for a long uphill section.

The shoulder starts to narrow before a zippy downhill stretch after the top of the climb, leading to the intersection with West Lake Drive. Cross the intersection into Montauk Harbor and follow the road to make a counterclockwise circle, past Gosman's Dock and a vista of craggy, rocky shores.

The road becomes West Lake Drive in the curve after the view, and then crosses Flamingo Avenue headed south. This section is built-up with car-centric commercial spaces, but maintains a wide shoulder and lower speed limits.

The First People of Long Island

Carbon dating establishes a tribal presence on Long Island as far back as 2000 B.C., but little is known about these early groups. When European settlers from New England arrived in eastern Long Island in the early seventeenth century, they found a wide-ranging group of people seemingly led by the Montaukett tribe, a group of fishers, hunters, and farmers, based on the South Fork. The Montauketts were actually part of the Lenape nation, but the Europeans referred to them by the place name they used for their area.

The Narragansett and Pequot frequently raided these lands, taking wampum and food from the resource-rich but peaceful people of the island. The ravages of war and illnesses brought by Europeans decimated their numbers, leading to an unpopular alliance with settlers from New England. Despite disagreements over land use and property, the Montaukett persisted as a recognized tribal group until a 1910 court decision declared them extinct, allowing a Brooklyn-based developer to annex their land and clear it to develop tracts for luxurious summer homes.

The development plan failed and the property was purchased by the US Army, which established Camp Wikoff as a quarantine for Army personnel returning from the Spanish–American War. The property would later be condemned by Robert Moses and preserved as state parks.

Today, the Montaukett Indian Nation is a federally unrecognized group of more than 600 people living in the Montauk area who claim a relation to the Shinnecock Indian Nation in Southampton. The group successfully reversed the 1910 decision and is actively seeking restoration of their state and federal recognition. The nation maintains an active web presence to share their history, activism, and events, at montaukett.org.

Take the left turn onto Old West Lake Drive, at the 6.6-mile mark, watching for faster through traffic.

This mile-long road passes some scenic views of Lake Montauk on the left before entering a quiet residential neighborhood. Bear left as it ends in a T-junction with NY 27 and carefully turn left, following NY 27 for a third of a mile.

Watching for through traffic again, take the left onto East Lake Drive for a quiet ride on a mostly flat road through the Montauk County State Park properties, detailed below in the attractions section. The road ends at Gin Beach, where the route turns around, and returns to NY 27.

Turn right onto NY 27 and follow it back to Montauk Village, climbing one little hill right before the end and then turning right onto South Edison Street in the descent, to arrive at the finish.

MILES AND DIRECTIONS

0.0 Start on South Edison Street and turn right onto Main Road (Montauk Highway / NY 27).

0.7 Right onto South Delrey Road then Second House Road.

1.6 Right onto Midland Road then Industrial Road.

2.3 Left onto Edgemere Street.

2.4 Slight left onto Flamingo Avenue / NY 49.

4.3 Cross West Lake Drive, continuing on Flamingo Avenue.

4.5 Left onto West Lake Drive.

5.0 Cross Flamingo Avenue, continuing on West Lake Drive.

6.6 Left onto Old West Lake Drive.

7.6 Left onto Montauk Point State Parkway / NY 27.

7.9 Left onto East Lake Drive.

10.8 Turn around.

13.7 Right onto Montauk Point State Parkway / NY 27.

15.8 Right onto South Edison Street to arrive at finish.

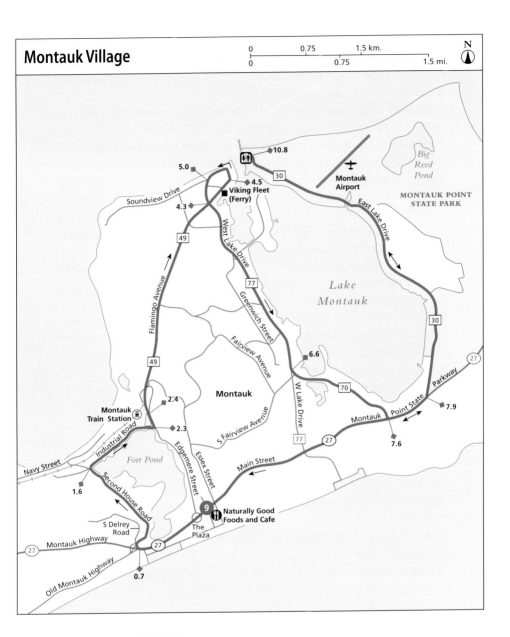

Montauk Village

0   0.75   1.5 km.

0   0.75   1.5 mi.

N

RIDE INFORMATION

Local Events/Attractions

Montauk Historical Society: The Montauk Historical Society manages the Montauk Lighthouse, featured in ride 8, and the Second House, the oldest structure in Montauk. First built in 1746, it burned down and was rebuilt in 1797. At the time, Montauk was being used as pastureland for farmers in

East Hampton, who brought their cattle and sheep to graze. First, Second, and Third House were built as places for the shepherds to stay. The Montauk Indian Museum is located on the grounds of the Second House Museum. Montaukhistoricalsociety.com.

Montauk County Park: Beach access, hiking, biking, and horseback riding are all permitted at this park, formerly known as the Theodore Roosevelt County Park. Historically, this site was home to the Third House and an American headquarters during the Spanish–American War. The site served as quarantine for ill yet victorious soldiers, including Teddy Roosevelt and his Rough Riders. This route passes two entrances to the park: The first is south of the airport, for the Big Reed Nature Trail; the second, near the end of East Lake Drive, north of the airport, where the park office is with easy beach access.

Montauk Beaches: This route passes near most of the beaches on Montauk. Ditch Plains Beach, Kirk Park Beach, and Gin Beach are all on or just off the main route. Visit the On Montauk site for more information about these popular beach spots, at onmontauk.com/montauk-beaches/.

Culloden Point: This little peninsula north of Montauk was named for the H.M.S. *Culloden*, a British warship that ran aground here about 60 years before the *Amistad* used it to anchor. The wreck is an underwater national archaeological site, first discovered in the 1970s.

Depot Gallery: The Montauk Artists' Association operates an art gallery and school in the original waiting room of the Montauk Station. montaukartistsassociation.org.

Restaurants

Naturally Good Foods & Cafe: 779 Montauk Hwy., Montauk; (631) 668-9030; naturallygoodfoodsandcafe.com

SagTown Coffee Montauk: 19 South Elmwood Ave., Montauk; (631) 668-8021; sagtown.com

Herb's Market: 778 Montauk Hwy., Montauk; (631)668-2335; herbsmontaukmarket.com

Goldberg's Famous Bagels: 28 South Etna Ave., Montauk; (631) 238-5976; goldbergsmontauk.com

La Brisa: 752 Montauk Hwy., Montauk; (631) 668-8338; tacombi.com/locations/Montauk

Montauk Brewing Company: 62 S Erie Ave., Montauk; (631) 668-8471; montaukbrewingco.com

Ben & Jerry's: 478 West Lake Dr., Montauk; (631) 668-9425

Gin Beach Market: 541 East Lake Dr., Montauk; (631) 668-3088

Restrooms

4.5: Gosman's Dock
10.8: Gin Beach

East Hampton Beaches

The Town of East Hampton stretches across most of the South Fork, from Sag Harbor, a hamlet it shares with Southampton, to Montauk Point, the eastern tip of Long Island. East Hampton was a remote farming community until the 1950s. It's now known as a playground for the rich and famous. Step up to the bar at one of the upscale taverns in downtown East Hampton though, and you're more likely to find yourself standing next to a local farmer than a celebrity. The village feels distinctly New England in style, due to preservation efforts that have maintained features dating to the 1648 settlement by colonists from Massachusetts and Connecticut. The iconic windmills, another distinctive regional feature, were a later addition, built in the early nineteenth century.

Start: The East Hampton Main Beach on Ocean Avenue

Length: 10.7 miles

Riding time: About 1 hour

Best bike: Road bike or hybrid

Terrain and trail surface: Asphalt

Traffic and hazards: This ride covers quiet back roads through the town of East Hampton and should be suitable for almost any cyclist. This would be a good ride for parents and children.

Things to see: Beautiful Hamptons' beaches, New England style mansions, and cute, historic sites along the route.

Fees: Parking is strictly monitored in East Hampton. Residents and non-residents can buy beach-parking passes, usually in advance, or pay for commercial parking in downtown, with a 2-hour maximum most of the year. On-street parking has a 1-hour maximum at most. For longer visits, park at the Lumber Lane lot, which charges a small fee for overnight parking.

Getting there: Follow the Southern State Parkway toward Eastern Long Island, and take exit 40 for Robert Moses Causeway South toward Oceans Beaches. Take exit RM1E to NY 27E/Montauk. Follow NY 27E to East Hampton; turn right onto Ocean Avenue and, with a permit, park at East Hampton Main Beach. For the commercial lots, follow NY 27 into East Hampton and follow local signs. For the Lumber Lane Lot, follow NY 27 into East Hampton village, and turn left onto Newtown Lane, then left again onto Railroad Avenue. Take the next left onto Lumber Lane; the parking lot will be in one block, where the road meets Gingerbread Lane. Once parked, retrace your steps to NY 27, and follow it to Ocean Avenue to East Hampton Main Beach. Transit users can take the Long Island Rail Road to the East Hampton station and ride to the beach following the instructions above.

GPS: N40 56.632' / W72 11.654'

THE RIDE

This is a flat, fairly easy ride, which takes you along quiet streets to some of the loveliest beaches on Long Island. It's a popular area for families to ride with children, and the short distance, lack of traffic, and beautiful scenery make this ride appealing to a variety of cyclists.

This ride starts at the East Hampton Main Beach, a gorgeous, wind-swept beach with clean sand and a great view south of Long Island into the Atlantic Ocean. East Hampton is popular but often secluded, thanks to the access restrictions and limited non-resident parking permits issued.

Follow Ocean Avenue away from the beach, through the quintessential Hamptons made familiar by popular media: Regal mansions tower over massive privet hedges, and private drivers smoke outside of limousines while they wait for their employers.

Approaching the fork, bear right onto James Lane, past a charming town pond up a little side street. On the left are the historic South End Cemetery and the Town Green, on the right, St. Luke Episcopal Church and several historical society buildings, including the Mulford Farm, built around 1680, and one of the many vintage windmills throughout the town.

After passing the farm, the route turns right onto Dunmere Avenue, a quiet, tree-lined road with more privet-fenced homes. Dunmere passes through Maidstone Club, a surprisingly attractive private golf course and club, before crossing a narrow creek from Hook Pond, onto Further Lane.

Gardiner Windmill

The route bypasses two beaches that can be visited with quick detours: Highway Behind the Pond, just after the bridge, leads to Wiborg Beach; and the next right onto Old Beach Lane leads to Egypt Beach.

Continuing on the mapped route, Further Lane is a neighborhood road bordered by lovely homes, with a mix of architectural styles including classic New England shingle-style buildings and graceful Italianate villas.

Further Lane ends in a T-intersection with Indian Wells Highway. Turn right onto this slightly busier, narrow road, then turn left at the next intersection onto Bluff Avenue. To make a quick detour to Indian Wells Beach, skip the left turn and travel another block to the end of Further Lane.

Continuing on the route, Bluff Road passes nature preserve land and the East Hampton Town Marine Museum before reaching the four-way intersection with Atlantic Avenue. Turn right to follow the route to Atlantic Avenue Beach, a quiet little beach in the middle of a dune preserve. The dunes are off-limits to visitors for the safety of nesting birds and the ecosystem. It is a smaller beach, but has seasonal concessions and restrooms. Atlantic Avenue is fairly safe and slow, but faster than the other roads this route covers. Even if riding with children, avoid the sidewalks, which are in poor condition and provide poor sight lines to the many driveways.

Atlantic Avenue Beach

Bike Shops

Bermuda Bikes Plus: 36 Gingerbread Ln., East Hampton; (631) 324-6688; bermudabikes.com

Khanh Sports: 60 Park Place, East Hampton; (631) 324-0703; khanhsports.com

The Amagansett Beach & Bicycle Company: 1 Cross Hwy., Amagansett; (631) 267-6325; amagansettbeachco.com

Sag Harbor Cycle Company: 34 Bay St., Sag Habor; (631) 725-1110; sagharborcycle.com

After visiting Atlantic Avenue Beach, turn around, follow Atlantic Avenue back to Bluff Road, and retrace the outbound route. Amagansett has some coffee and deli offerings in a small village district, easily accessible by continuing an additional block up Indian Wells Highway past Further Lane. East Hampton has a much larger downtown district brimming with cute boutiques and cafes, primarily near the intersection of Newtown Lane and Main Road (NY 27), just a half-mile up Main Road after turning right off of Dunemere Lane.

MILES AND DIRECTIONS

0.0 Start at East Hampton Main Beach on Ocean Avenue.

0.6 Right onto James Lane.

1.0 Right onto Dunemere Lane.

1.8 Continue on Further Lane.

East Hampton Beaches

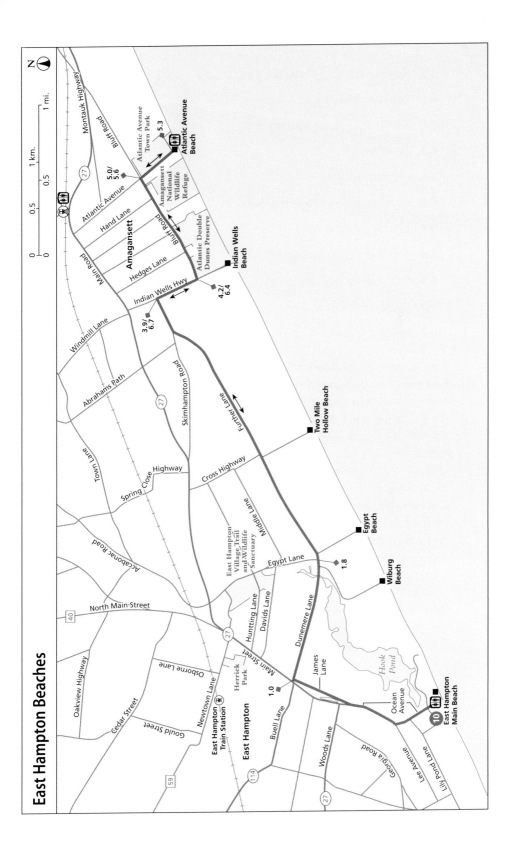

3.9 Right onto Indian Wells Highway.

4.2 Left onto Bluff Road.

5.0 Right onto Atlantic Avenue.

5.3 Turn around.

5.6 Left onto Bluff Road.

6.4 Right onto Indian Wells Highway.

6.7 Left onto Further Lane.

8.8 Continue on Dunemere Lane.

9.6 Left onto James Lane.

10.0 Continue on Ocean Avenue.

10.7 Arrive at finish.

Events and attractions

East Hampton Historical Society: The Society maintains a number of properties: the Mulford Farm, the Osborn-Jackson House, the Clinton Academy, the East Hampton Town Marine Museum, the Town House, and the Hook Schoolhouse. The Mulford Farm is one of the most significant English Colonial farmsteads, built around 1680; the other properties date to the eighteenth century. All of the properties are open to visitors. Hours and more information are available on the Society website, at easthamptonhistory.org.

East Hampton Beaches: East Hampton has a number of beautiful beaches in the north and south of the region. North beaches are on the Peconic Bay, and the southern beaches are on the Atlantic Ocean. Many of the southern beaches appear on this route or are accessible via quick detours. Current information is available on the East Hampton town website, at easthamptonvillage.org/beaches.htm.

Pollock-Krasner House and Study Center: This home was inhabited by Lee Krasner and Jackson Pollock; Pollock was considered the leader of the Abstract Expressionist movement, and Krasner was an influential artist known for work that spanned many different styles. The couple purchased the home shortly after marrying, and lived and worked there until their deaths. The home and studio are open to tours and visitors on a seasonal basis. sb.cc.stonybrook.edu/pkhouse.

Amagansett Farmers Market: Local farmers sell their produce every weekend in June, and daily from July to Aug, at 367 Main St. in Amagansett.

East Hampton Farmers Market: Open on Fridays in the summer at 136 North Main St. in East Hampton.

Sag Harbor Whaling and Historical Museum: This architectural beauty is full of artifacts and exhibits on the history of the whaling industry in Sag Harbor. sagharborwhalingmuseum.org.

Restaurants

Citarella Gourmet Market: 2 Pantigo Rd., East Hampton; (631) 283-6600; citarella.com

Golden Pear Cafe: 34 Newtown Ln., East Hampton; (631) 329-1600; goldenpearcafe.com

Scoop Dujour: 35 Newtown Ln., East Hampton; (631) 329-4883

Goldberg's Famous Bagels: 100 Pantigo Place, East Hampton; (631) 329-8300; goldbergsbagels.org

Mary's Marvelous: 207 Main St., Amagansett; (631) 267-8796; marysmarvelous.com

Jack's Stir Brew Coffee: 146 Montauk Hwy., Amagansett; (631) 267-5555; jacksstirbrew.com

La Fondita: 74 Montauk Hwy., Amagansett; (631) 267-8800; lafondita.net

Brent's General Store: 8 Montauk Hwy., East Hampton; (631) 267-3113; brentsgeneralstore.com

Starbucks: 39 Main St., East Hampton; (631) 329-8645; starbucks.com

Restrooms

0.0: East Hampton Main Beach

5.3: Atlantic Avenue Beach

11

Springs: Parks and Beaches

The quiet hamlet of Springs differs considerably from its governing town of East Hampton. Where East Hampton is wealthy and exclusive, Springs is home to working-class residents who live in modest homes on quiet neighborhood streets and commute into New York City to work in a variety of fields, from construction to personal finance to maintenance. The area features several beautiful bay front parks, with quiet, calm waters and sandy, dune-covered beaches.

Start: Amagansett municipal parking lot, behind the library and town hall

Length: 18.9 miles

Riding time: About 1 hour 30 minutes

Best bike: Road bike

Terrain and trail surface: Asphalt

Traffic and hazards: This route primarily follows quiet, back roads. Use caution when crossing the busier roads, which may not have stop signs.

Things to see: Wildlife in natural marshland environments, historic buildings, and scenic views of Gardiners Bay.

Fees: None. Parking is free in the municipal lot of Amagansett. Follow posted signs, as some spots are limited to 2 hours.

Getting there: Follow the Southern State Parkway toward Eastern Long Island, and take exit 40 for Robert Moses Causeway South toward Oceans Beaches. Take exit RM1E to NY 27E/Montauk. Follow NY 27E through Amagansett; the municipal lot behind the library is on the left. Transit users can take the Long Island Rail Road to the Amagansett station, then follow NY 27 to the municipal lot behind the library where the ride starts.

GPS: N40 58.523' / W72 08.475'

THE RIDE

This 18.9-mile loop starts in the East Hampton hamlet of Amagansett then heads to the northwest for a clockwise tour of Springs, the quiet hamlet to the northeast. Most of the route is fairly flat, with only two climbs of any real consequence, for a total elevation gain of 495 feet.

The route starts at the library on Main Road (Montauk Highway / NY 27). Exit the parking lot and turn right onto Main Road, a fairly busy stretch of road with a generous shoulder, then take the first right onto Windmill Lane, a quieter, pleasant road that heads uphill past the historic Oak Grove Cemetery. The next several streets make up the first climb of the route, which will cover more than 100 feet of climbing over the next two miles, before a long downhill to the Harbor Creek area.

Windmill Lane ends at a T-junction with Town Lane, across from Balsam Farm Stand to the right. Turn left onto Town Lane for the next third of a mile, then take the first right onto Abrahams Path, at the four-way intersection.

Abrahams Path is another quiet road, starting off in a heavily wooded area, passing the East Hampton Golf Club property before crossing Accabonac Road at a busy intersection. Traffic on Accabonac has no stop, so proceed with caution. The road reaches max elevation on the next short stretch, then heads downhill, to Springs Fireplace Road (CR 41). Turn right and take the first left to continue on Abrahams Path.

At the end of Abraham's Path, the route turns right onto Three Mile Harbor Hog Creek Road, possibly the least prosaic street name throughout Long Island. This slightly busy road fronts the Three Mile Harbor, and passes a number of marinas and seafood restaurants. Traffic is busy by the intersection, by the view of the harbor, but traffic volume and speeds decline after the second marina, near Gardiners Lane.

At the 5.9-mile mark, with the Maidstone Market & Deli visible across the intersection on the right, turn left onto Flaggy Hole Road, following signs for the beach and Camp Blue Bay. Take the first left, onto Maidstone Park Road, just before a no outlet sign, following the sign for the beach.

Bear right at the fork to enter the park, just after Michael's Restaurant. The park road continues counterclockwise around a sports field then down a short descent with an amazing view of Gardiner's Bay, a large, open body of water beyond a grassy beach. The road curves around a quarter-mile stretch through a salt marsh and nature preserve, with hiking trails and osprey platforms.

The park road exits right, back onto Maidstone Park Road. Backtrack on the road, turning right onto Flaggy Hole Road, to the earlier intersection with Three Mile Harbor Hog Creek Road. Turn left, passing the general store on your right, and continue on a section of road bordered by nature preserve land, heading northeast into Springs.

The road curves sharply to the right, meriting a caution sign, and becomes Hog Creek Road. Turn immediately left onto Kings Point Road, then left again onto Fenmarsh Road, a tiny connecting street that ends at Water Hole Road. Turn left for a short stretch until the route turns right at the small intersection with Hog Creek Lane.

Hog Creek Lane is a relatively quiet road with a small shoulder running through a neighborhood of both seasonal homes and year-round cottages. When Hog Creek Lane ends at the stop sign, turn right onto Springs Fireplace Road, along the white slatted fence.

This long road curves and winds through a quiet neighborhood full of nature preserves and sanctuary land. Just before Old Stone Highway, the Pollock-Krasner House appears on the left. This significant art landmark is detailed below in the Ride Information section.

After passing the Pollock-Krasner House, the route turns left onto Old Stone Highway, at the 12.0-mile mark, through a historic town green surrounded by a series of historic buildings: The Parsons Blacksmith Shop, the old town hall, and on the left, the Springs Community Presbyterian Church, dating to 1882. After the church, the road passes the Springs General Store, a deli and market, which also served as the first post office in Springs, built in 1844.

Old Stone Highway is a fairly quiet road, primarily bordered by parks and preserve land, with very few homes. Turn left to stay on Old Stone Highway where it intersects with Neck and Accabonac Roads in a slightly confusing collection of forks and grassy triangles.

Turn left onto Louse Point Road at the next triangle. This narrow little road circles around the East Harbor, through a marshy woodland section and then into open, gorgeous tidal marshes and wetlands. This is a haven and nesting area for shorebirds, which dash crustacean shells against the road to open them. The cracked and broken shells can be quite sharp, and will easily puncture most tires, so use caution riding here.

Bear right to follow the road as it approaches the water, up to Louse Point Town Beach. Swimming is prohibited, but this is an excellent spot for birding and

Bike Shops

Bermuda Bikes Plus: 36 Gingerbread Ln., East Hampton; (631) 324-6688; bermudabikes.com

Khanh Sports: 60 Park Place, East Hampton; (631) 324-0703; khanhsports.com

The Amagansett Beach & Bicycle Company: 1 Cross Hwy., Amagansett; (631) 267-6325; amagansettbeachco.com

Sag Harbor Cycle Company: 34 Bay St., Sag Harbor; (631) 725-1110; sagharborcycle.com

View of Accabonac Harbor from Louse Point

nature watching. After sightseeing, turn around and retrace the route back to Old Stone Highway, turning left at the intersection.

Old Stone Highway features the steepest climb of the ride, a 100-foot effort with grades from 3.0 to 6.0 percent, before the route bears right onto Town Lane, a quiet rural road through farmland and forests, heading downhill. When the Balsam Farm Stand appears on the right, turn left, back onto Windmill Lane, for a short distance into Amagansett.

Turn right onto Main Road, finishing the ride back at the municipal lot behind the library.

MILES AND DIRECTIONS

0.0 Start on Montauk Point State Parkway / NY 27 / Main Road.

0.1 Right onto Windmill Lane.

0.8 Left onto Town Lane.

1.1 Right onto Abrahams Path.

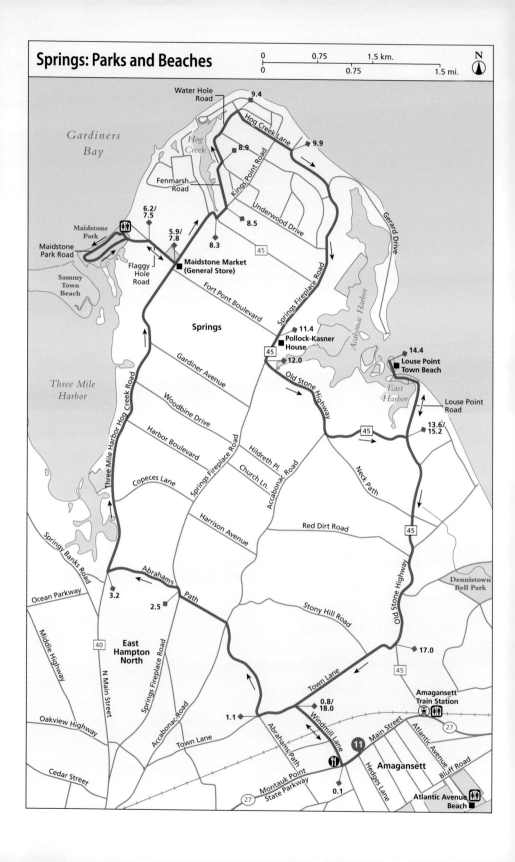

Springs: Parks and Beaches

0   0.75   1.5 km.

0   0.75   1.5 mi.

N

Gardiners Bay

Hog Creek

Water Hole Road

9.4

Hog Creek Lane

8.9

9.9

Fenmarsh Road

Kings Point Road

Underwood Drive

6.2/7.5

Maidstone Park

Maidstone Park Road

5.9/7.8

8.5

8.3

Flaggy Hole Road

Maidstone Market (General Store)

45

Gerard Drive

Sammy Town Beach

Fort Pont Boulevard

Springs

Springs Fireplace Road

Acabonac Harbor

Three Mile Harbor

11.4

Pollock-Kasner House

14.4

Louse Point Town Beach

45

12.0

Old Stone Highway

East Harbor

Louse Point Road

Gardiner Avenue

Three Mile Harbor Hog Creek Road

Woodbine Drive

Harbor Boulevard

Springs Fireplace Road

Hildreth Pl.

Church Ln.

Accabonac Road

Neck Path

45

13.6/15.2

Copeces Lane

Harrison Avenue

Red Dirt Road

45

Springy Banks Road

Dennistown Bell Park

Ocean Parkway

Abrahams

3.2

Path

2.5

Stony Hill Road

Old Stone Highway

Middle Highway

N Main Street

East Hampton North

40

Springs Fireplace Road

17.0

Amagansett Train Station

45

Oakview Highway

Accabonac Road

Town Lane

Town Lane

0.8/18.0

27

1.1

Windmill Lane

11

Main Street

Atlantic Avenue

Amagansett

Bluff Road

Cedar Street

Abrahams Path

Hedges Lane

0.1

Montauk Point State Parkway

27

Atlantic Avenue Beach

2.5 Right onto Springs Fireplace Road then left to continue on Abrahams Path.

3.2 Right onto Three Mile Harbor Hog Creek Road.

5.9 Left onto Flaggy Hole Road.

6.2 Left onto Maidstone Park Road.

7.5 Right onto Flaggy Hole Road.

7.8 Left onto Three Mile Harbor Road.

8.2 Right onto Hog Creek Road.

8.3 Left onto Kings Point Road.

8.5 Left onto Fenmarsh Road.

8.9 Left onto Water Hole Road.

9.5 Right onto Hog Creek Lane.

9.9 Right onto Springs Fireplace Road / CR 41.

12.0 Left onto Old Stone Highway.

12.9 Left to continue on Old Stone Highway.

13.6 Left onto Louse Point Road.

14.4 Turn around.

15.2 Left onto Old Stone Highway.

17.0 Right onto Town Lane.

18.0 Left onto Windmill Lane.

18.7 Left onto Montauk Point State Parkway / NY 27 / Main Road.

RIDE INFORMATION

Events and Attractions

Maidstone Beach: This quiet beach on the bay is a hidden gem, primarily visited by locals and families. It isn't heavily developed, but it has both lifeguards and restrooms.

Louse Point Town Beach: This no-swimming beach is a protected wildlife habitat, full of shellfish and shorebirds.

Pollock-Krasner House and Study Center: This home was inhabited by Lee Krasner and Jackson Pollock; Pollock was considered the leader of the Abstract Expressionist movement, and Krasner was an influential artist known for work that spanned many styles. The couple purchased the home shortly after marrying and lived and worked there until their deaths. The home and studio are open to tours and visitors on a seasonal basis. sb.cc.stonybrook.edu/pkhouse.

Ashawagh Hall and Parsons Blacksmith Shop: These historical buildings in Springs offer a variety of events. The Ashawagh Hall property maintains a webpage with a calendar of upcoming events at ashawagh-hall.org.

Leiber Collection: This museum and gallery, in a Renaissance style Palladian structure, was built by Gerson and Judith Leiber in 2005, to house their collective multi-disciplinary art. The museum is surrounded by six planted gardens and a seventh garden of sculptural works. leibermuseum.org.

Restaurants

Maidstone Market & Deli: 514 Three Mile Harbor Hog Creek Rd., East Hampton; (631) 329-2830

Springs General Store: 29 Old Stone Hwy., East Hampton; (631) 329-5065; springsgeneralstore.com

Old Stone Market: 472 Old Stone Hwy., East Hampton; (631) 267-6244; oldstonemarket.com

Restrooms

6.3: Maidstone Beach

Southampton Beaches

The Town of Southampton, named for one of the British Earls of Southampton, is the oldest English settlement in New York. Puritans from the Massachusetts Bay Colony settled the area in 1640, and were said to have lived in peace with the already established Shinnecock Nation, who today still live in Southampton on the oldest reservation in America. The town comprises eleven beaches, seven miles of oceanfront, four historic districts, and a dizzying array of upscale boutiques and fine dining restaurants.

Start: Agawam Park in Southampton

Length: 13.0 miles

Riding time: About 1 hour

Best bike: Road bike or hybrid

Terrain and trail surface: Asphalt

Traffic and hazards: Most of this ride takes place on narrow, low-speed roads with bike-friendly signage. Meadow Lane can get flooded at its lowest points along the Shinnecock Bay. Be attentive when navigating parked cars on the very short stretch through downtown Southampton.

Things to see: Some of the most popular beaches on Long Island, impressive Hamptons mansions, many historic sites, and lovely water views.

Fees: None. There is ample free parking in the municipal lots in Southampton. Automobile parking is strictly regulated at the beaches, but bicycles are free.

Getting there: Follow the Southern State Parkway toward Eastern Long Island, and take exit 40 for Robert Moses Causeway South toward Oceans Beaches. Take exit RM 1E to NY 27E/Montauk. From NY 27E, turn right onto Tuckahoe Lane, then left onto County Rte. 80. Turn right onto Jobs Lane to arrive at Agawam Park. Follow local signs for parking: There is a municipal lot behind Jobs and Windmill Lane, near Rotations Bicycle Center. Transit users can take the Long Island Rail Road to the Southampton station. Turn right from the plaza onto Railroad Plaza, then left onto North Main Street, then left again onto Main Road at the junction. Follow Main Road to Jobs Lane. Turn right to arrive at Agawam Park.

GPS: N40 52.978' / W72 23.572'

THE RIDE

This route connects nearly every beach in Southampton while passing a number of historically significant sites and scenic views over 13.0 miles of pancake-flat road riding. The roads are narrow, slow speed, and bike-friendly. With the total elevation gain at 56 feet and the stops so frequent and so beautiful, this is a perfect sightseeing ride for cyclists of any level.

Starting by Agawam Park in downtown Southampton, exit Jobs Lane left, onto Pond Lane, and ride past the Cultural & Civic Center of Southampton, in an attractive brick building on the right. Agawam Lake provides scenic water views on the left, until the road curves to the right, becoming Ox Pasture Road, a neighborhood full of exclusive mansions behind privet hedge and ornate fencing.

Turn left onto First Neck Lane at the next stop sign to continue riding past more Hamptons mansions. Note the architecturally significant "White Fence," the Samuel L. Parrish house, at 409 First Neck Lane, on the left. This symmetrical Colonial Revival shingled home features a wrap-around porch and many other distinctive elements. At the second stop sign, continue straight onto Meadow Lane. This 4.2-mile long stretch passes more mansions, beach cottages, and marshy beachfront property, and (5) Southampton Beaches. The first is Coopers Beach, the only fully developed beach on this route. Second is Halsey Neck Lane, which is easy to miss: Look for the small parking lot and "Village Permit Required" signs.

After Halsey Neck, the view on the right opens up as the road heads along Heady Creek and Shinnecock Bay. When the houses start to fill in again the ride is near Road D, the third beach, and then another long stretch of bay front opens up as the ride passes Dune Beach and Road F beach, both easy to miss on little side lanes to the left.

The road ends at Shinnecock East County Park, an undeveloped beach at the tip of the peninsula into the bay. After a stop, turn around, and follow

Meadow Lane back to the intersection with First Neck Lane and Gin Lane, turning right onto Gin Lane.

The road passes Cryder Beach almost immediately, on the right, then St. Andrew's Dune Church, a historic free church housed since 1879 in a lovely pink Arts and Crafts-style building with Tiffany stained glass windows. The building was once a life-saving station for the beaches beyond. Next door, the Bathing Corporation of Southampton is an exclusive East Coast beach club in a lovely Spanish Revival style building. Just after the corporation building, note the driveway and parking for Gin Lane beach access.

Continue on Gin Lane, curving past more beachfront mansions, up to and past Little Plains Road, with that beach on the right. At the next stop sign, the road continues through Wyandanch Lane, past the beach on the right, before curving left onto Old Town Road, between Old Town Pond, left, and Old Town beach, right.

Bike Shops
Rotations Bicycle Center: 32 Windmill Ln., Southampton; (631) 283-2890; rotationsbicyclecenter.com
Sag Harbor Cycle Company: 34 Bay St., Sag Harbor; (631) 725-1110; sagharborcycle.com

Quiet Southampton beach on a windy day

Follow the road along the pond, making a hairpin left turn onto Old Town Crossing to Toylsome Lane, through a lovely, tree-lined neighborhood. Toylsome Lane ends in a T-junction with South Main Street, and the route turns right, toward downtown Southampton.

At the intersection with Jobs Lane, turn left into the thriving downtown district, and carefully bear left around the monument triangle to the finish at Agawam Park.

MILES AND DIRECTIONS

0.0 Start at Agawam Park on Jobs Lane, left onto Pond Lane.

0.3 Right onto Ox Pasture Road.

0.5 Left onto First Neck Lane.

1.2 Continue onto Meadow Lane.

5.4 Turn around.

9.7 Right onto Gin Lane.

11.9 Left onto Old Town Crossing and continue onto Toylsome Lane.

12.5 Right onto South Main Street.

12.8 Left onto Jobs Lane.

13.0 Arrive at finish.

RIDE INFORMATION

Local Events/Attractions

Agawam Park: This well-manicured public park sits on lovely Agawam Lake. It features Monument Square, which contains two outstanding monuments: The World War Memorial is a beautiful open structure with Grecian columns; the Pyrrhus Concer Marker honors a notable Southampton resident whaler who rescued Japanese sailors in 1845. Cannons are a common feature around the park and the rest of downtown, reflecting the naval history of the village.
Southampton Beaches: Southampton's beaches are among the best in the United States. Most are undeveloped. Coopers Beach is the only fully developed one, offering concessions, restrooms, and other amenities. This ride passes ten of the eleven beaches Southampton maintains: Coopers Beach, Halsey Neck Lane, Road D, Dune Beach, Road F, Cryder, Gin Lane, Little Plains, Wyandanch, and Old Town.

Southampton Beaches

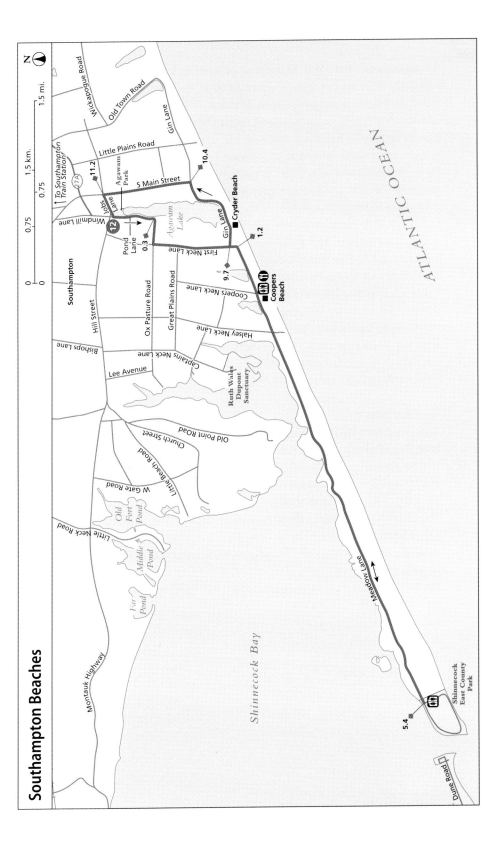

N

1.5 mi.

1.5 km.

ATLANTIC OCEAN

Shinnecock Bay

Wickapogue Road

Old Town Road

Gin Lane

Little Plains Road

To Southampton
Train Station

11.2

Agawam
Park

S Main Street

10.4

Cryder Beach

Jobs Lane

Windmill Lane

12

Pond
Lane

0.3

Agawam
Lake

Gin Lane

1.2

First Neck Lane

9.7

Coopers Neck Lane

Coopers
Beach

Southampton

Hill Street

Ox Pasture Road

Great Plains Road

Halsey Neck Lane

Bishops Lane

Lee Avenue

Captains Neck Lane

Ruth Wales
Dupont
Sanctuary

Old Point Road

Church Street

Little Beach Road

W Gate Road

Old
Fort
Pond

Little Neck Road

Middle
Pond

Far
Pond

Montauk Highway

Meadow Lane

Shinnecock East County
Park

5.4

Dune Road

Southampton Historical Society: Organized as the Colonial Society in 1898, the Society operates three museums: The Thomas Halsey Homestead, Pelletreau Shop, and Rogers Mansion. The Halsey Homestead, built in 1660, is believed to be the oldest English home in the state of New York. The Pelletreau Shop offers tours of the only seventeenth-century business in continuous operation in America: Currently, the space is occupied by a master jeweler who offers workshops on jewelry-making in addition to tours. The final structure, Rogers Mansion, is a historic mansion full of Victorian and Edwardian pieces, on the grounds of Old Southampton Village, complete with blacksmith and cobbler shops, a one-room schoolhouse, a Colonial-era barn, and a nineteenth-century paint store. Learn more at southamptonhistoricalmuseum.org.

Parrish Art Museum: Founded in 1897, this major museum has the largest collection of William Merritt Chase's work, along with an extensive, varied collection focused on American paintings of the twentieth and twenty-first centuries. Works by Roy Lichenstein, Jackson Pollock, Lee Krasner, and Willem de Kooning are included in the permanent collection. The museum moved from Southampton to nearby Watermill in 2012 into a new Herzog & de Meuron-designed building. Learn more at parrishart.org.

Restaurants

Coopers Beach Cafe: 268 Meadow Ln., Southampton; (631) 283-0003
Blue Duck Bakery Cafe: 30 Hampton Rd., Southampton; (631) 204-1701; blueduckbakerycafe.com
The Village Gourmet Cheese Shop: 11 Main St., Southampton; (631) 283-6949; villagecheeseshoppe.com
The Golden Pear Cafe: 99 Main St., Southampton; goldenpearcafe.com
Sip 'N Soda: 40 Hampton Rd., Southampton; (631) 283-9752; sipnsoda.com
Citarella Gourmet Market: 20 Hampton Rd., Southampton; (631) 283-6600; citarella.com
Starbucks: 29 NY 27A, Southampton; (631) 461-0246; starbucks.com

Restrooms

0.0: Agawam Park
1.8: Coopers Beach
5.4: Shinnecock Park

Big Fresh Pond Loop

North Sea is a quiet community on the Peconic, stretching from Sag Harbor to Southampton Town. The area is notable for its natural beauty, including the bucolic Big Fresh Pond, Wolf Swamp Sanctuary, Scallop Pond, North Sea Harbor, and lovely beachfront on Gardiners Bay. The area is primarily residential, and technically a hamlet of larger, more touristy, Southampton. This tightlyknit community wasn't always a sleepy hamlet, however: It was once home to Captain John Scott, the infamous polymath who rose to the title of President of Long Island following a successful career as a privateer, royal advisor, attorney, land speculator, and spy. His seventeenth-century home is believed to have been located where the historic estate of Colonel H. H. Rogers stands today.

Start: Intersection of Millstone Brook Road and Scotts Road in North Sea

Length: 5.7 miles

Riding time: About 30 minutes

Best bike: Road bike or hybrid

Terrain and trail surface: Asphalt

Traffic and hazards: Use caution when turning left onto North Sea Road from Parrish Road: Through traffic has no stop and North Sea Road is a busy thoroughfare.

Things to see: Lovely views of Big Fresh Pond, coastal views of Gardiners Bay at the northernmost point of the ride, views of North Sea Harbor, and stretches of conservation land fields and forests.

Fees: None. Roadside parking is free and none of the attractions charge admission.

Getting there: Follow the Southern State Parkway toward Eastern Long Island and take exit 40 for Robert Moses Causeway South toward Oceans Beaches. Take exit RM 1E to NY 27E/Montauk. From NY 27E, turn left onto Paumanok Path / Tuckahoe Road. Continue on Barkers Island Road.

Turn right at Millstone Brook Road to the intersection with Scotts Road. While not specifically a parking lot, this is where out-of-town visitors park to hike the trails through the Emma Rose Elliston Park and Wolf Swamp Sanctuary.

The nearest train station is the Long Island Rail Road station in Southampton, 4.0 miles away. From the train station, exit Railroad Plaza in a right turn onto North Main Street. Turn left at the T-intersection with North Sea Mecox Road, then left onto North Sea Road and an immediate right onto West Neck Road. Turn right onto Millstone Brook Road ahead to the ride start.

GPS: N40 55.388' / W72 25.507'

THE RIDE

The highlight of this ride is 64-acre Big Fresh Pond and the quiet back roads that tie the park around the pond to the north coast of the hamlet. This ride is short and flat and would be ideal for recreational riders and nature lovers. If planning to hike into the park properties near the ride start, make sure to wear or bring a pair of flat shoes.

From the triangle, head south on heavilyshaded Millstone Brook Road, passing between the Wolf Swamp Sanctuary property on the right and the Emma Rose Elliston Park on the left.

Turn left onto Big Fresh Pond Road at the first chance. This curvy road runs through a quiet neighborhood that offers several views of the pond and heavy tree cover. After a mile or so, bear right onto Parrish Road at a fork, which ends just ahead in a T-junction with busy North Sea Road.

Carefully turn left onto North Sea Road. This is a major local thoroughfare with higher speeds, but the shoulder should make it comfortable for riding. North Sea doesn't have the type of downtown restaurant district that Southampton does, but two excellent local delis are near this turn on the right side of the route: Schmidt's Market, specializing in gourmet foods and seafood, is first, and second, the North Sea General Store, a humble deli and snack stop.

This road passes a number of historic attractions. Just off the route, on Millstone Brook Road to the left, is the historic North Sea Burial Grounds. After Millstone Brook Road, and before Noyac Road, the Rose-Elliston House is on the right and the Captain John R. Rose House on the left.

The shoulder narrows approaching the stop sign at the intersection with Noyac Road, although traffic volume and speed should decrease as well. After the stop sign, the A. Rose House appears on the left, diagonally across from a

View of Big Fresh Pond

marina. After a short residential stretch, the road approaches the Conscience Point area about a half-mile from the Noyac Road intersection. The J. Reeve House appears on the left, followed by the Tupper Boat House on the right, next to the Conscience Point Road. This is a nice tiny detour to view North Sea Harbor; the road ends at the water in about 400 feet.

After the Conscience Point area, North Sea Road becomes incredibly scenic, with beautiful vistas of marsh and wetlands on the left. The road passes one more point of interest before ending at the water. The North Sea Beach Colony, a 100-year old summer community founded by working-to-middle class vacationers whose grandchildren come back every year, is denoted on the right by a historic sign.

Bike Shops

Rotations Bicycle Center: 32 Windmill Ln., Southampton; (631) 283-2890; rotationsbicyclecenter.com
Sag Harbor Cycle Company: 34 Bay St., Sag Harbor; (631) 725-1110; sagharborcycle.com

The road ends just ahead at a beach on a scenic section of Peconic Harbor. Directly ahead is Nassau Point, where Albert Einstein vacationed from 1937 to 1939. To the left is Robins Island, a 435-acre private island owned by hedge fund manager Louis Bacon.

After a beach break, turn around and ride a half-mile back on North Sea Road, bearing right onto Scotts Road at the fork just before a lovely open field. The Port of Missing Men, a historic estate, is minimally visible on the right. One of the structures, sadly not visible from the road, is believed to be the 1661 residence of Captain John Scott.

Scotts Road continues through forest and conservancy lands, only sparsely developed for residential use, on a slight uphill section before arriving back at the start where Millstone Brook Road intersects.

MILES AND DIRECTIONS

0.0   Start on Millstone Brook Road.

0.2   Left onto Big Fresh Pond Road.

1.3   Right onto Parrish Road.

1.4   Left onto North Sea Road.

3.8   Turn around.

4.3   Right onto Scotts Road.

5.7   Left onto Millstone Brook Road, arrive at finish.

RIDE INFORMATION

Local Events/Attractions

Emma Rose Elliston Memorial Park: The Rose family has been in North Sea since the area was settled by Europeans and the family members are still active members of the community. They bequeathed this property in 1951 and have since grown it into more than 100 acres of undeveloped land. The park provides access to Big Fresh Pond, the second largest lake on Long Island and a popular local swimming hole. Hiking trails abound. Members of the Rose family still live in their historic homes throughout the hamlet, while other houses have been sold. These are private residences, although many can be viewed from the road on this route. They include A. Rose House, a lovely brownstone foundation two-story farmhouse built in 1873; the Captain John R. Rose House, a Greek Revival-style farmhouse still inhabited by the Captain's descendants; and the Rose-Elliston House, a modest one-story home believed to be a temporary residence when the Captain John house was in construction.

North Sea Burial Grounds: This cemetery dates to 1782. It's bordered by lovely decorative fencing, and features the headstones of many members of the Rose family.

Conscience Point and Conscience Point National Wildlife Refuge: The first European settlers are believed to have landed here, before establishing a thriving port town. Many of them would relocate east and form Sag Harbor, which quickly overtook North Sea as the primary port town on the bay. Conscience

Big Fresh Pond Loop

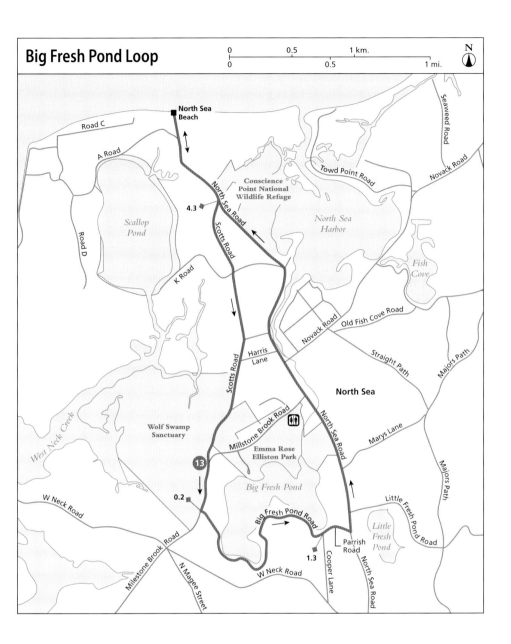

Point is a 6-acre park open for hiking and recreation. A 20-ton boulder marks the historic significance, much like the marker in Plymouth, Massachusetts.
Tupper Boathouse: This landmark is currently being renovated for historic preservation. It was originally a workshop for boat-builders at the end of the Roaring Twenties, and was later used as a nightclub.

Robins Island: Ownership of this island was in contention for decades. Lawsuits by the heirs of the original owner, Parker Wickham, kept it off the market. In 1993, it was purchased by hedge Fund manager Louis Bacon, who would later set aside all of the land under an easement to The Nature Conservancy, preventing development.

Little Fresh Pond: This route travels near Little Fresh Pond, accessible via Fresh Pond Lane with a quick detour right off of Parrish Road. The small pond is a popular swimming hole and one of the cleanest in the region, with an active and invested waterfront community. The only public access point is from Fresh Pond Lane.

Restaurants
Schmidt's Market: 1282 North Sea Rd., Southampton; (631) 702-2612
North Sea General Store: 1360 North Sea Rd., Southampton; (631) 283-1826
BOA Thai: 129 Noyac Rd., Southampton; (631) 488-4422; boathai.com
North Sea Tavern & Raw Bar: 1271 North Sea Rd., Southampton; (631) 353-3322; northseatavernrawbar.com

Restrooms
2.8: Conscience Point Marina

North Sea to Noyac

North Sea and Noyac, quiet hamlets of Southampton, are full of beautiful back roads and authentic country stores, making for convenient stops throughout a long tour of the area. This area borders two other Southampton hamlets, Sag Harbor and North Haven, and a glorious 1.5-mile causeway linking Noyac and North Haven. Outsiders spell the hamlet as Noyack, but local roads and residents prefer the alternative, and will usually write the name without the k. We'll go with the locals—no k.

Start: Intersection of Millstone Brook Road and Scotts Road in North Sea.

Length: 19.3 miles

Riding time: About 1 hour 45 minutes

Best bike: Road bike

Terrain and trail surface: Asphalt

Traffic and hazards: Use caution when turning left across many of the roads on this route. Oncoming traffic may not have a stop sign. A few sections along Noyac Road contain long parking lots that require careful attention.

Things to see: Harbor views, lovely back roads through forests and farmlands.

Fees: None.

Getting there: Follow the Southern State Parkway toward Eastern Long Island and take exit 40 for Robert Moses Causeway South toward Oceans Beaches. Take exit RM 1E to NY 27E/Montauk. From NY 27E, turn left onto Paumanok Path / Tuckahoe Road. Continue on Barkers Island Road. Turn right at Millstone Brook Road to the intersection with Scotts Road. While not specifically a parking lot, this is where out-of-town visitors park to hike the trails through the Emma Rose Elliston Park and Wolf Swamp Sanctuary.

The nearest train station is the Long Island Rail Road station in Southampton, 4.0 miles away. From the train station, exit Railroad Plaza in a right turn onto North Main Street. Turn left at the T-intersection with North Sea Mecox Road, then left onto North Sea Road and an immediate right onto West Neck Road. Turn right onto Millstone Brook Road ahead to the ride start.

GPS: N40 55.388' / W72 25.507'

THE RIDE

This ride starts in familiar territory but features a very different type of route from the previous chapter. Instead of gentle roads around the water, the route follows Millstone Brook Road to the east, past the Emma Rose Elliston Park, and then turns onto long, hilly, country roads, passing through forested sections of North Sea into nearby Noyac. Total elevation gain is 1,048 feet, nearly ten times that of the previous chapter, making this one of two hilly routes in the South Fork section.

From the fork with Scotts Road, turn left onto Millstone Brook Road for more than a half-mile of quiet back road before the road reaches the North Sea Burial Grounds, a lovely historic cemetery, and then ends in a T-junction with North Sea Road. Turn right onto this busier road, past car dealerships and local retail, then carefully turn left, shortly after passing the North Sea General Store, onto Little Fresh Pond Road. It's easy to miss this turn: If you see Schmidt's Market, you've just passed it.

Cross the intersection with Majors Path at the stop sign and continue on Edge of Woods Road ahead. This road is aptly named: It's surrounded by forest on a long, tranquil section of road. Other sights over the next 2.4 miles include pastoral fields and rustic split rail fences. Of historical interest to cyclists, Spencer Wright operated Traffic Circle Design, a bicycle frame shop here from 2008 to 2011. While his shop is no longer open, he maintains a Flickr gallery showcasing the high-end commuter frames he built at flickr.com/photos/trafficbikes/sets.

At the stop sign, cross 7 Ponds Town Road and continue on Edge of Woods Road, just ahead to the left, bordered on each side by the horse enclosures of Meadow View Farms. After the farm, turn left at the stop sign onto Water Mill Town Road, where the road heads gently uphill. Bear right after a half-mile back onto Edge of the Woods Road, continuing slightly uphill, until the road ends, across from a nursery, in a T-junction with Deerfield Road.

Turn left onto a shaded, pretty road that has a narrow shoulder and slightly faster traffic. After 1.5 miles, turn right onto Middle Line Highway, another quiet country road that heads quickly downhill on a long, straight descent.

At the stop sign at the bottom of the last hill, turn right onto Millstone Road, a busier road with a generous shoulder. Just after the sweeping vista of farmland, take a quick left onto Old Sag Harbor Road, a tiny little side street, while watching for oncoming traffic.

Old Sag Harbor Road winds around, mostly flat, until ending in a stop at Brick Kiln Road. Carefully turn left onto this sometimes-busy road headed downhill to a stop sign. Brick Kiln Road turns right, but the route continues onward, onto Stoney Hill Road.

Stoney Hill Road heads downhill for another quick descent before ending at the intersection with Noyac Road. Continue straight ahead, past a farm stand on the right, onto Noyac Road.

> ### Bike Shops
> **Rotations Bicycle Center:** 32 Windmill Ln., Southampton; (631) 283-2890; rotationsbicyclecenter.com
> **Sag Harbor Cycle Company:** 34 Bay St., Sag Harbor; (631) 725-1110; sagharborcycle.com

Use caution continuing past the traffic circle ahead on the right and head uphill, following Noyac Road as it curves to the left. A quick detour is possible here, too. While the Noyac–North Haven causeway, on the right, is featured in the next chapter (Sag Harbor Loop), it provides a glorious 3-mile round-trip detour on this route. Simply turn right into the traffic circle, taking the first exit, and ride along the water until the causeway ends, then turn around and ride back to the intersection to continue on the mapped route.

The road heads into the village center of Noyac, which primarily consists of a market, deli, liquor store, and small, single-family homes. There may be on-street parking, so watch for car doors, and be attentive passing the suburban-style parking lots for the half-dozen businesses. After passing the marina on the right, the shoulder opens up again as the road continues into a scenic section over the creek that feeds Trout Pond to the south.

Just ahead is the Elizabeth A. Morton National Wildlife Refuge, an important ecological site detailed below, across from the Noyac Golf Club. The route continues along Noyac Road, bearing right at the fork with Deerfield Road for nearly 2 miles of tree-lined road, mostly headed downhill.

Use caution around the Peconic Marina on Wooley Pond, near the 16.3-mile mark, which has some picturesque water views and a high-volume parking lot fully open to the road. Just ahead on another forested section of road, the route passes another farm stand on the left and then a deli on the right.

The next landmark is a vista of the North Sea Harbor, opening up to the right, near the 17.6-mile mark. After the harbor, the road enters the little downtown of North Sea, which mostly consists of a volunteer firefighter station, community association, and Thai restaurant. Just ahead, the road ends in a T-junction with North Sea Road. Turn right and follow North Sea Road for a quarter-mile, turning left onto Harris Lane, then left again onto Scotts Road, a quiet road through nature preserve land. The route ends in a half-mile, back at the triangle where Scotts Road and Millstone Brook Road meet.

MILES AND DIRECTIONS

0.0   Start on Millstone Brook Road.

0.5   Right onto North Sea Road.

1.2   Left onto Little Fresh Pond Road.

1.8   Cross Majors Path and continue on Edge of Woods Road.

4.2   Left onto Water Mill Town Road.

4.7   Right onto Edge of Woods Road.

5.2   Left onto Deerfield Road.

6.7   Right onto Middle Line Highway.

8.0   Right onto Millstone Road.

8.5   Left onto Old Sag Harbor Road.

9.9   Left onto Brick Kiln Road.

10.1   Continue onto Stoney Hill Road.

11.0   Continue on Noyac Road.

18.5   Right onto North Sea Road.

18.7   Left onto Harris Lane.

18.8   Left onto Scotts Road.

19.3   Arrive at finish at intersection of Scotts Road and Millstone Brook Road.

RIDE INFORMATION

Local Events/Attractions

Emma Rose Elliston Memorial Park: This ride passes the Emma Rose Elliston Memorial Park, featured in the previous chapter.

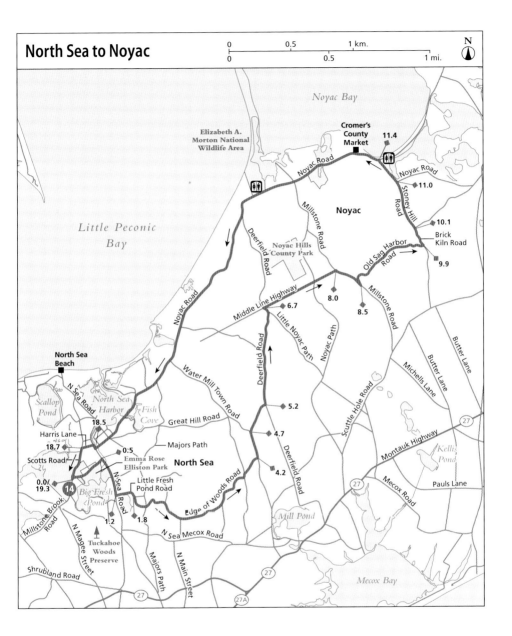

North Sea to Noyac

North Sea Burial Grounds: This cemetery dates to 1782. It's bordered by lovely decorative fencing, and features the headstones of many members of the Rose family.

Little Fresh Pond: This route travels around Little Fresh Pond, hidden from view by the homes around the shore. The small pond is one of the cleanest in the region, with an active and invested waterfront community. Swimming access is on Fresh Pond Lane, just off of North Sea Road, a quarter of a mile from the turn onto Little Fresh Pond Road.

Elizabeth A. Morton National Wildlife Refuge: Donated by the Morton family, this 187-acre refuge is an ecological treasure with a wide-range of habitats, from saltwater to freshwater. The park uses a self-serve system to collect fees, reduced for cyclists. Bicycles are not permitted on the picturesque hiking trails.

Restaurants

Serene Green Farm Stand and Seafood Market: 3980 Noyac Rd., Sag Harbor; (631) 334-6311; serenegreeninc.com

Cromer's County Market: 3500 Noyac Rd., Sag Harbor; (631) 725-9004; cromersmarket.com

Jimmy Jims Deli: 3348 Noyac Rd., Sag Harbor; (631) 725-1930; jimmyjimsdeli.com

North Sea Farms: 1060 Noyac Rd., Southampton; (631) 283-0735;

Country Deli: 926 Noyac Rd., Southampton; (631) 283-4900

Schmidt's Market: 1282 North Sea Rd., Southampton; (631) 702-2612

North Sea General Store: 1360 North Sea Rd., Southampton; (631) 283-1826

BOA Thai: 129 Noyac Rd., Southampton; (631) 488-4422; boathai.com

North Sea Tavern & Raw Bar: 1271 North Sea Rd., Southampton; (631) 353-3322; northseatavernrawbar.com

Sag Harbor Loop

The village of Sag Harbor developed around its namesake, a draw for the original settlers from nearby North Sea. The deeper body of water helped expand a lucrative whaling and shipping industry, bringing wealth and prestige to the settlers. The historic character has been maintained to the present day, although the waterfront is more centered on recreation and tourism than serious industry; and the traders markets have been replaced with luxury retail boutiques.

Start: Intersection of Bridge Street, West Water Street, and Long Island Avenue, at the municipal parking lot in downtown Sag Harbor

Length: 7.6 miles

Riding time: About 30 minutes

Best bike: Road bike or hybrid

Terrain and trail surface: Asphalt

Traffic and hazards: Watch the densely parked cars on Main Road in downtown, and use caution on the few stretches outside of bike lanes on Noyac Road and Brick Kiln Road.

Things to see: A breathtaking vista along the harbor, historically significant architecture, and the usual sights of a quaint harbor village turned shopping destination.

Fees: None.

Getting there: Follow the Southern State Parkway toward Eastern Long Island and take exit 40 for Robert Moses Causeway South toward Oceans Beaches. Take exit RM 1E to NY 27E/Montauk. From NY 27E, turn left onto Scuttle Hole Road. At the traffic circle, take the second exit and stay on Scuttle Hole Road. Turn left onto Bridgehampton–Sag Harbor Turnpike and continue onto Main Road. Near the end of Main Road, turn left onto West Water Street. The entrance to the municipal lot is on Bridge Street, right by the intersection with Water Street and Long Island Avenue.

The nearest train station is the Long Island Rail Road station in Bridge-hampton, nearly five miles away. From the train station, turn left onto Maple Lane, left onto Lumber Lane and then right onto Narrow Lane. Turn left onto Sagg Road until Middle Line Highway. Cross Middle Line onto Madison Street to Main Road, turning left at the end of Main Road onto Water Street.

GPS: N41 00.103' / W72 17.858'

THE RIDE

This short and mostly flat ride starts in the quaint downtown village district of Sag Harbor, then loops around Sag Harbor Cove. Along the way, it travels through North Haven, along a gorgeous causeway, and then on little back roads from Noyac back into Sag Harbor. The route continues for a tiny extra loop to explore the rest of the village district before returning to the municipal lot off of West Water Street.

Starting at the intersection of three streets, follow West Water Street toward the village center and the intersection with Main Road. Use caution when crossing the bustling road, turning left once and then left again onto Ferry Road, passing the historic Long Wharf and a Hamptons windmill on the right.

Ferry Road, a narrow road with a painted lane for bicycles, immediately crosses a bridge, featuring spectacular views of Sag Harbor Bay and Sag Harbor Cove. At the 1.3-mile mark, exit the bike lane into the traffic circle, and turn right at the third exit into the painted bike lane on Short Beach Road. This is the highlight of the ride, as the road becomes Noyac–Long Beach Road and continues over a 1.5-mile causeway with gorgeous vistas of Noyac Bay on the right and Sag Harbor Cove on the left.

The beach on the right, Foster Memorial Town Beach, requires a town-parking permit for automobiles, but no restrictions on cyclists. The beach has restrooms and, usually, a food stand.

At the end of the causeway, enter the traffic circle and take the second exit onto Noyac Road. This road has no bike lane, but it has a fairly wide shoulder, so should remain comfortable for riding.

Noyac Road bears left after 0.4 mile. Oncoming traffic has a stop sign, but be cautious, mindful of drivers behind you that may bear right. Just at the intersection is a popular family farm stand, Serene Green, offering fresh local fruit, produce, and baked goods.

Noyac Road continues for another 1.3 miles through a suburban neighborhood with 30-mph speed limits and a narrow shoulder. At the stop sign, turn left onto Brick Kiln Road, a slightly narrower, busier, shoulderless road, for just 0.2 mile until it reaches a major intersection with Main Road.

Water view from Sag Harbor

Take a left onto Main Road, keeping Mashashimuet Park and Otter Pond on the right. Shortly ahead is the Cove Delicatessen on the right and Canio's Books on the left, a hot spot for local literati. As Main Road continues, it passes historic homes of architectural distinction, including several grand Federal homes and examples of Greek and Italianate Revival. The Sag Harbor Whaling Museum is especially noteworthy, housed in an imposing Greek Revival house with a temple front.

Past the Civil War Memorial, continue on Main Road, paying close attention to the nose-in parking along the right, back to the intersection with Bay Street. Turn right this time, and follow Bay Street through a slightly cluttered waterfront area, which passes the short access road to Havens Beach, a Sag Harbor hidden treasure. To take in the sights, turn left and follow Havens Beach Road roughly 700 feet to the beach. This is an unprotected beach where swimming is prohibited, but it's quiet and has beautiful views of Sag Harbor Bay.

> **Bike Shops**
> **Sag Harbor Cycle Company:** 34 Bay St., Sag Harbor; (631) 725-1110; sagharborcycle.com
> **Bermuda Bikes Plus:** 36 Gingerbread Ln., East Hampton; (631) 324-6688; bermudabikes.com
> **Khanh Sports:** 60 Park Place, East Hampton; (631) 324-0703; khanhsports.com

After a stop at the beach, continue on Bay Street to the stop sign and turn right onto Hempstead Street through a quiet side neighborhood. At the next stop sign, turn right again onto Hampton Street, which curves right, and onto Division Street as it passes Christ Episcopal Church and then St. Andrews Roman Catholic Church. Just ahead, Division Street enters the busy downtown, passing a number of boutiques and upscale cafes before the road ends at Bay Street. Turn left onto Bay Street and follow it to the intersection with Main Road just ahead, then left onto Main Road, and immediately turn right onto West Water Street to arrive at the finish.

MILES AND DIRECTIONS

0.0 Start on West Water Street, left onto Main Street.

0.1 Left onto Ferry Road / NY 114.

1.3 3rd exit from traffic circle onto Short Beach Road.

3.1 2nd exit from traffic circle onto Noyac Road.

3.5 Left to stay on Noyac Road.

4.8 Left onto Brick Kiln Road.

5.0 Left onto Main Street.

5.9 Right onto Bay Street.

6.6 Right onto Hempstead Street.

6.7 Right onto Hampton Street.

7.1 Right onto Division Street.

7.4 Left onto Bay Street then cross Main Road onto West Water Street.

7.6 Arrive at finish.

RIDE INFORMATION

Local Events/Attractions
Sag Harbor Beaches: The beaches on this route are Foster Memorial Beach, known locally as Long Beach, and Havens Beach, an undeveloped beach popular for lounging and sunset watching.

Sag Harbor Whaling Museum: This home belonged to a prominent whaling family when it was built in 1845, but also served as a summer home for a wealthy philanthropist and as a Masonic Temple before it was purchased and repurposed into a whaling museum. The museum showcases the history of Sag Harbor and is open for tours seven days a week for a modest fee.

Sag Harbor Loop

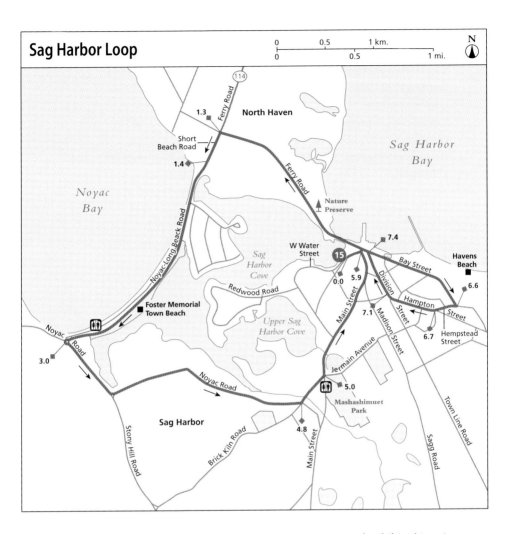

Sag Harbor Historical Society: The Society maintains and exhibits historical properties spanning 300 years of local history. Among these, include the Annie Cooper Boyd House on Main Road, and the Old Jail House Museum on Division Street. More information, and a gallery of historical photos, is available on their website at sagharborhistorical.org.

Bookstores: Sag Harbor has two bookstores, both of them popular gathering places for literary talks and readings. Canio's is on the outskirts of town, and Harbor Books is on Main Road near the start of this route. Sadly, this is a low number for a village that once boasted of five bookstores.

Sag Harbor Farmer's Market: This farmer's market on Bay Street by the harbor is open every Saturday from the end of May to the beginning of October. More information on their website at sagharborfarmersmarket.org.

Restaurants

SagTown Coffee: 78 Main St., Sag Harbor; (631) 725-8696; sagtown.com

Sag Harbor Baking Co.: 51 Division St., Sag Harbor; (631) 899-4900

Golden Pear Cafe: 111 Main St., Sag Harbor; (631) 725-2270; goldenpear.com

Cavaniola's Gourmet: 80 Division St., Sag Harbor; (631) 725-0095; cavaniolas.com

Bagel Buoy Market: 3 Bay St., Sag Harbor; (631) 725-7690; bagelbuoy.com

LTBurger: 62 Main St., Sag Harbor; (631) 899-4646; ltburger.com

Serene Green Farm Stand and Seafood Market: 3980 Noyac Rd., Sag Harbor; (631) 334-6311; serenegreeninc.com

Restrooms

2.9: Foster Memorial Town Beach
5.0: Mashashimuet Park

Westhampton Beach

*The village of West Hampton Dunes is situated on a barrier island that was origi-
nally part of Fire Island. A nor'easter split Fire Island in two in 1931, followed by
a hurricane in 1938; the two storms widened Moriches Inlet and devastated the
resort town of Westhampton Beach, whose residents moved farther inland. West
Hampton Dunes would struggle as a small village of the no-longer contiguous
Brookhaven, now 20 miles away via a land route through Southampton, and
would be nearly obliterated by a string of powerful storms and hurricanes in the
1991, 1992, and 1993. Fearing for their future, residents incorporated it as an independent village in 1993 and elected their first and to-date only mayor, who over-
saw the rebuilding of the beach. The project was so successful that it is now used
as a model for other restoration works, and the beach is considered one of the top
restored beaches in America.*

Start: Visitor center on Glovers Lane, in the village of Westhampton
Beach.

Length: 29.4 miles

Riding time: About 2 hours and 30 minutes

Best bike: Road bike

Terrain and trail surface: Asphalt

Traffic and hazards: The roads are fairly slow and safe. Use caution
on Main Road around the nose-in parking spots. Steel deck bridges
can be dicey in wet weather; this ride crosses two, on Jessup Lane and
Beach Lane. Dune Road, particularly at the western end, can get flooded
during high tide or inclement weather. Watch for sand on windy days.

Things to see: Scenic bay views, beaches on the Atlantic Ocean, and
preserved wetlands.

Fees: None. Both the visitor center and the larger municipal lot behind
it on Glovers Lane offer free parking.

Getting there: Follow the Southern State Parkway toward Eastern Long Island, and take exit 40 for Robert Moses Causeway South toward Oceans Beaches. Take exit RM1E to NY 27E/Montauk. From NY 27E, take exit 61 for County Road 51N toward Riverhead/Eastport. Turn right onto Eastport–Manor Road, following signs for Eastport, then left onto Old Country Road into Westhampton. Turn right onto Mill Road to the municipal lot at the intersection with Glovers Lane.

Transit users can take the Long Island Rail Road to the Westhampton station. Turn left onto Depot Lane until Montauk Highway. Cross the road onto Oneck Lane then left onto Mill Road to the intersection with Glovers Lane to begin the ride.

GPS: N40 48.680' / W72 38.614'

THE RIDE

The final ride in the Hamptons starts in Westhampton Beach, crosses lovely Moneyboque Bay, and follows a long road on a barrier island, known locally as Dune Road. The route heads east to visit Shinnecock West County Park, companion to the East Park visited in the Southampton Beach ride (Rte. 12), then backtracks west. Visit Cupsogue Beach County Park, a developed park with restrooms, food concessions, and a swimming pool, on the western end, before heading back to the village to finish the ride. Cyclists looking for a shorter, easier ride may wish to skip the eastern leg, cutting off 16.7 miles for a total distance of only 12.7 miles. The eastern leg has more scenic water views, but Cupsogue Beach is the real highlight of the ride and should not be missed.

From the visitor center, turn left onto Glovers Lane, then right onto Mill Road at the stop sign. Turn left onto Main Road at the end of Mill Road, by the town green, and use caution navigating around the nose-in parked cars.

Turn right ahead onto Beach Lane, a quiet neighborhood street with a narrow shoulder. Privet hedge and antique fences border the road until a tiny section of nose-in parking, adjacent to the Moneyboque Bay Tidal Wetlands Area, before a picturesque steel deck bridge. Turn left after the bridge onto Dune Road, across from the entrance to Rogers Beach, and head east.

The road enters Quoque just ahead, passes Ogden Pond on the left, and then Quogue Village Beach on the right, with views of the Penniman Creek and then Shinnecock Bay along the left. Houses are sparse on the east side of the island, although a number of exclusive resorts are primarily on the right side of the road.

Views open up around 3 miles before the end, as the road passes Tiana Beach and enters the Shinnecock West County Park area. The next 3 miles pass

Atlantic Ocean view in West Hampton Dunes

views of dunes and marshes, over a sandy, sometimes wet road. Restaurants and other amenities are open seasonally.

After a break, turn around and follow Dune Road back toward the west. The road gets more developed after Beach Lane, with homes and resorts often blocking views. On the left, the route passes another public beach, Lashley Beach, about 2 miles west from Rogers Beach.

The road enters the Village of West Hampton Dunes ahead, but there are few stops here. It's primarily a resort town, and residents drive to nearby villages for groceries. Pikes Beach is just ahead, the last point of interest before the road ends at Cupsogue County Park. After stopping, turn around, and follow Dune Road back through West Hampton Dunes until

Bike Shops

Bike 'n Kite: 112 Potunk Ln., Westhampton Beach; (631) 288-1210; bikemanforu.com
East End Bicycles: 2873 Montauk Hwy., Brookhaven; (631) 399-7390; eastendbikes.com
Twin Forks Bicycles: 121 East Main St., Riverhead; (631) 591-3082; twinforksbicycles.com
Rotations Bicycle Center: 32 Windmill Ln., Southampton; (631) 283-2890; rotationsbicyclecenter.com

View of Westhampton Beach from the island

reaching the first bridge back to the main island. Turn left onto Jessup Lane and cross another steel deck bridge with lovely views of boats parked in the bay.

Bear right onto Stevens Lane ahead, then immediately bear left onto Potunk Lane for a quarter of a mile. After the country club property, turn right onto Main Road, into downtown Westhampton Beach, along a street lined with historically significant buildings. Many of the structures were moved following the storms that separated Dune Road Island from Fire Island. Take the second left, following signs for parking and restrooms, onto Glovers Lane to arrive at the finish.

MILES AND DIRECTIONS

0.0 Start by the visitor center and municipal lots on Glovers Lane, right onto Mill Road.

0.2 Left onto Main Road.

0.3 Right onto Beach Lane.

South Fork and the Hamptons

Westhampton Beach

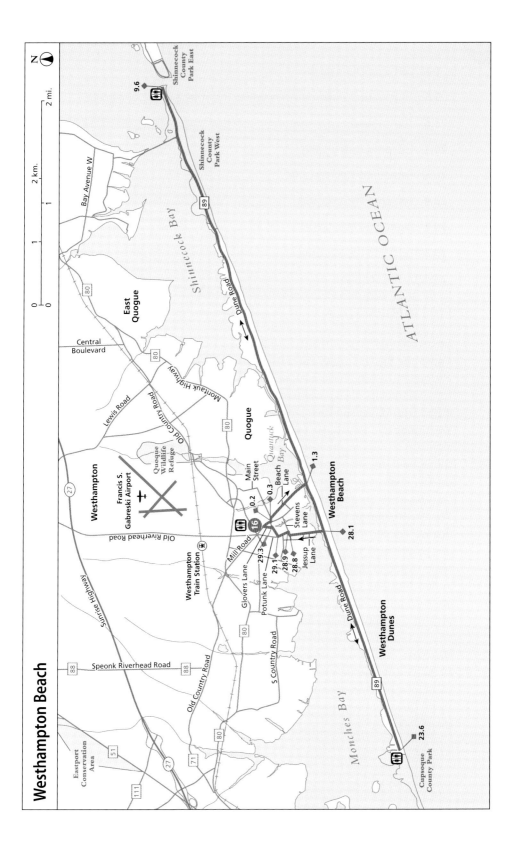

1.3 Left onto Dune Road.

9.6 Turn around. Ride southwesterly to the other end of Dune Road.

23.6 Turn around.

28.1 Left onto Jessup Lane.

28.8 Right onto Stevens Lane.

28.9 Left onto Potunk Lane.

29.1 Right onto Main Road.

29.3 Left onto Glovers Lane.

29.4 Arrive at finish.

RIDE INFORMATION

Local Events/Attractions

Cupsogue Beach County Park: This nearly 300-acre park is rich in amenities and natural beauty, making it one of the more popular beaches in the Hamptons. Swimming, diving, camping, and fishing are permitted and amenities include restrooms, showers, concessions, lifeguards, and EMT service.

Westhampton Beach Historical Society: This group was founded to maintain records on the history of the area. They manage several buildings throughout the village, offering tours of several houses at their main campus on Mill Road near the start of this ride. For more information, visit their website, at whbhistorical.org.

The Westhampton Beach Farmers' Market: Open every Saturday from the first weekend in May to the last weekend in November, local farmers, fishers, and bakers staff this market. More than forty vendors sell everything from dog treats to pound cakes made with local ingredients.

Juried Arts and Crafts Shows: On the first weekend in August every year Westhampton Beach hosts the Mary O. Fritchie Juried Art Show and a spring art and craft show on the first weekend of June, both on the village green, near the ride start on Glovers Lane.

Beaches: This ride passes a number of beaches, most of them minimally developed. Rogers Beach, Tiana Beach, Lashley Beach, and Pikes Beach are all quiet local beaches open to the public. Two of the beaches are more developed, Quogue Village Beach and Cupsogue Beach, both of which have lifeguards and restrooms.

Restaurants

Eckart's Luncheonette: 162 Mill Rd., Westhampton Beach; (631) 288-9491

Beach Bakery Cafe: 112 Main St., Westhampton Beach; (631) 288-6552; beachbakerycafe.com

Post Stop Cafe: 144 Main St., Westhampton Beach; (631) 288-9777

Hampton Coffee Company: 194 Mill Rd., Westhampton Beach; (631) 288-4480; hamptoncoffeecompany.com

Sydney's Taylor Made Cuisine: 32 Mill Rd., Westhampton Beach; (631) 288-4722; sydneysgourmet.com

Goldberg's Famous Deli & Restaurant: 65 Main St., Westhampton Beach; (631) 998-3878; goldbergsfamouswhb.com

Ben & Jerry's: 121 Main St., Westhampton Beach; (631) 288-5753; benjerry.com

John Scott's Surf Shack: 540 Dune Rd., Westhampton Beach; (631) 288-5810

Restrooms

0.0: Visitor Center
9.6: Shinnecock West County Park
23.6: Cupsogue County Park

Brookhaven and Southwestern Suffolk

Originally a collection of agricultural hamlets, Brookhaven is the largest and most populous town in Suffolk County, following a large period of growth fueled by a nineteenth-century shipbuilding industry, the post-war population boom, and the highway and railroad expansions planned by New York City planner Robert Moses. Three lines of the Long Island Rail Road and a ferry connection to Bridgeport, CT, serve the area along with more than a dozen major roads.

The region has retained much of its authentic colonial character in the St. James and Three Villages area, especially in the area around Stony Brook; other sections were built in the 1900s, as part of a colonial-revival effort funded by a major philanthropist.

Brookhaven also includes Port Jefferson, although none of the routes in this book visit the historic shipbuilding village. Despite its charm and character, this bustling suburban town does not have a variety of bicycle routes. Connecticut cyclists sometimes bike through the town, primarily on NY 25A headed east, after arriving via the Bridgeport & Port Jefferson ferry.

Rides in this section feature Wildwood State Park, a preserve set on high bluffs over a long beach, and two rides through the quaint hamlets of Brookhaven's North Shore. In the middle of Brookhaven comes Cathedral Pines, a mountain bike park in a forest of towering old pine trees offering miles of singletrack. A route from the Wertheim National Wildlife Refuge visits Fire Island then detours through the village of newly incorporated Mastic Beach on the return route. The last three routes leave Brookhaven, visiting the towns of Islip and Babylon in southwestern Suffolk. Islip includes Glacier 8, a mountain bike trail at Hidden Pond Park, and a scenic bay ride in Sayville, starting at the Long Island Maritime Museum. The final ride starts in Babylon, at Argyle Lake, and follows a four-mile linear trail past Southards Pond to Lake Belmont.

Wildwood

Wildwood State Park resembles the West Coast more than the East. This 600-acre park includes 2 miles of beach beneath high, rocky bluffs, hundreds of camping sites, and a forest of oaks, maples, and other hardwood trees. The park does not have extensive bike paths, but it's in a prime spot for heading out on this road bike ride.

Start: North Wading River Road, by the entrance to Wildwood State Park in Wading River.

Length: 27.7 miles

Riding time: About 2 hours 15 minutes

Best bike: Road bike

Terrain and trail surface: Asphalt

Traffic and hazards: Use caution crossing the train tracks on River Road and Mill Road. This ride has three left turns over busy, multilane roads. The first from Panamoka Trail onto NY 25, and the second and third at Edwards Avenue after Mill Road. Watch for oncoming traffic at these spots.

Things to see: Rocky bluffs overlooking the Long Island Sound, lovely back roads through hardwood forests, past parks, farms, and pastoral pond views.

Fees: Wildwood Park charges for admission by car from May 27 to September 2, but free parking spots are usually available outside of the park. Follow all posted rules and notices.

Getting there: Take the Long Island Expressway (I-495E) to Riverhead and exit 68 for William Floyd Parkway toward County 46 / Shirley / Wading River. Follow signs for NY 25A E / Wading River and then turn left onto Randall Road. Turn right onto North Country Road into Wading

River Village, then bear left onto North Wading River Road to the ride start at Wildwood State Park. The nearest train station is about 11 miles away in Riverhead, and it may be easiest to ride to the intersection of Mill Road and Edwards Avenue and start the ride there, at the 15.7-mile mark. From the station, take Railroad Avenue to a left onto Cedar Street, then right onto Court Street. Continue onto Center Drive then right onto Nugent Drive, a busy road with a painted bike lane, for 3.7 miles until it becomes Edwards Avenue. At the intersection with Mill Road, follow the mapped route back to this point.

GPS: N40 57.772' / W72 48.538'

THE RIDE

Starting at the entrance to Wildwood State Park, this route follows quiet roll-ing roads through parkland and preserves, exploring a quiet spot on the North Shore, dotted by farm stands and general stores.

From the entrance, bear right onto North Wading River Road, heading uphill into a residential neighborhood. The hill crests after a mile and the road heads down on a fast stretch to a stop sign at the intersection with North Country Road.

Use caution as through traffic has no stop sign. Turn left onto the wide-shouldered road for another quick uphill climb, then descend to the fork, where the route bears right onto Wading River Manor Road.

In less than half a mile, the route approaches a busy suburban commer-cial development and a signalized intersection with NY 25A. Cross to continue on Wading River Manor Road, passing a big box store and then a sprawling farm on the right and a tree nursery on the left.

Turn right at the first stop sign, onto Long Pond Road. This low-volume street becomes Lakeside Trail through a neighborhood of rustic bungalows and cottages situated on Lake Panamoka. Follow Lakeside as it curves through the neighborhood, past cul-de-sacs and no outlet signs, and numerous views of the water.

Bear left at each fork until Panamoka Trail appears on the right, at the 5.5-mile mark, and turn up into the short climb. Follow Panamoka Trail until the road ends in a T-junction with Middle Country Road (NY 25).

Traffic can be fast here; use caution turning left to continue on the route. Just after the turn, a pastoral view of Horn Pond may be visible on the right, depending on the season and foliage. While traffic here can be fast, Middle Country Road has a wide shoulder converted to a painted bike lane, and should be comfortable for the next eight-tenths of a mile. The route passes Fink's Country Farm and then a trailer and R.V. dealer just before turning right onto Wading River Manor Road.

This is a long, mostly straight, stretch of beautiful country roads, bordered by heavily forested parkland. This area is almost completely undeveloped and has low traffic volumes, but speeds can be fast. At the fork, continue straight onto Schultz Road for nearly two more miles of similar riding.

Turn left onto North Street at the intersection, past Sheila's Sweet Shoppe, a bakery operating out of a residence on the corner. In the summer, the family sells Italian ice out front. Continue on North Road through a more inhabited area until the route bears right at the fork, following the bike route sign onto Mill Road. Use caution crossing the railroad tracks just ahead on this almost entirely undeveloped street.

Cross the four-way intersection with Connecticut Avenue and Halsey Manor Road to continue on Mill Road. The next 2.8 miles pass a few homes but the area is still minimally developed and heavily forested. An access spot for the Peconic River is on the left just before Mill Road ends at the intersection with Edwards Avenue, where the route turns left. Be mindful of oncoming traffic on this busy route both here and just ahead where the route turns left again onto River Road.

River Road has some rough patches of asphalt, but is otherwise a lovely route through farmland and protected Peconic River property. Use caution on the two train crossings, and turn left in a half-mile after the second crossing to continue on River Road.

River Road passes through the Swan Lake Golf Club before the next fork. Turn right to follow the route onto Old River Road, a very narrow, minimally maintained road of cracked asphalt through a beautiful, quiet area with horse enclosures and only a few homes. If the road surface looks too dicey, bear left to stay on River Road.

Bike Shops

Rocky Point Cycle Inc.: 669 NY 25A, Rocky Point; (631) 744-5372; Rockypointcycles.com

Carl Hart Bicycles: 620 Middle Country Rd., Middle Island; (631) 924-5850; carlhart.com

Twin Forks Bicycles: 121 East Main St., Riverhead; (631) 591-3082; twinforksbicycles.com

Both roads end at Wading River Manor Road, where the route turns right. Turn right to continue on Wading River Manor Road, retracing the outbound route back to the signalized intersection with Middle Country Road (NY 25). The route follows this narrow-shouldered road, mostly uphill, and passes the Deep Pond Conservation Area on the right.

Wildwood Beach

Turn right at the intersection of Sound Avenue (NY 25A), into the painted bike lane, and follow the road past a number of farm stands and markets over the next 2.1 miles. At the intersection, turn left onto Hulse Landing Road, past the farmland and then a series of cul-de-sacs and suburban developments. Bear right onto Wildwood Road at the 27.5-mile mark, arriving at the finish just ahead.

By continuing along the park road for another half-mile from here, riders can visit the Wildwood Beach, which has food concessions and a restroom.

MILES AND DIRECTIONS

0.0 Start in Wildwood and proceed on North Wading River Road.

2.3 Left onto North Country Road.

2.7 Right onto Wading River Manor Road.

3.5 Right onto Long Pond Road.

4.8 Left onto Lakeside Trail.

5.5 Right onto Panamoka Trail.

6.3 Left onto Middle Country Road (NY 25).

Wildwood

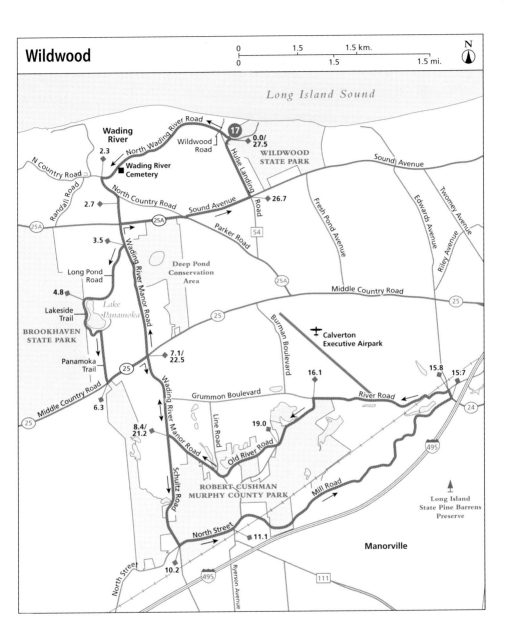

7.1 Right onto Wading River Manor Road.

8.4 Continue on Schultz Road.

10.2 Left onto North Street.

11.1 Right onto Mill Road.

15.7 Left onto Edwards Avenue.

15.8   Left onto River Road.

18.1   Left to continue on River Road.

19.0   Right onto Old River Road.

20.1   Right onto Wading River Manor Road.

24.6   Right onto NY 25A / Sound Avenue.

26.7   Left onto Hulse Landing Road.

27.5   Right onto Wildwood Road.

27.7   Arrive at finish.

RIDE INFORMATION

Local Events/Attractions
Wildwood State Park: This beautiful park is a popular campsite, drawing visitors for the natural beauty and amenities. For more information and booking, visit their website, at nysparks.com/parks/68/.

Deep Pond Conservation Area: A Boy Scout council owns this property, but permits responsible anglers to use it with some limitations. It's a beautiful spot and one of the only completely undeveloped ponds in Long Island. For more information, visit the website at dec.ny.gov/outdoor/24157.html.

Restaurants
Angelo's Deli: 737 Hulse Landing Rd., Wading River; (631) 929-4616
Sheila's Sweet Shoppe: 127 North St., Manorville; (631) 369-0885; sheilassweetshoppe.com
My Creperie: 2 Sound Rd., #B, Wading River; (631) 886-2527; my-creperie.com
North Fork Bacon & Smokehouse: 1 Sound Rd., Wading River; (631) 886-2220; northforkbacon.com
Wading River Deli: 6263 NY 25A, Wading River; (631) 929-5694
Lewin Farms: 812 Sound Ave., Calverton; (631) 929-4327; lewinfarm.com
Fink's Country Farm: 6242 Middle Country Rd., Wading River; (631) 886-2272; finksfarm.com
Davis Peach Farm: 561 Hulse Landing Rd., Wading River; (631) 929-1115; Restrooms
Condzella's Farm: 6233 North Country Rd., Wading River; (631) 929-5058; condzellasfarm.com

Restrooms
0.0: Wildwood State Park

North Shore

The Town of Brookhaven comprises more than sixty communities, including nine separate villages, spanning from the north to the south of Suffolk County. Wading River, the first village on this route, consists of a tiny cluster of stores and restaurants situated around a pastoral pond, settled by eight families from New England on the North Shore of Long Island. The layout and architecture of Wading River bears strong resemblance to quintessential New England villages, particularly evident in the lovely, steepled, Congregational Church and village green.

Adjacent to the west is the slightly older Shoreham. Once closely linked to Wading River by the Long Island Rail Road, the villages share a school district and small community-centered lifestyle. Shoreham is most notable as the site of Nikola Tesla's Wardenclyffe Tower, a failed wireless transmission station dismantled in 1917. Locals purchased the property in 2013 and are working on bringing a museum dedicated to Tesla to the site.

Start: Village center of Wading River, near the green and pond.

Length: 20.7 miles

Riding time: About 2 hours

Best bike: Road bike

Terrain and trail surface: Asphalt

Traffic and hazards: NY 25A on the return leg of the ride includes a chaotic, high-speed intersection. Bypass this entirely by following the directions below to take a few hundred-feet of sidewalk to the turn onto Westchester Drive. Most of the roads are designated bicycle routes with "Share the Road" signage, but may not have wide road shoulders or bike lanes.

Things to see: Two optional detours, visit Shoreham and Wading River beaches, both lovely scenic spots for viewing Long Island Sound. Other views include country roads, quaint village centers, and historic architecture.

Fees: None. There is ample free parking in Wading River Village.

Getting there: Take the Long Island Expressway (I-495E) to Riverhead and exit 68 for William Floyd Parkway toward County 46 / Shirley / Wading River. Follow signs for NY 25A E / Wading River then turn left onto Wading River Manor Road. Turn left onto North Country Road to the ride start in Wading River Village. The nearest train station is more than 11 miles away, in Riverhead. It might be easier for transit users to ride the route in reverse, starting at the Port Jefferson train station. Turn left from the station onto Highlands Boulevard, then left onto North Columbia Street. Turn right just ahead onto North Country Road, which picks up the mapped route by the intersection of Lower Rocky Point Road and North Country Road. Follow the route, clockwise, adjusting the mileage points by +4.0 miles.

GPS: N40 57.293' / W72 51.060'

THE RIDE

This mild road ride follows North Country Road through the quaint villages of Brookhaven, on 20.7 miles of rolling terrain, with a total elevation gain of 1,000 feet. The ride starts on North Country Road at the intersection with Sound Road, adjacent to the lovely pond and green, location of the Wading River Historical Society. Follow North Country Road past the creperie and smokehouse, toward the Town of Brookhaven historical sign.

The shoulder is very narrow, but outside of typical commute hours, it should be a safe and comfortable cycling road. After a signalized intersection at Lilco Road, the route heads sharply downhill, curving left past the reno-vated historic Woodhull House on the right.

A gated park road on the right, 0.6 mile ahead, provides access to Shore-ham Beach. A detour to this quiet and picturesque spot is less than a mile down the drive. Access to the beach is obtained by walking down a short, steep hill, not suitable for bicycling. This undeveloped beach has great views of the Sound and long stretches of white sand for beach walks.

From the beach drive, the route continues on North Country Road for another long stretch of scenic backcountry roads and scattered homes, first passing a lovely split-rail fence and horse field.

After the intersection with Southgate Road, the shoulder widens and traffic speed and volume increase. Turn right just as North Country Road approaches NY 25, onto Briarcliff Road, a quieter, unpainted neighborhood

Shoreham Beach

road bordered by trees and single-family homes. The road narrows as it heads northwest, up a slight hill, and back down to the end of Briarcliff Road, by a small park at the intersection of a cul-de-sac and a private road for Shoreham village residents.

Turn left onto Woodville Road, similar to the last road, but with some interesting architecture. Here are several neo-classical homes with Ionic columns, shingle-style houses, and lovely examples of the Arts and Crafts movement.

The road passes under a vine-covered historic train overpass, used in the first decade of the twentieth century by the Long Island Rail Road for a Shoreham to Wading River spur, shortly before reaching North Country Road. Turn right onto this slightly busier stretch of road, with a wide shoulder, but bordered by car-centric suburban style commercial spots.

Bear right onto Rocky Point Landing Road, running behind the Joseph A. Edgar Intermediate School, after the local hardware store and just before the gas station. This road passes through a quiet neighborhood with sidewalks and narrow road shoulders heading northwest.

Road under tunnel from Shoreham

Bear left at the 8.1-mile mark, up a short hill, to continue onto Lower Rocky Point Road, adjacent to the Suffolk County Park. This undeveloped section of forest borders the road and, through the woods, a private beach for area residents.

Lower Rocky Point Road curves and winds through wooded neighborhoods after the forest, ending in a wide intersection with North Country Road in Miller Place. For an old-fashioned ice cream parlor, bear right for a detour of a quarter-mile to McNulty's, otherwise, follow the mapped route by turning left and continuing on North Country Road.

At the fork, bear left to stay on North Country Road, continuing through the signalized intersection with Echo Avenue on a flat to downhill section of well-maintained and quiet road.

North Country Road turns left onto NY 25A, which is not as bike-friendly as other stretches of this road. Long Island is in the midst of a dramatic expansion of bike lanes. Whenever a road is repaved or repaired, if possible, it is repainted with bike lanes or sharrow markings. Unfortunately, this section is lagging behind on repair, and the traffic is fast and chaotic. This route immediately turns left, onto Westchester Drive, to avoid the fast and dangerous section ahead. Some riders will prefer to take the sidewalk, turning onto it just before the road curves right to the intersection. This is legal here and probably safer than navigating the intersection. Just use caution in crossing the parking lot entrances and in turning left onto Westchester Drive, about 400 feet ahead. Remember to be courteous and respectful toward pedestrians.

Westchester Drive is a wide, unpainted road. Follow the loops and curves, mostly uphill, past new developments and cul-de-sacs until the road ends back at Rocky Point Landing Road. Turn right, into familiar territory, and backtrack to the intersection with North Country Road behind the Joseph A. Edgar School. Carefully turn left, mindful of cross traffic, and follow North Country Road out of the busy commercial strip and past Woodville and Briarcliff roads.

> ### Bike Shops
> **Rocky Point Cycle Inc.:** 669 NY 25A, Rocky Point; (631) 744-5372; Rockypointcycles.com
> **Carl Hart Bicycles:** 620 Middle Country Rd., Middle Island; (631) 924-5850; carlhart.com

Follow the road back through this scenic stretch until the route finishes back at the quaint village center of Wading River. Among a number of places to rest post-ride is Wading River Beach, a public beach with restrooms and food concession, just up Sound Avenue.

MILES AND DIRECTIONS

0.0 Start in Wading River Village on North Country Road.

1.7 **Optional**: Right onto the unnamed road to visit Shoreham Beach (+1 mile round-trip).

2.9 Right onto Briarcliff Road.

4.2 Left onto Woodville Road.

5.1 Right onto North Country Road.

6.3 Right onto Rocky Point Landing Road.

8.1 Left onto Lower Rocky Point Road.

10.4 Left onto North Country Road.

11.0 Left to stay on North Country Road.

12.8 Left onto Westchester Drive.

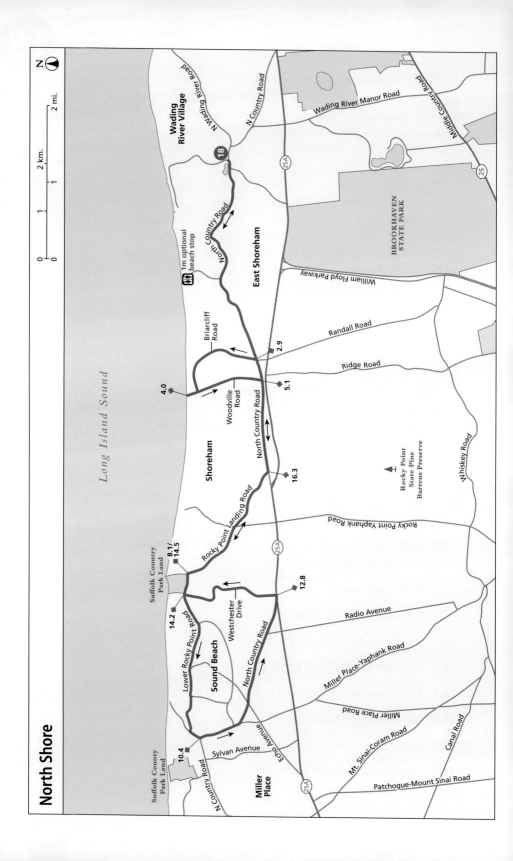

North Shore

14.2 Right onto Lower Rocky Point Road.

14.5 Right onto Rocky Point Landing Road.

16.3 Left onto North Country Road.

19.0 **Optional**: Left onto the unnamed road to visit Shoreham Beach (+1 mile round-trip).

20.7 Arrive at finish.

RIDE INFORMATION

Local Events/Attractions

Wading River Historical Society: Since 1947, this society has maintained records and documents related to the history of the village. They operate the History House, a museum with exhibits and artifacts, in the village center by the start of this ride. For more information, visit their website, at wadingriverhistoricalsociety.weebly.com.

Tesla Science Center: The Friends of Science East are currently renovating this property to serve as a museum dedicated to Nikola Tesla. The center is not open yet, but the group posts updates and information on their website, at teslasciencecenter.org.

Restaurants

My Creperie: 2 Sound Rd., #B, Wading River; (631) 886-2527; my-creperie.com
North Fork Bacon & Smokehouse: 1 Sound Rd., Wading River; (631) 886-2220; northforkbacon.com
Sweets of the Spoon: 597 NY 25A, Rocky Point; (631) 849-4771; sweetsofthespoon.com
B&M Prestano Bakery: 593 NY 25A, Rocky Point; (631) 849-3475

Restrooms

4.2: Municipal park

The Three Villages

Part of the historic Three Village area, St. James comprises a mix of modern homes, woodlands, and a cluster of preserved and restored nineteenth-century structures. The extensive historic district offers a rare view into the past of an early agricultural community. In the 1850s, villagers named the hamlet for the Episcopal Church of St. James. The church still exists today, just one of twenty-one historic buildings, mostly along a narrow stretch of North Country Road, many of which are still operational. The St. James Railroad Station is an active stop on the Long Island Rail Road, and the St. James General Store, near the start of the route, is the longest continuously operated general store in America.

Start: Deepwells Farm County Park, across from the Saint James General Store, at the intersection of Moriches and Harbor Hill Roads in Saint James.

Length: 22.0 miles

Riding time: About 1 hour 45 minutes

Best bike: Road bike

Terrain and trail surface: Asphalt

Traffic and hazards: The back roads are quiet, but may not be well maintained, so watch for cracks and potholes. Both Christian Avenue and Main Road in Stony Brook can be quite busy.

Things to see: Beautifully preserved nineteenth-century architecture, beaches, and long stretches of quiet roads along scenic rivers.

Fees: May to Labor Day. Park for free in the Deepwells Park lot, across the street from the general store.

Getting there: Take Northern State Parkway to NY 347/NY 454 E in Hauppauge. Bear left at the fork, following signs for 347 / Port Jefferson, then slight right toward Hauppauge Road and then a left onto Hauppauge. Continue onto North Country Road, then left onto Moriches Road. The General Store is just ahead, and the parking lot for Deepwells Park is on the left. Transit users can take the Long Island Rail Road to the St. James station, just a half-mile away. Turn left from the platform onto Norwood Avenue, then left onto Lake Avenue. At the intersection, turn left onto Moriches Road. St. James General Store is just ahead.

GPS: N40 53.255' / W73 09.709'

THE RIDE

This is the hilliest route in the book, with more than 1,500 feet of climbing, and a peak elevation of 208 feet. None of the climbs are very long; they are broken into roughly seven 100-foot climbs, with the most challenging climb just before the final turn to end the ride back at St. James General Store. Elevation profiles make this ride look more intimidating than it is thanks to the relative flatness of Long Island.

To start, carefully cross Moriches Road from the Deepwells Farm property and turn left to follow Moriches Road through a neighborhood of post-war housing and past the sign marking the boundary of the village of Head of the Harbor.

Near the Nissequogue Village sign, the scenery becomes more thickly forested and rural, passing a scenic pond and horse stables before reaching a left turn onto Old Mill Road, just after a section of split rail fencing. This low-volume, 25-mph road climbs through a manicured neighborhood before a fast, steep descent to the intersection with Nissequogue River Road below.

Turn right onto Nissequogue River Road, up a short steep climb, and then along a gently rolling 1.5-mile stretch of riverfront through the trees and occasional home on the left. Turn left onto Moriches Road just after the simple post-and-rail fence along the open field, and then right, following the road as it becomes Horse Race Lane.

At the end of Horse Race, bear left onto Short Beach Road, bordered by the David Weld Sanctuary lands, then the Nissequogue River on the left. At the end is Short Beach, a sandy peninsula beach projecting into Smithtown Bay and the Sound to the north, and the river to the west and south.

After a visit to the beach, turn around, retracing past the Sanctuary and continuing onto Boney Lane, passing the intersection with Horse Race Lane. Near the end, bear right past Triple Oak Road, then immediately left onto Long Beach Road.

St James General Store

This quiet road climbs and then plateaus as it passes a boarding school's horse pasture, before a fast, curving descent to a scenic view of Stony Brook Harbor and Long Beach Town Park. Follow the road as it continues to the marina and yacht club, then turn around, retracing Long Beach Road past Boney Lane until Long Beach ends at a T-junction with Moriches Road, turning left along the corner with the pastoral Horse on a Hill Farm.

This twisty, winding road has no shoulder, but is low in speed and volume. After 1.4 miles and a small pond on the right, turn left onto Cordwood Path, a narrow, steeply-downhill road ending with a view of Cordwood Park and the southern shore of Stony Brook Harbor. To continue on Harbor Road, turn right, then left at the stop sign. The next two miles won't have many views of the titular harbor; scenery consists of hardwood trees and shingle-style homes.

After a stop sign, Harbor Road continues downhill past a historic gristmill and the Mill Pond Park on the right. The road ends in a T-junction with Main Road just ahead and turns left into the Stony Brook Village Center. The Long Island Museum, detailed below, is less than a quarter-mile in the opposite direction on Main Road.

Mill Pond in Stony Brook

Use caution traveling through the Stony Brook Village Center. Despite the historic buildings and quaint shops, it's very car-centric and traffic can be heavy. Turn left to enter the traffic circle ahead and then right to exit onto Shore Road, following the water until the road turns right at Stony Brook Beach, becoming Sand Street.

Sand Street ends just ahead. Turn left onto the much busier Christian Avenue, a wider, shouldered road, and climb a short hill before bearing right onto Cedar Street. The route loops through this little neighborhood until within sight of the Stony Brook School, then turns right onto Hollow Road for 0.8 mile before ending back at Main Road.

> ### Bike Shops
>
> **Bike Discounters:** 438 Lake Ave., Saint James; (631) 862-0940; thebikeoutlet.com
>
> **The Cycle Company:** 564 West Jericho Turnpike, Smithtown; (631) 979-7078
>
> **Campus Bicycle:** 1077 NY 25A, Stony Brook; (631) 689-1200; campusbicycle.com

Retrace the outbound route, turning left onto Main Road, then right onto Harbor Road in less than a half-mile. Turn left onto Bacon Road after passing vineyards and farmlands for just over a half-mile of rolling hills. Bear left onto Hitherbrook Road at the end of Bacon Road, then right onto Three Sisters Road, turning wide around Gate Road.

This narrow, twisty road winds downhill to a stop sign. Turn left onto Harbor Hill Road and into the final climb of the ride: Harbor Hill Road ends in an intersection with Moriches Road, back at the ride start.

MILES AND DIRECTIONS

0.0 Start on Moriches Road near the St. James General Store.

1.4 Left onto Old Mill Road.

2.6 Right onto Nissequogue River Road.

4.4 Left onto Moriches Road.

4.5 Right onto Horse Race Lane.

4.9 Left onto Short Beach Road.

5.8 Turn around.

6.7 Continue on Boney Lane.

7.2 Left onto Long Beach Road.

9.6 Turn around.

12.3 Left onto Moriches Road.

13.7 Left onto Cordwood Path.

14.2 Right onto Harbor Road.

16.8 Left onto Main Street.

17.0 Second exit from traffic circle onto Shore Road.

17.3 Continue on Sand Street.

17.5 Left onto Christian Avenue.

17.8 Right onto Cedar Street.

18.3 Right onto Hollow Road.

19.1 Left onto Main Street.

19.5 Right onto Harbor Road.

20.3 Left onto Bacon Road.

20.9 Continue on Hitherbrook Road.

The Three Villages

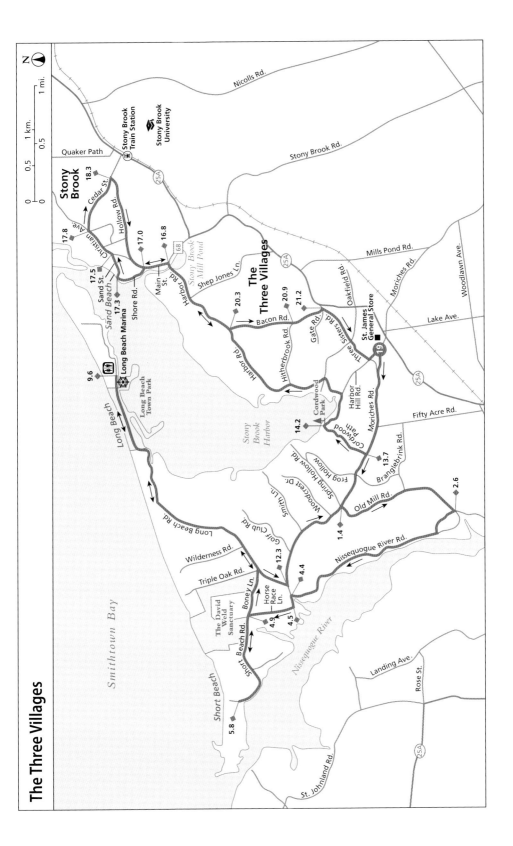

21.2 Right onto Three Sisters Road.

21.8 Left onto Harbor Hill Road.

22.0 Right onto Moriches Road, arrive at finish.

RIDE INFORMATION

Local Events/Attractions

Deepwells Farm County Park: This former estate was built for a descendant of Richard Smith, the founder of Smithtown, and would go through a number of hands, including those of William J. Gaynor, Mayor of New York City from 1910 to 1913. The property contains two 125-foot wells, inspiring the name, and a nineteenth-century Greek-Revival mansion. The property is managed by the Deepwells Historical Society, which lists events on their website, at deepwells.org.

St. James General Store: This general store is still in operation, and even offers a post office sub-station for area residents. The property has been saved from conversion to a residence many times, and has been acquired by Suffolk County and New York State as a historic preservation site. Reflecting a 30-year period from 1880-1910, the store is staffed by women in Gibson Girl outfits who serve as tour guides, interpreters, and salespeople. The store hosts book signings, historical talks, and skilled craftspeople sharing their trades.

Three Villages Historical Society: This society operates a museum, historic home site, and archives, exploring the history of Stony Brook, St. James, and the other areas that make up the Three Villages. They list events, photos, and more information about area history on their website, at threevillagehistoricalsociety.org.

The Long Island Museum of American Art, History, and Carriages: This 9-acre open-air museum contains seven buildings and barns and an extensive collection of carriages from the 1800s. The Museum's permanent collection includes a massive catalogue of Hudson River School painter William Sidney Mount. longislandmuseum.org.

Restaurants

Crazy Beans: 97 Main St., Stony Brook; (631) 675-6964; crazybeansrestaurant.com

Fratelli's Italian Eatery: 77 Main St., Stony Brook; (631) 751-4445; fratellisitalianeatery.com

Robinson's Tea Room: 97 Main St., Stony Brook; (631) 751-1232

Restrooms

5.8: Short Beach

9.6: Long Beach

Cathedral Pines

Cathedral Pines County Park is a 320-acre forest park located in the hamlet of Middle Island, at the headwaters of the Carmans River. One of the highlights of this park is the smell: The forest is composed of towering pine trees, many planted in the mid-nineteenth century, and the trails are coated with the fragrant needles. The park offers camping, hiking, bridle paths, and mountain biking, with support from volunteers who maintain and clean the trails following storms. Like most mountain biking sites on Long Island, the park is supported by the volunteer organization CLIMB, the Concerned Long Island Mountain Bicyclists. Helmets and eye protection are required on this route.

Start: Trailhead at edge of parking lot in Cathedral Pines State Park

Length: 8.2 miles

Riding time: 75–90 minutes

Best bike: Mountain bike

Terrain and trail surface: Single track, hard-packed dirt covered in pine needles

Traffic and hazards: This route includes a number of optional Black Diamonds and double Black Diamonds, but none of them are too challenging for an intermediate mountain bike rider. Stay off the trails if they are wet to avoid damaging them. Extensive tree roots are one of the main concerns, making this a less-than-ideal park for limited suspension bikes.

Things to see: Quiet trails through hardwood forest comprising tall nineteenth-century pine trees. Deer are a common sight.

Fees: There is a fee to park at Cathedral Pines on weekends, from Memorial Day to Labor Day. Entrance on bicycle is free, and Suffolk County Green Key bearers receive a hefty discount.

Getting there: Take I-495E to exit 66 Sills Road. (Patchogue Yaphank Road), bear left at Expressway Drive South. Turn left at Patchogue Yaphank Road, then bear right at Mill Road. Bear left at Yaphank-Middle Island Road. Park entrance is on the left. Transit users can take the Long Island Rail Road to the Yaphank station, nearly 3.5 miles away. Turn right from the station onto Yaphank Avenue, then left onto Main Road. At the end of Main Road, turn right, onto Yaphank-Middle Island Road. The park will be on the left in about 2.0 miles.

GPS: N40 51.917' / W72 56.354'

THE RIDE

Mileage readings on this ride are inconsistent: Wheel sensors clock it around 9 miles, while Garmins and other GPS devices come closer to 8.2 or 8.4. The map and mileage below were calculated using multiple passes with a Garmin, but may still come up inaccurate. Regardless, the route is very well marked, and is easy to follow even if mileage readings are inconsistent.

The main route is the Blue Trail, an easy, hard-packed dirt path, perfect for novices and experts alike. As is generally the case with singletrack, this route must be ridden counterclockwise. Additional, more difficult trails are marked, and should be ridden as described below and on the map. Every point on the route is within a half-mile or less of the campsites.

This route is not particularly technical, but it does have some strenuous climbs for novices. The route is popular with single speed riders, so none of the hills are too difficult. There are only a few obstacles, and all of them can be easily bypassed.

From the parking lot, turn right onto the Blue Trail, headed north. Cross the park road and continue around a curve, then turn right onto Big Pines, with one large log obstacle on this optional Black Diamond section. Big Pines has a fast descent followed by a steep ascent. The side path exits close to the entrance, and the route continues right, back on the Blue Trail.

After another mile, turn right onto Campsite Six, an optional stretch on a bridge over the Carmans River. The ramp is angled to make this a non-technical ride.

Turn right, back onto the Blue Trail, and then left onto Black Diamond, a curvy, tricky side trail that ends in a rocky spot. This is one of the only convoluted trails on the course, but it's easy to find your way back to the Blue Trail. At the end, turn left, back onto the Blue Trail, until a left turn onto the Carmans River Path, up a short, very steep climb. There are logs on this uphill section,

Trail through Cathedral Pines

but less experienced riders can bypass these obstacles.

Cross the Blue Trail ahead and hang right, up Kitty Litter Hill, then into a fast descent before an ascent of Cemetery Hill, the most challenging climb on the route. The route plateaus ahead and winds side to side before it crosses a fire road and continues right, onto Boundary Line, beginning a long, beautifully flowing section of trail. Despite some exposed roots, the ride for the next 2 miles or so is very smooth and fluid, looping around on a wide wood rail, then curving right back to the Blue Trail through a long, easy section before a right onto Berm and Burn, with easy, well-banked turns for another fast and flowing section.

Cross the Blue Trail again to continue northward on Berm and Burn, which loops back and rejoins the Blue Trail. Turn right for the last, unnamed, Black Diamond, for one last fast descent before ending the ride at the trailhead.

Some riders will do a second lap, solely following the Blue Trail, to increase distance and keep the ride fresh. This would add about 5 miles to the total distance.

Bike Shops

Carl Hart Bicycles: 620 Middle Country Rd., Middle Island; (631) 924-5850; carlhart.com

20 Cathedral Pines

MILES AND DIRECTIONS

0.0 Start at the trailhead at edge of parking lot and follow Blue Trail right and north.

0.3 Cross the park road.

0.7 *Option:* Right for Big Pines (Black Diamond).

0.9 Right onto Blue Trail.

2.2 Right onto Campsite Six (Double Black Diamond).

2.3 Right onto Blue Trail.

2.8 Left onto Black Diamond (Double Black Diamond).

2.9 Left onto Blue Trail.

3.1 Left onto Carmans River Path (Black Diamond) then cross Blue Trail onto Kitty Litter Hill (Black Diamond) followed by Cemetery Hill.

3.4 Right onto Blue Trail.

3.9 Cross fire road. (*Option:* Turn right onto Boundary Line [Black Diamond].)

4.9 Right onto Blue Trail.

6.1 Right onto Barlette Loop (Optional) (Double Black Diamond).

6.6 Right onto Blue Trail, then right onto Berm and Burn (Double Black Diamond).

7.3 Cross Blue Trail to continue on Berm and Burn.

7.7 Left onto Blue Trail.

7.8 Right onto Black Diamond Loop (Optional).

7.9 Right onto Blue Trail.

8.2 Arrive at finish.

RIDE INFORMATION

Local Events/Attractions

CLIMB (Concerned Long Island Mountain Bicyclists): This nonprofit organization maintains trails and organizes mountain bike events all over Long Island. Check their website to learn about local events to Cathedral Pines, at climbonline.org. Local riders use the CLIMB forums to coordinate group rides,

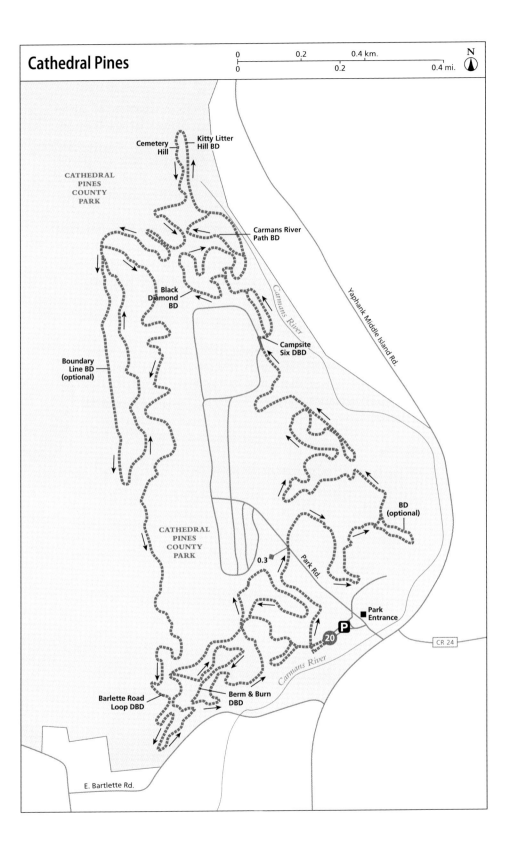

Cathedral Pines

0 0.2 0.4 km.
0 0.2 0.4 mi.

N

Kitty Litter
Hill BD

Cemetery
Hill

CATHEDRAL
PINES
COUNTY
PARK

Carmans River
Path BD

Carmans River

Yaphank Middle Island Rd.

Black
Diamond
BD

Campsite
Six DBD

Boundary
Line BD
(optional)

CATHEDRAL
PINES
COUNTY
PARK

BD
(optional)

0.3

Park Rd.

Park
Entrance

20 P

CR 24

Barlette Road
Loop DBD

Berm & Burn
DBD

Carmans River

E. Bartlette Rd.

too, which may be of interest to visitors. This park is popular, with a beginner ride and an advanced ride organized most weeks.

Six Hours of Cathedral Pines: This endurance race is organized by Something Wicked, a local group promoting mountain bike racing. Originally accredited with USA Cycling Event, the race used to require a license, but organizers left USACE to open the event to riders regardless of license or affiliation. The race is held annually in November and covers all of the optional loops on this course. Find out about the upcoming race on the organization website, at somethingwickedevents.com.

Fat Tire Festival: CLIMB organizes this one-day event with camping the night before and an assortment of rides starting the next morning. Rides are organized in a number of categories and offer something for everyone. Admission is free to CLIMB members. Dates vary by year. Check the CLIMB website, at climbonline.org, for current information.

Restaurants
Millhouse Inn: 284 Mill Rd., Yapahank; (631) 345-0361
The Cook Room: 25 Middle Country Rd., Middle Island; (631) 696-4260
Yaphank Deli: 908 Main St., Yaphank; (631) 924-9587
Tropical Smoothie Café: 267 Middle Country Rd., Selden; (631) 696-4780; tropicalsmoothie.com

Restrooms
0.3: Just up the park road crossed at this point.

Mastic Beach

Proudly referred to as the AntiHamptons by at least one local, via her civic boosting Twitter account, the little village of Mastic Beach is situated on a peninsula in gorgeous Moriches Bay. Locals describe their village as a quiet, low-key place to raise a family or enjoy middle-class life in a scenic area without the pressures and costs of living in a tourist destination like the Hamptons. The area is rich in natural beauty, bordered by the 2,550-acre Wertheim National Wildlife Refuge to the east, wide bays to the south, and, to the west, a picturesque inlet. Although part of the larger Town of Brookhaven, Mastic Beach was only incorporated in 2010. Local residents felt disconnected from their town government, and were struggling to deal with absentee landlords and blighted property. The process has been rocky and more expensive than initially thought, but the village continues to move forward in their goal of improving the economy and infrastructure of their beloved community.

Start: The Wertheim National Wildlife Refuge entrance property on Smith Road

Length: 13.3 miles

Riding time: 1 hour 15 minutes

Best bike: Road bike

Terrain and trail surface: Asphalt

Traffic and hazards: The William Floyd Parkway has a painted bike lane, but can be a bit busy and fast. Use caution especially on the left turn off the parkway on the return trip. The bridge to Fire Island has one short section of steel grating. Use caution on this in inclement weather.

Things to see: Diverse wildlife in a variety of habitats, scenic bay views from a long, picturesque bridge, and a breathtaking ocean beach.

Fees: None. The refuge does not charge for parking, and beach access is free for cyclists.

Getting there: Take the Long Island Expressway (I-495E) to exit 68S to William Floyd Parkway. Turn right onto Montauk Highway then left onto Smith Road. The refuge entrance will be on the right. Transit users can take the Long Island Rail Road to the Mastic–Shirley station, approximately 1 mile east of the visitor center. From the station, bike on Surrey Circle to the William Floyd Parkway and cross, continuing on Surrey Circle, until Northern Boulevard. Turn left, then left again on Smith Road where Northern Boulevard ends. The entrance will be on the right in about 0.25 mile.

GPS: N40 47.785' / W72 53.117'

THE RIDE

This mostly flat ride crosses a scenic bay onto Fire Island, visits Smith Point County Park and the Atlantic Ocean, then returns with a detour into downtown Mastic Beach on the way back to the ride start at Wertheim National Wildlife Refuge. With a maximum elevation of 34 feet, this 13.3-mile ride should be comfortable and easy even for novice cyclists.

From the refuge entrance, turn right onto Smith Road, a narrow street bordering the preserve forest on the right and a neighborhood on the left. Turn left at the end of Smith Road, onto Ranch Drive, and cross two side streets before the right turn onto Margin Drive West when Ranch Drive ends.

Margin Drive West is a very wide, quiet road, parallel to the William Floyd Parkway. It's designated as a bike route, but doesn't have a lane or other in-street markings. Regardless, traffic speed and volume are both low, making this a better route than the very busy parkway.

Turn left onto Robinwood Drive, at the end of Margin Drive West, then right into the painted bike lane on this stretch of the William Floyd Parkway. Traffic speeds can be quick here, but cyclists are expected and should feel comfortable in the painted lane. After a mile, past the Smith County Marina on the right, the lane merges with a wide shoulder, just before a narrow bridge with beautiful views to both sides. The shoulder disappears and bike-friendly signage declares that bikes have priority over automobiles.

Use caution crossing the short steel deck drawbridge section in the middle of the bridge. When wet, the grates can be slippery and treacherous for cyclists. At the end of the bridge, continue on the Parkway and enter the traffic circle ahead. The first turn exits to the Wilderness visitor center, which offers exhibits on area flora and fauna and other resources for Fire Island visitors.

The route continues past the visitor center, turning right at the second exit from the circle onto Fire Island Beach Road and continuing past the Smith Point Beach Hut and TWA Flight 800 Memorial, turning around at the Smith Point Park Campgrounds and heading back through Smith Point Park toward the traffic circle and William Floyd Parkway.

There are two beachfronts here: the southern front, past the visitor center or the beach hut, is an Atlantic Ocean beach, and the northern is a quieter, protected bay beach. The beach hut has restrooms and food concessions. Once finished here, continue to the traffic circle and turn right at the first exit, back onto William Floyd Parkway.

From the traffic circle, this is a 1.8-mile ride on the Parkway, most of which has the same bike lane as the outbound route. At the signs for historic Mastic Beach village, turn right, onto Neighborhood Road, a quieter and less-well maintained street full of patched asphalt and some potholes.

This road enters into the commercial section of Mastic Beach, with delis, ice cream parlors, and neighborhood businesses. Turn left onto Elder Drive

Narrow Bay from Smith County Point Park

just after Mastic Beach Village Hall, which doubles as a visitor welcome center, and then immediately left onto Commack Road.

Commack Road crosses Neighborhood Drive and passes through a neighborhood of small, modest homes before ending at Palmetto Drive. Turn right and follow the road until returning to William Floyd Parkway, where the route turns right, continuing north in the bike lane for just over a half-mile.

At a signalized intersection, turn left onto Robinwood Drive then right onto Margin Drive West, retracing the outbound route. Turn left onto Ranch Drive, then right onto Smith Road, ending the ride back at the Wertheim National Wildlife Refuge parking lot.

Bike Shops

East End Bicycles: 2873 Montauk Hwy., Brookhaven; (631) 399-7390; eastendbikes.com
Kreb Cycle: 10 Bell St., Bellport; (631) 286-1829; krebcycle.com

MILES AND DIRECTIONS

0.0 Start at the Wertheim National Wildlife Refuge entrance going south on Smith Road.

1.0 Left onto Ranch Drive.

1.5 Right onto Margin Drive West.

2.6 Left onto Robinwood Drive, then right onto William Floyd Parkway.

4.9 Second exit from traffic circle onto Fire Island Beach Road.

5.5 Turn around.

6.1 First exit from traffic circle onto William Floyd Parkway.

7.9 Right onto Neighborhood Road.

8.8 Left onto Elder Drive.

8.9 Left onto Commack Road.

9.8 Right onto Palmetto Drive.

9.9 Right onto William Floyd Parkway.

10.5 Left onto Robinwood Drive then right onto Margin Drive West.

11.7 Left onto Ranch Drive.

12.6 Right onto Smith Road.

13.3 Arrive at finish.

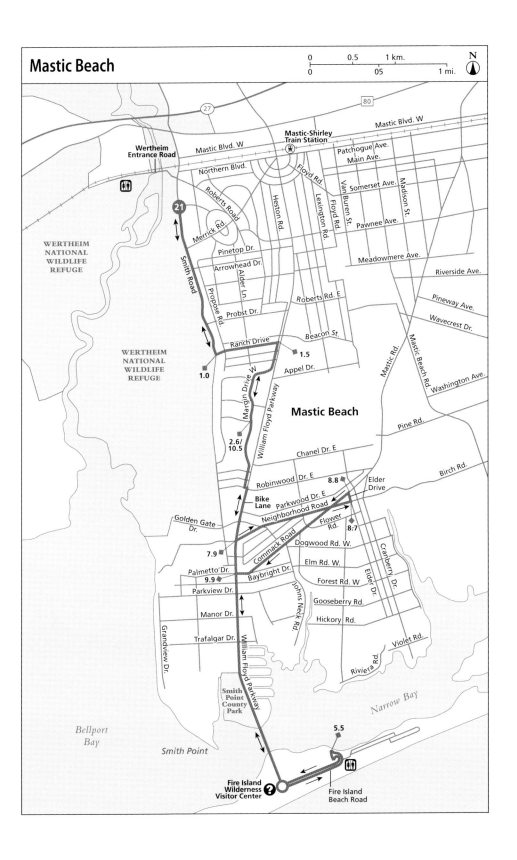

RIDE INFORMATION

Local Events/Attractions

Smith Point County Park: Smith Point County Park offers camping, swimming, scuba diving, fishing, and other outdoor recreation along the oceanfront. The park operates the Smith Point Beach Hut, a concession with a diverse menu and raw bar. The National Park Service publishes events and notices on their park website, located at nps.gov/fiis/planyourvisit/smith-point-county-park.htm.

The Wertheim National Wildlife Refuge: One of the last undeveloped estuaries on Long Island, this preserve provides habitats for an assortment of wildlife, including box turtles, osprey, wild turkey, white-tailed deer, muskrats, foxes, and even nesting bald eagles. The refuge also preserves habitats, including pitch pine and pine-oak woodlands and hundreds of acres of healthy wetlands. The park maintains a visitor center and hiking trails. Learn more on their website, at fws.gov/refuge/wertheim.

Fire Island National Seashore: Fire Island is a beautiful, preserved natural barrier island, serving as a barrier for the bays and inlets of southern Long Island. The National Park Service offers camping, beach spots, educational programs, and maritime history with a variety of year-round services. Learn more on their website, at nps.gov/fiis/index.htm.

Restaurants

Smith Point Beach Hut: Fire Island Beach Road, Fire Island; (631) 281-7789; thebeachhuts.com

EmpanadaVille: 374 Neighborhood Rd., Mastic Beach; (631) 399-3526; empanadaville.net

Hero Haven: 478 Neighborhood Rd., Shirley; (631) 399-3802

Paradise Ice Cream Parlor: 410 Neighborhood Rd., Mastic Beach; (631) 657-3331

Handy Pantry: 321 Neighborhood Rd., Mastic Beach; (631) 399-0821; handypantrystores.com

Mastic Deli & Market: 234 County Rd. 46 #2, Shirley; (631) 281-7210

Town & Country Deli: 157 Commack Rd., Mastic Beach; (631) 399-1172

Restrooms

0.0: Wertheim National Wildlife Refuge
5.5: The Beach Hut at Smith Point County Park
8.8: Mastic Beach Village Hall

Glacier 8 at Hidden Pond Park

The hamlet of Hauppauge is believed to derive its name from an Algonquian word meaning "sweet waters." A high water table and plentiful natural springs support the theory. This ride explores the mountain bike trails of Hidden Pond Park, a forested area with swampy sections fed by those underground water sources. In addition to being a fantastic mountain bike location, Hauppauge may also be known to cyclists as the corporate headquarters of White Lightning Co., developers of a popular wax-based chain lubricant advertised as the "first and only chain lube that would self-clean."

Start: The trailhead at Hidden Pond Park, in Woodbury

Length: 4.0 miles

Riding time: About 30 minutes

Best bike: Mountain bike

Terrain and trail surface: Single track, short section of two-way trail

Traffic and hazards: This ride takes place in a car-free park. Use caution around hikers and dog walkers, who are likely to follow the fire road through the blue-blazed trail. The descent on the orange-blazed trail can be treacherous. Other challenges include a few log features and exposed tree roots. As with any singletrack park, do not ride the trails if wet, to prevent damaging them.

Things to see: Scenic overlook from the peak of the blue blaze trail, hardwood trees, and several species of small, migratory birds.

Fees: None. Hidden Pond Park does not charge for admission. Park near the handball and tennis courts.

Getting there: Take the Long Island Expressway (I-495E) to exit 58 North on Old Nichols Road to Terry Road. Turn left at the entrance to Hidden Pond Park. Follow the park road until it ends at a parking lot near the handball and tennis courts. Transit users could take the Long Island Rail

Road to Central Islip station, about 4 miles from the ride start, and follow the bike route in a wide shoulder on East Suffolk Avenue until the left turn onto Terry Road to the park entrance on the left. Unfortunately, no local buses exist to complete the route, making for a less than ideal 8-mile round-trip of road riding on a mountain bike.

GPS: N40 49.150' / W73 10.087'

THE RIDE

This short singletrack route was renovated and expanded in 2013 by CLIMB, the Concerned Long Island Mountain Bicyclists, a group of mountain bike enthusiasts who manage and maintain nearly two dozen trails on Long Island. This route is popular particularly among climbers for its challenging hills and the banked turns on the descents. The trail doesn't have many technical obstacles: Outside of a handful of log features, the challenges on this trail come from three steep climbs. If a log feature is outside of your abilities, dismount and walk the bike around it to avoid braiding the trail. All singletrack routes are one-way; follow the directions and posted signage carefully. Although these trails should be avoided if wet, many ride them in the winter on fat tire bikes, and the trails are maintained for this activity.

Starting by the handball and tennis courts, follow the dirt road to the fence at the end, and turn right onto the Yellow / Blue Dot trail, on a flat section through hardwood trees with exposed tree roots. This path is two way, so watch for oncoming riders and stay to the right. The blazes for this section are a field of yellow with blue dots.

When the route forks, bear right onto the Mellow Yellow loop, a gentle counterclockwise circle blazed with yellow markings, through a pretty section of marshy forests back to the Yellow / Blue Dot trail.

Head south, passing some golf course property on the right, to continue warming up before the first climb. Shortly after the entrance, bear right onto the singletrack Blue Cruzer loop. Blazings for this trail are blue. The trail crosses the fire road, blazed with white markings, then heads uphill into hardest climb of the ride, a 100-foot elevation gain with sections as steep as 10 percent. After the peak, the path levels out and approaches a scenic overlook toward the north offering views of the treetops below.

During the descent, turn right onto the Orange-Palooza Black Diamond trail, a curvy, winding downhill path with banked sides. This is a fast, technical descent, and riders who know how to bank on berms will be able to attain high speeds. This section of trail is blazed with orange markings, and runs parallel to the Motor Parkway, out of sight but audible, to the right.

When the Orange-Palooza trail bottoms out and curves left, stay right to rejoin the Blue Cruzer, near the 2.5-mile mark, following the blue blazes. After a lovely narrow section, turn left, following the pink blazes of the Pink-alicious Black Diamond trail, a gnarly, curvy series of climbs winding around and around until rejoining the Blue Cruzer, on a left turn, near the 3.5-mile mark. Follow the route north, back to the Yellow / Blue Dot trail, and turn right near the 3.8-mile mark to arrive back to the ride start.

The park has a snack bar and restroom at the Rinx facility. Otherwise, options are mostly limited to national chains within a mile or two of the park entrance, detailed below. None of these destinations are particularly bike-friendly, being located in car-centric suburban areas.

> ## Bike Shops
>
> **The Cycle Company:** 564 West Jericho Turnpike, Smithtown; (631) 979-7078
> **The Bike Cave:** 194 Commack Rd., Commack; (631) 499-2453
> **Bike Depot East:** 75 West Main St., East Islip; (631) 581-5557; thebikedepoteast.com
> **Sayville Bike Works:** 75 Main St., Sayville; (631) 589-0009; sayvillebike.com/main.shtml

MILES AND DIRECTIONS

0.0 Start at trailhead on Yellow / Blue Dot Trail then right to stay on Yellow / Blue Dot Trail.

0.3 Right onto Yellow Blaze loop.

0.8 Continue onto Yellow / Blue Dot Trail.

1.0 Continue onto Blue Blaze Trail.

1.2 Continue on Blue Blaze Trail.

1.4 Pass White Blaze Trail.

1.6 Cross White Blaze Trail.

1.7 Right onto Orange Blaze Trail.

2.3 Right onto Blue Blaze Trail.

2.5 Left onto Pink Blaze Trail.

3.5 Left onto Blue Blaze Trail.

3.8 Right onto Yellow / Blue Dot Trail.

4.0 Arrive at finish.

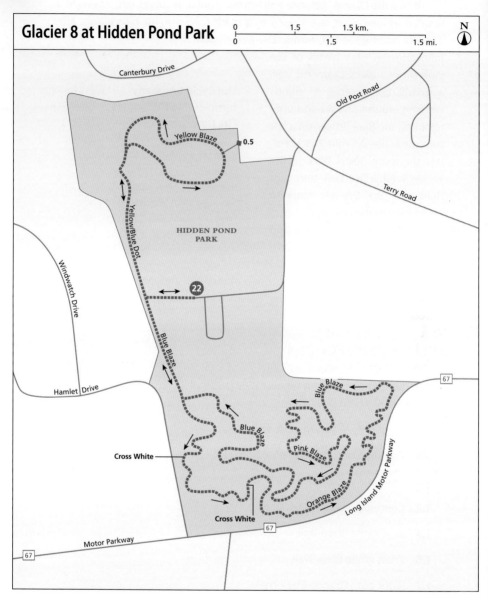

Glacier 8 at Hidden Pond Park

RIDE INFORMATION

Local Events/Attractions

Hidden Pond Park: The Town of Islip owns this park, which is operated in collaboration with local volunteers, associations, and companies. The mountain bike trails are managed by CLIMB, the section of the Long Island Greenbelt hiking trail by the trail conference group, and the developed attractions by

The Rinx, a private corporation. They offer a snack bar with grilled foods and cheap bites, skating rink, day camp, cross fit gym, and a pool. Parking, restrooms, and the snack bar are free, and the other entertainments are accessible with an inexpensive daily pass. The park has two ponds, but they're closer to swamps: Depending on rainfall and heat, they may or may not be full of water.

CLIMB (Concerned Long Island Mountain Bicyclists): This nonprofit organization maintains trails and organizes mountain bike events all over Long Island. Check their website to learn about local events to Glacier 8, at climbonline.org. Local riders use the CLIMB forums to coordinate group rides, too, which may be of interest to visitors.

Long Island Greenbelt Trail: Consisting of more than 200 miles of hiking paths on Long Island, the LI Greenbelt runs through Hidden Pond Park, on the white-blazed fire road. More information on the hiking trail system is available from the Long Island Greenbelt Trail Conference website, at ligreenbelt.org.

Restaurants
Crazy Crepe Cafe: 71 East Main St., Smithtown; (631) 656-8866; crazycrepecafe.com
Starbucks: 3701 Expressway. Dr. North, Islandia; (631) 553-3706; starbucks.com
Hauppauge Palace Diner: 525 Smithtown Bypass, Hauppauge; (631) 724-1775; hpdiner.com
Panera Bread: 399 Nesconset Hwy., Hauppauge; (631) 979-2028; panerabread.com
Starbucks: 513 NY 111, Hauppauge; (631) 724-0928; starbucks.com
Starbucks: 465 Smithtown Blvd., Nesconset; (631) 979-3093; starbucks.com

Restrooms
0.0: North of parking lot
0.6: Just south of trail on White/Red Dot trail to park entrance trailhead

South Shore

The hamlets of Sayville and Bayport are two charming historic communities in Brookhaven, on the South Shore of Suffolk County. The first of these, Sayville, was originally a logging and oyster-farming site for neighboring communities, and wasn't settled until 1761. The community would forgo a name until the US Postal Service requested one after nearly 80 years of habitation. Residents were split between Greensville and Edwardsville, honoring two early settlers, so they compromised on Seaville. Why Sayville, then? Local historians claim the filing clerk misspelled sea as say because his only spelling reference was an old Bible. The residents appealed to the Postmaster General to change the spelling back, but he refused, citing a surplus of Seavilles and a dearth of Sayvilles. This plausible-sounding legend is interesting trivia, but the historicity is hard to determine. Neighboring Bayport is probably best known as being home to the fictional mystery-solving Hardy Boys, from the eponymous young adult series by Franklin W. Dixon.

Start: West Avenue by the Long Island Maritime Museum parking lot.

Length: 9.1 miles

Riding time: About 45 minutes

Best bike: Road bike or hybrid

Terrain and trail surface: Asphalt

Traffic and hazards: The first section of Main Road is car-centric, with large, open parking lots. The second is a bustling downtown, with curbside parking and heavy foot traffic. Use caution and good judgment navigating this area.

Things to see: Lovely views of Great South Bay and several picturesque views of marshland and creeks. Several points of historical interest are here including the John E. Roosevelt Estate and other architecturally distinctive homes.

Fees: None. The Long Island Maritime Museum charges for admission but not parking.

Getting there: Take the Long Island Expressway (I-495E) to exit 59 South. Continue on Lakeland Avenue, crossing Veterans Highway and Sunrise Highway, until Lakeland Avenue becomes Railroad Avenue. Turn right onto West Main Street then left onto West Avenue to the ride start at the museum parking lot. Transit users can take the Long Island Rail Road to Sayville. Follow Depot Street west to Greeley Avenue, and turn left. Turn right onto West Main Street and continue until the left turn onto West Avenue to the museum parking lot.

GPS: N40 43.367' / W73 05.687'

THE RIDE

Starting on West Avenue, this ride heads toward downtown Sayville then turns onto quiet neighborhood streets, visiting a beach and marina before heading into nearby Bayport to visit Bayport Beach. Bayport is a quiet town compared to Sayville, but the town green is picturesque and the beach lovely.

From West Avenue, turn right onto West Main Street (Montauk Highway) along a very commercial strip with big box stores, car dealerships, and a preponderance of gas stations. The route also passes Sayville Bike Works, on the left, just after the initial turn.

After crossing a little creek, take the second right onto Sunset Drive, just before a liquor store. The road passes through a residential neighborhood of modest homes before curving right along the water.

Turn left just ahead onto Jones Drive until the road ends in a T-junction with Handsome Avenue. Turn right, then left onto Elm Street at the 1.5-mile mark. These roads all travel through quiet neighborhoods, with low traffic volumes and speeds. When Elm Street ends, turn right onto Foster Avenue, to the Sayville Beach and Park and Port of Call, the Marina site.

Turn left onto Browns River Road, then left again onto River Road, after 0.2 mile of beachfront road. Follow River Road to Terry Street, where the route turns left, then immediately right to continue on River Road, past The Cull House restaurant.

Ahead, River Street finally comes into view of the river, and then turns curves around a parking lot to continue heading north before ending at a stop sign at the intersection with Hamilton Street. Turn left and follow this short neighborhood road to the right turn onto Foster Avenue just ahead.

From Foster, turn right onto Middle Road (CR 65) into a wide shoulder, and head away from Bayport. On the left, the ride passes an Episcopal Church in a pretty, low-profile stone building, and then the historic Meadow Croft

Bird houses at The Long Island Maritime Museum grounds

estate, formerly the John E. Roosevelt Estate, before crossing through a section of picturesque marshland.

Bike Shops

Sayville Bike Works: 75 Main St., Sayville; (631) 589-0009; sayvillebike.com
Bike Depot East: 75 West Main St., East Islip; (631) 581-5557; thebikedepoteast.com

After 1.5 miles on Middle Road, the route reaches a lovely green with a gazebo, the Bayport Memorial Park. Tiny downtown Bayport is just 400 feet ahead on Middle Road, with a few shops and the Golden Sparrow coffee house, for a short detour.

Continuing on the mapped route, turn right just before the green onto Esplanada, then right again onto Gerritsen Avenue. At the edge of the bay, turn left onto William Street, and up to Bayport Beach. The beach has a shaded gazebo, boardwalk, and restrooms.

After a break, continue onto Paulanna Road, back to Esplanada, and retrace the outbound route, following Middle Road toward Sayville. At Foster Avenue, turn right, then left onto North Main Street. From here, the ride heads through the thriving downtown of Sayville, past a number of coffee shops, bakeries, and cafes, on a sometimes hectic stretch of road.

Gazebo on the beach

Just past Sayville Bike Works, turn left onto West Avenue, and finish the ride back at the Long Island Maritime Museum.

MILES AND DIRECTIONS

0.0 Start at the Long Island Maritime Museum and exit left onto West Avenue.

0.4 Right onto West Main Street.

0.7 Right onto Sunset Drive.

1.2 Left onto Jones Drive.

1.4 Right onto Handsome Avenue.

1.5 Left onto Elm Street.

2.0 Right onto Foster Avenue.

2.1 Left onto Browns River Road.

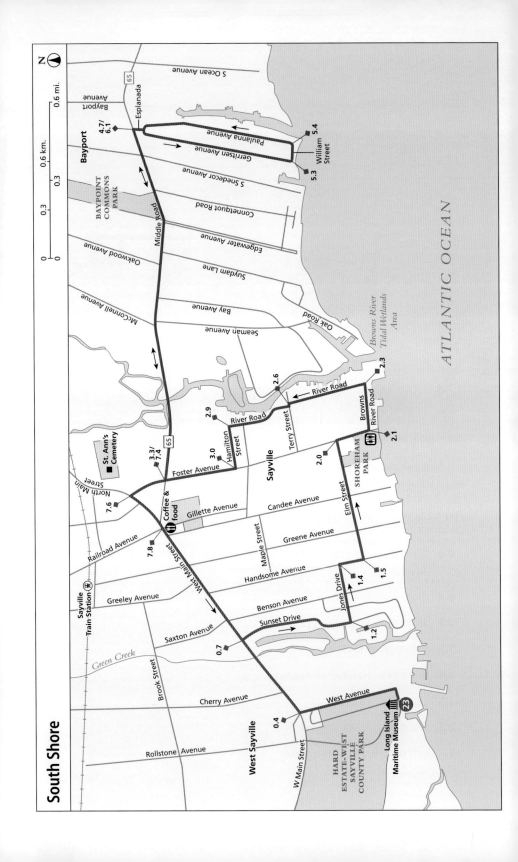

South Shore

ATLANTIC OCEAN

N

0   0.3   0.6 km.

0   0.3   0.6 mi.

Bayport

BAYPOINT COMMONS PARK

Oakwood Avenue

McConnell Avenue

Middle Road

65

Esplanada

Bayport Avenue

S Ocean Avenue

Paulanna Avenue

Gerritsen Avenue

S Snedecor Avenue

Connetquot Road

Edgewater Avenue

Suydam Lane

Bay Avenue

Seaman Avenue

Oak Road

4.7/6.1

5.3

5.4

William Street

Browns River Tidal Wetlands Area

St. Ann's Cemetery

65

3.3/7.4

3.0

Foster Avenue

Hamilton Street

River Road

River Road

2.9

2.6

2.3

Browns River Road

Terry Street

Sayville

2.0

SHOREHAM PARK

2.1

North Main Street

Coffee & food

7.6

7.8

Railroad Avenue

Sayville Train Station

Gillette Avenue

Candee Avenue

Greene Avenue

Maple Street

Elm Street

1.5

1.4

Jones Drive

Handsome Avenue

Benson Avenue

Greeley Avenue

West Main Street

Saxton Avenue

Sunset Drive

0.7

Green Creek

Brook Street

1.2

Cherry Avenue

West Avenue

Rollstone Avenue

W Main Street

West Sayville

0.4

HARD ESTATE–WEST SAYVILLE COUNTY PARK

Long Island Maritime Museum

23

2.3   Left onto River Road.

2.6   Left onto Terry Street then right onto River Road.

2.9   Left onto Hamilton Street.

3.0   Right onto Foster Avenue.

3.3   Right onto Middle Road / CR 65.

4.7   Right onto Esplanada then right onto Gerritsen Avenue.

5.3   Left onto William Street.

5.4   Left onto Paulanna Avenue.

6.0   Left onto Esplanada.

6.1   Left onto Middle Road.

7.4   Right onto Foster Avenue.

7.6   Left onto North Main Street.

7.8   Continue on West Main Street.

8.7   Left onto West Avenue.

9.0   Right at LI Maritime Museum Entrance.

9.1   Arrive at finish.

RIDE INFORMATION

Local Events/Attractions

Long Island Maritime Museum: Over 200 years of Long Island maritime history is collected and told in the nine historic buildings and 14 acres that comprise the museum grounds. Visitors can walk the grounds for free. A nominal fee is charged for tours and entrance to the museum, which contains a massive collection of artifacts, photographs, and documents.

Area Beaches: This route visits Sayville Beach and Park, a lovely sandy beach on Great South Bay, and the Sayville Marina Park, a long pier with scenic views. In Bayport, the ride passes the Bayport Memorial Park and visits the Bayport Beach at the turning point.

Sayville Historical Society: The local historical society offers tours of the Edwards Homestead, a museum containing artifacts from early Sayville families, named after the family of town founder John Edwards. Schedule a tour on their website, sayville.com/historicalsociety.

Sayville Ferry Service: This ferry runs trips to nearby Fire Island. Bicycles are not permitted. Routes, cost, and schedule are on their website, at sayvilleferry .com.

Sayville Farmers Market: Every Saturday at the Islip Grange, located at the intersection of Broadway Avenue and Montauk Highway.

Telefunken / Sayville Wireless: A German firm built this wireless facility in 1911, and later used it to transmit information on the Lusitania and to ask Mexico for a military alliance against the United States. The British intercepted and decoded these messages, leading America into World War I. The station was decommissioned and abandoned, but a local group of historians has sought to restore the site for a future museum exploring the history of the wireless and Long Island. More on the history of the wireless station can also be found at the Long Island Maritime Museum.

Islip Grange Park: North of the route, the Islip Grange Park is a collection of historic buildings from early European settlers. A church, barn, and windmill are among the structures preserved in the park at 10 Broadway Ave., Sayville.

Restaurants

Cornucopia Natural Foods: 39 North Main St., Sayville; (631) 589-9579; cornucopiahealthfoods.com

Sayville Sandwich: 291 West Main St., Sayville; (631) 750-9298

Starbucks: 59 Main St., Sayville; (631) 244-8983; starbucks.com

Fritzsche's Bakery: 56 Main St., Sayville; (631) 589-0586

Blackbirds' Grille: 553 Old Montauk Hwy., Sayville; (631) 563-4144; blackbirdsgrille.com

The Golden Sparrow: 570 Middle Rd., Bayport; (631) 472-1857

The Cull House: 75 Terry St., Sayville; (631) 563-1546; cullhouse.com

Bagels Delox: 372 Montauk Hwy., Sayville; (631) 563-2716

Off The Block: 501 Montauk Hwy., Sayville; (631) 573-6655; offtheblockmeats.com

Restrooms

0.0: LI Maritime Museum
2.1: Sayville Beach and Park
5.4: Bayport Beach

Babylon to Lake Belmont

Babylon: Ancient city-state of Mesopotamia, Rastafarian euphemism for wickedness, and a healthy, thriving Suffolk County town on the South Shore. When Nathaniel Conklin's influential family moved to Huntington South, into a home next to a tavern, his mother called the area "another Babylon." At the time, it was a stopover for travelers, who came to harvest salt hay from the lagoons for their cattle ranches and homes on the North Shore. Mrs. Conklin was determined to improve the character of the region and make it a "New Babylon," words Nathaniel would later etch into a stone tablet to be incorporated in the fireplace he built for his own home.

Although the town would go through many changes, the name and moral aspirations stuck. Huntington South became Babylon in 1872, when it passed its first resolution setting aside an appropriation of $1,500 for impoverished residents. The salt hay industry declined, but travelers kept coming, transported by a new rail system and welcomed by a booming hotel industry. Instead of cattle ranchers, these new visitors were well-heeled New Yorkers, seeking the natural beauty of barrier beaches and Fire Island.

Start: Argyle Park trailhead in Babylon Village

Length: 8.0 miles

Riding time: 30–45 minutes

Best bike: Hybrid

Terrain and trail surface: Asphalt, hard packed dirt, and gravel

Traffic and hazards: Use caution on the road crossings over Trolley Line Road, Park Avenue, and Locust Avenue, all near the start. Ride carefully and considerately around riders on horseback on the Southards Pond trails.

Things to see: Rustic trail meandering around scenic two lakes and a pond. The water crossings are especially picturesque, over rustic bridges and causeways.

24

THE RIDE

This easy off-road ride visits a series of interlinked recreational paths, starting in Babylon Village Park, continuing through Southards Pond Park, and completing a lap around Belmont Lake in West Babylon before embarking on the return trip. The route can easily be ridden in reverse, or from various entry points along the route.

Starting at the southernmost portion, on Argyle Lake, follow the hardpack gravel clockwise, passing over a lovely dam and bearing right over a short causeway. At the northernmost point, turn right onto the sidewalk, and then carefully exit the sidewalk down a short ramp to Trolley Line Road, on the left, just before the bridge. Cross the street into the parking lot and follow a small paved trail under the railroad bridge.

This stretch of trail follows the tranquil feeder creek of Argyle Lake past a dog park and ball field, then crosses Locust Avenue on a green-painted crosswalk. Use caution and watch for oncoming vehicles as you navigate onto the next section of trail, past another ball field and the tennis courts, to the next painted crossing over Park Avenue. Follow the route past the basketball courts then bear left, diagonally away from the basketball court, onto a hardpacked dirt trail into the woods of Southards Pond Park. This wide, open pathway is popular for horseback riding, so give riders and horses plenty of space.

Horseback riding at Southards Pond Park

Follow the trail, bearing left at the next fork, and wind around until a tunnel under NY 27 above.

The next 2.5 miles of the path intertwine with the Carlls River, one of the largest river systems on the island, in a scenic stretch of forestland. Near the end of this area, the path separates in three directions: Right and left exit onto Sylvan Road. Continue straight, through the tunnel, with more scenic views of the river to the left.

The trail continues through a very low tunnel just ahead, beneath the Southern State Parkway. Tall riders may wish to dismount; the ceiling is just over 6 feet tall. Exit the tunnel onto the paved Belmont Lake State Park trail, turning left, over a picturesque stone bridge with views of the lake along the right. In 400 feet, bear right, passing the Belmont Cannons. As the sign explains, these were captured by Commodore Oliver Hazard Perry, who won the Naval Battle of Lake Erie and wrote President James Madison with the quote, "We have met the enemy and they are ours...." The cannons were placed here in tribute to the Commodore by his niece, Caroline Slidell Perry, who lived here with her husband, August Belmont, the famous German–American politician and namesake of the Belmont Stakes horse race.

Trail south of Lake Belmont

Bike Shops

Babylon Bike Shop: 218 East Main St., Babylon; (631) 587-6709; babylonbikeshop.com

The Vicious Cycle: 213 Higbie Ln., West Islip; (631) 669-3174; viciouscycleny.com

Sunrise Tri: 520 Sunrise Hwy., West Babylon; (631) 587-6200; sunrisecyclery.com

Lindenhurst Bike Works: 27 West Montauk Hwy., Lindenhurst; (631) 956-0225

The estate was later purchased by the State of New York and the mansion converted into park headquarters until 1935, when it was torn down and replaced with the present structure, visible beyond the cannons and just to the right.

Continue on the trail, heading north, with more views of the park on the right. Cross a rustic wooden bridge and turn left onto a wide dirt path for a tiny side loop that rejoins the path just ahead, before the second bridge.

Exit the loop, left, and continue over this second bridge, then turn right, following the water into the main area of the park. The trail passes restrooms, picnicking spots, a playground, snack concessions, and a boat launch with paddleboats and rowboats.

Continue following the water southward, back to the stone bridge, and turn left, out of the park. Watch your head again under the low-clearance tunnel and continue along the same route as before, back to Southards Pond Park. This time, turn left toward the pond for a scenic view of the water and follow the route nearly to the entrance, then turn right to continue on the trail.

The trail exits behind the small park on Park Avenue. Cross Park Avenue, continuing behind the tennis courts and the water, continuing down and across Locust Avenue to Trolley Line Road. Turn left at the lake, taking the path along the water, past the Babylon Panthers baseball and football fields. The fields are named after the first African–American baseball team, the Babylon Black Panthers, made up of people who may have worked in service at the Argyle Hotel. When they went on the road, they renamed the team the Cuban Giants. None of the players were Cuban, but they claimed to be in order to avoid violence and discrimination based solely on their race. Today, the high school baseball team remembers this groundbreaking group in their name, the Babylon Panthers.

MILES AND DIRECTIONS

0.0 Start at Argyle Park and head left, around Argyle Lake.

0.4 Exit the park onto Trolley Line Road, then left onto the trail behind the parking lot, along the creek.

0.7 Cross Locust Avenue, continue on the trail.

0.8 Cross Park Avenue, continue on the trail to the left behind basketball courts through Southards Pond Park.

1.8 Pass through the tunnel under NY 27.

3.3 Pass through two tunnels, the first under Sylvan Avenue, the second under the Southern State Parkway, then turn left onto the trail around Belmont Lake.

3.9 Turn left to follow the smaller side trail.

4.4 Turn left onto the main trail.

4.8 Turn left to follow the trail back under the series of tunnels.

6.3 Pass through the tunnel under NY 27.

6.7 Turn left into Southards Park along the pond.

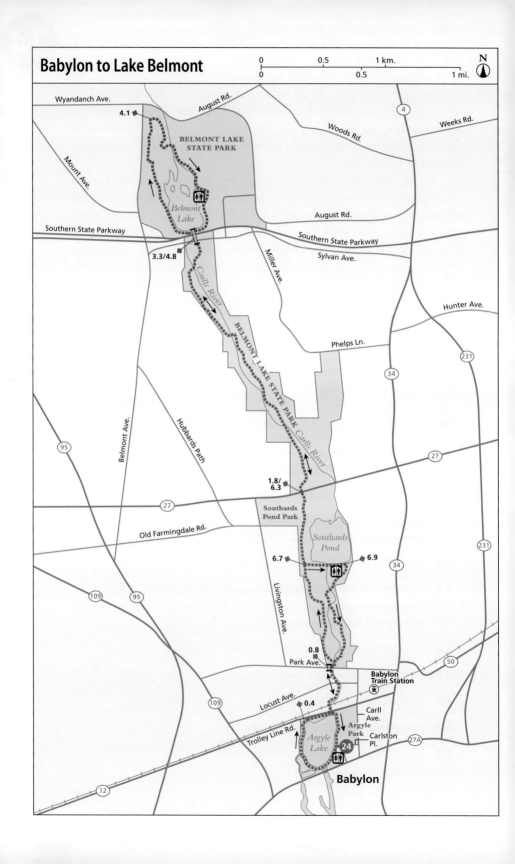

6.9 Turn right to follow the trail south.

7.5 Ride the trail to the basketball court and cross Park Avenue, following the trail beside the tennis courts.

7.6 Cross Locust Avenue, continue on the trail.

7.8 Left onto Trolley Line Road and onto trail east of Argyle Lake.

8.0 Arrive at finish.

RIDE INFORMATION

Local Events/Attractions
Belmont Lake State Park: The highlight of this ride is the 463-acre Belmont Lake State Park, a day park where August Belmont once lived and kept horses. The park charges a vehicle use fee for entry by automobile most weekends from Apr to Oct.

Argyle Park: This municipal park in the village of Babylon is situated around the 25-acre eponymous lake. Popular with anglers and recreational users, the park also offers a number of events, including a popular annual country fair organized by the Babylon Beautification Society. See its website for more information at babylonbeautification.org/county-fair.html.

Southards Pond: This 19-acre pond is a natural part of the Carlls River system. The area is a scenic refuge, composed of undeveloped parkland, woods, and marshes.

Nathaniel Conklin House: This historic site holds events and offers tours of the gardens and home of the influential resident who reputedly named the town Babylon. The village maintains a website listing events, hours, and other information necessary for a visit, at villageofbabylonny.gov/conklin-house.

Village of Babylon Historical Society: The society maintains a museum in the former offices of Henry Livingston (1837–1906), editor and publisher of the *Southside Signal,* a newspaper in the late nineteenth century. The building later was occupied by the library and now serves as a museum depicting life in the village from the nineteenthcentury to the 1940s.

Restaurants
Babylon Bean Coffee House: 17 Fire Island Ave., Babylon; (631) 587-7729; thebabylonbean.com

Jack Jack's Coffee House: 223 Deer Park Ave., Babylon; (631) 526-9983; jackjackscoffeehouse.com

Bagelicious: 114 Deer Park Ave., Babylon; (631) 539-9893; bagelicious.com

Glen's Dinette: 23 East Main St., Babylon; (631) 669-4700; glensdinette.com

Karinia's Deli: 80 West Main St., Babylon; (631) 482-1912; karinasdeli.com
Juice 'N Blendz: 17 Deer Park Ave., Babylon; (631) 482-9550; juicenblendz.com
The Villager: 262 Deer Park Ave., Babylon; (631) 482-8585; thevillagerbabylon.com
Starbucks: 1238 Deer Park Ave., North Babylon; (631) 667-1647; starbucks.com

Restrooms

0.0: Argyle Park
3.6: Belmont Lake State Park
6.9: Southards Pond Park

Oyster Bay and Northwest Suffolk

Oyster Bay is the easternmost Nassau County town, comprising some thirty-six villages and hamlets. The 169-square mile town spans the entire height of the island, bordering Long Island Sound to the north, Suffolk County to the east, and the Atlantic Ocean to the south. Although separated by county and town borders, the locations in this section have much in common, starting with a shared history dating back to their foundings, and courtroom battles initiated over territorial overlaps.

This section starts in northwestern Suffolk, with three rides beginning in parts of Huntington. The first heads east, through Smithtown, visiting the extensive park system along the Nissequogue River in the hamlet of Kings Park. The second starts in the Huntington Hamlet of Cold Spring Harbor and visits the northern border on Lloyd Neck, detouring through a grand estate turned State park and nature preserve. The third starts in Huntington and visits the North Shore Hamlet of Oyster Bay. The next ride circles the eponymous bay of Oyster Bay, starting in the hamlet and staying within the township; the last ride visits the small city of Glen Cove, which is entirely surrounded by the Town of Oyster Bay. Glen Cove is small, but it has three important history museums featured in this ride. The last route revisits the Nassau/Suffolk border, following Bethpage Bikeway, a 13-mile linear trail through a surprisingly verdant area.

Oyster Bay is served by the Oyster Bay branch of the Long Island Rail Road, a spur from the Main Line, which has stations in Bethpage and Hicksville. The region is crisscrossed with major highways and automobile routes.

Kings Park Loop

The Kings Park Psychiatric Center, built in 1885, was founded on the then novel idea that overcrowded, gloomy hospitals were not conducive to recovery. The State of New York operated this hospital as an agrarian farm colony, where patients fed livestock and grew produce. The hamlet was named for the hospital, which served as the primary employer and economic-driver for the region. Following cutbacks in mental health care spending and advances in pharmacology, the center closed in 1996 after 111years of continuous operation. Today, most of the hospital is part of the sprawling Nissequogue River State Park, a 521-acre park overlooking the river and forming the eastern border of Kings Park. To the north, the hamlet is bordered by an environmentally protected stretch of Long Island Sound. Limited commercial development and a commitment to preservation make the area a prime spot for outdoor recreation.

Start: Bellerose Avenue at the Northport Station in East Northport

Length: 22.4 miles

Riding time: About 1 hour 45 minutes

Best bike: Road bike

Terrain and trail surface: Asphalt

Traffic and hazards: Use caution on the busy stretches of NY 25A in downtown Smithtown and Northport.

Things to see: Long country roads through preserved forests, several tranquil parks just off the route, the controversial Whisper the Bull statue in Smithtown and other historical points-of-interest.

Fees: None. Parking is free at the Northport Station.

Getting there: Take exit 42 from I-495 E onto the Northern State Parkway toward Hauppauge, then exit 42N for CR 66 N toward Northport onto Deer Park Road. Bear right onto East Deer Park Road, then left onto Elwood Road. Turn right onto Bellerose Avenue to the ride start at the train station. Transit users can take the Long Island Rail Road to the Northport Station at the start of the ride.

GPS: N40 52.885' / W73 19.620'

THE RIDE

This loop starts in East Northport, a hamlet of Huntington, and heads east, through Kings Park into Smithtown, before heading north toward Nissequogue River and Sunken Meadow State Parks. The last quarter of the ride travels just outside the historic maritime village of Northport before turning southward to the ride finish in East Northport.

From the start, head east on Bellerose Avenue, crossing the major intersection where Vernon Valley and Larkfield Roads meet, to continue on Bellerose through a neighborhood with a comfortable road shoulder and low traffic volumes. Bellerose becomes Wren Court at the 1.1-mile mark, curving slightly left, and then ending at Old Bridge Road, where the route turns right. The road follows a bridge over the train tracks below, then crosses Pulaski Road before ending at a T-junction with 5th Ave. Turn left then right onto Stoothoff Road, a twisty road that seems to have been built after the houses it winds around.

At the end of Stoothoff Road, turn sharply left onto Town Line Road, a wider, shouldered road leading to a right turn onto Old Northport Road. The route passes through an industrial area bordered by construction supply companies and stone companies before crossing a bridge over a highway, then turning left, onto Old Commack Road, into a tree-lined neighborhood.

At the service station, turn right onto Pulaski Road, a busy main thoroughfare with a wide shoulder. Pulaski ends just ahead at the intersection with NY 25A (Main Road) where the route crosses over to continue on Old Dock Road, then right onto Church Street, then left at the next signalized intersection, onto East Main Street. This slight detour skips a tight, congested quarter-mile stretch of Main Road.

After a post office and high school, the shoulder becomes a painted bike lane, and the road continues to a signalized intersection. Turn right to stay on NY 25A, on a fast descent past little ponds and parkland, past the larger-than-life statue of Whisper the Bull. Bear left onto West Main Street on a bridge over the Nissequogue, into a built-up and very busy section of downtown Smithtown, and turn left after 0.4 mile onto Edgewood Avenue. After the hill, turn left onto Landing Avenue. The next 6.7 miles are the most scenic on the

This larger-than-life statue of Whisper the Bull has both supporters and detractors

route, first passing Landing Avenue Park on the right, then over a picturesque bridge and past Sweetbriar Park on the left. The road climbs a fairly steep section after passing the historic Smithtown Landing Methodist Church and cemetery.

The climb peaks along a golf course property, then descends rapidly along the border of Arthur Kunz County Park. The entrance is on the right, after the stop sign, where the route turns left to continue on Landing Road, then immediately goes right onto Longfellow Drive.

From Longfellow, turn right onto Rosewood Road, which ends with a view of the river at the junction with Violet Road. Turn left onto Violet, then right onto Highland

Bike Shops

Bike Depot North: 82 Larkfield Rd., East Northport; (631) 754-2151
Adam's Cyclery: 270 Larkfield Rd., East Northport; (631) 261-2881; adamscyclery.com
Bourget's Bike Works: 1960 Jericho Turnpike, East Northport; (631) 493-0416
The Cycle Company: 564 West Jericho Turnpike, Smithtown; (631) 979-7078
Bike Discounters: 438 Lake Ave., Saint James; (631) 862-0940; thebikeoutlet.com

Drive, then left onto Riviera for a meandering ride with an uninterrupted view of the Nissequogue.

Riviera becomes Birch Road just before the route turns right onto St. Johnland Road. Follow the road slightly uphill, past Harrison Pond and the Obadiah Smith House historic home museum, and then around the entrance to the Nissequogue River State Park.

Cross Old Dock Road and continue onto Sunken Meadow Road, another long stretch of quiet road bordering more parkland, until the route turns right at a signalized intersection onto Fort Salonga Road (NY 25A). Outside of a few suburban-style shopping plazas and a busy built-up section in Northport, the wide shoulder and straight lines of this faster country road should make for comfortable cycling.

At the 21.3-mile mark, turn left onto Laurel Road. This road passes through the Genola Cemetery, a historic burying ground still in use, before ending at the intersection with Bellerose Avenue, Vernon Valley Road, and Larkfield Road. Turn left onto Bellerose Avenue and finish back at the train station.

MILES AND DIRECTIONS

0.0 Start on Bellerose Avenue.

1.1 Continue on Wren Court.

1.4 Right onto Old Bridge Road.

1.9 Left onto 5th Ave.

2.0 Right onto Stoothoff Road.

2.7 Left onto Town Line Road.

3.5 Right onto Old Northport Road.

4.1 Left onto Old Commack Road.

5.2 Right onto Pulaski Road.

5.5 Cross Main Road onto Old Dock Road.

5.7 Right onto Church Street.

5.9 Left onto East Main Street / NY 25A.

7.6 Right onto St. Johnland Road / NY 25A.

9.5 Left onto West Main Street / NY 25A.

9.9 Left onto Edgewood Avenue.

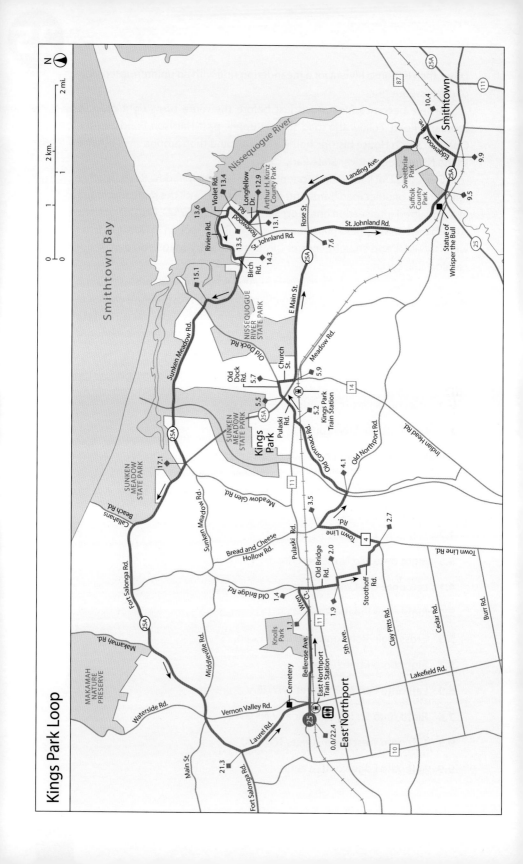

Kings Park Loop

Smithtown Bay

Nissequogue River

Smithtown

East Northport

Kings Park

N

0   1   2 km.

0   1   2 mi.

10.4   Left onto Landing Avenue.

12.9   Left onto Landing Road then right onto Longfellow Drive.

13.1   Right onto Rosewood Road.

13.4   Left onto Violet Road.

13.5   Right onto Highland Drive.

13.6   Left onto Riviera.

14.2   Continue on Birch Road.

14.3   Right onto St. Johnland Road.

15.1   Cross Old Dock Road and continue onto Sunken Meadow Road.

17.1   Right onto Fort Salonga Road / NY 25A.

21.3   Left onto Laurel Road.

22.4   Right onto Bellerose Avenue to arrive at finish.

RIDE INFORMATION

Local Events/Attractions
Kings Park Heritage Museum: This is the only school-managed community museum in the United States, planned by two residents, some high school students, and their teacher. The museum holds events, operates a store, and maintains records of important town and psychiatric center history. kpheritagemuseum.net.

Sunken Meadow State Park: This 1,287-acre park affords stunning views of Long Island Sound and the Connecticut coastline. Millions of people visit to swim and walk the 3-mile beach, bordered by majestic bluffs in the west. The park offers access to the Long Island Greenbelt, golf courses, and food concession.

Smithtown Historical Society: The society operates from a 22-acre parcel used as a museum and park in the Village of the Branch, with four historic buildings and two barns. The society manages several other properties throughout the area. smithtownhistorical.org.

Restaurants
Deli Button: 12 Laurel Rd., East Northport; (631) 261-2802
Edelweiss Delicatessen: 86 Main St., Kings Park; (631) 544-5404; edelweissdelicatessen.com
Bagel King: 5 Main St., Kings Park; (631) 269-6049
Nino's Deli: 75 West Main St., Smithtown; (631) 382-2424

Legendary Smithtown

This monument commemorates the founding of Smithtown, Long Island, N. Y., by Richard Smythe "The Bull Rider" who was granted in 1665 all the land he could cover on the back of a bull in 24 hours.

The larger-than-life statue of Whisper the Bull in downtown Smithtown serves as a monument to a larger-than-life tale about Richard Smythe, the founder of the town. The legend claims Smythe rescued the daughter of a grateful Grand Sachem Wyandanch, who then offered him any land he could encircle in one day while riding on the back of a bull. Smythe picked the longest day of the year, the Summer Solstice, to maximize his gains.

The anatomically correct statue has been a source of controversy for years, both for aesthetic reasons and because the story isn't true. Smythe's friend Gardiner actually saved Wyandanch's daughter, by negotiating a ransom price from the Narragansett tribe that had kidnapped her and taken her to Connecticut. In gratitude, Wyandanch gifted the region to Gardiner in the last year of his life, 1659, with Smythe as witness. Before Gardiner would die four years later, he signed over the property to Smythe. The bull story itself is certainly false, and it seems unlikely that the wealthy Smythe would have ever ridden a bull, a practice exclusive to poor farmers who couldn't afford horses. This aspect of the story seems at least partially inspired by the legend of Dido, Queen of Carthage, who was also reputed to possess great cunning. After leading her people in retreat from their former kingdom of Phoenicia, she entered a contract to purchase as much land as a bullhide could cover. Legend holds that Dido cut a hide into thin strips and encircled a territory that would become the great city of Carthage. Smythe had a reputation for being similarly crafty and tactical, and would outmaneuver his neighbors in nearby Huntington, using litigation to greatly expand the property Gardiner gifted him.

Crazy Crepe Cafe: 71 East Main St., Smithtown; (631) 656-8866; crazycrepecafe.com

Restrooms
0.0: Northport Train Station
10.7: Landing Avenue Park
12.9: Arthur Kunz County Park
14.7: Nissequogue River State Park
15.9: Sunken Meadow State Park

Two Harbors Ride

Cold Spring Harbor is a tiny maritime village on the North Shore of Long Island. The town successfully transitioned from an economy based on whaling to tourism after the decline of the former in the 1860s. The town would later be associated with Cold Spring Laboratory, located in a neighboring hamlet, but it may be best known to music fans as the title of Billy Joel's first studio album, recorded when the now famous singer was an unknown 22-year-old. The village also inspired novelist Richard Yates, whose final novel, titled Cold Spring Harbor, *tells a story of human restlessness and family secrets, partially set in the small hamlet.*

Start: Harbor Road by Cold Spring Harbor State Park

Length: 20.3 miles

Riding time: 90–105 minutes

Best bike: Road bike

Terrain and trail surface: Asphalt

Traffic and hazards: Downtown Cold Spring Harbor can be busy, but is overall a quiet, safe road. Use caution bearing left onto Goose Hill Road, because through traffic has right of way.

Things to see: Harbor views near the start of the ride, and from the causeway onto Lloyd Neck and along the road on the peninsula. Caumsett State Park includes historic buildings from a self-sufficient Gilded Age estate and bird habitats with more than 200 species present. Target Rock National Wildlife Refuge offers vernal ponds, birds, and diverse wildlife.

Fees: Target Rock refuge, at the end of the ride, charges a small fee to cyclists and pedestrians. Caumsett State Park is free for cyclists. Cold Spring Harbor Park offers free parking and admission, but spots are limited. If full, you may be able to pay for a spot at the Billy Joel Park and Boat Ramp across the street.

THE RIDE

This ride starts in Cold Spring Harbor and travels north, visiting Lloyd Harbor, and crossing a causeway onto the peninsula of Lloyd Neck for a detour into Caumsett State Park, a 1,750-acre park covering most of the peninsula. After the spin through a historic preservation site, the route follows the water to the Target Rock National Wildlife Refuge, before turning around to retrace back to the start. This route overlaps slightly with the next ride. To combine the two for a 40.2-mile ride, follow this ride out and back, then turn left onto Main Street and pick up the Huntington through Oyster Bay ride (NY 27).

This ride begins on Harbor Road, between Cold Spring Harbor Park on the right and Billy Joel Park and Boat Ramp on the left. Harbor Road heads uphill into the small downtown area of the village and becomes Main Street, just after passing the fire department on the right.

As the shops thin out, bear left at the fork onto Goose Mill Road. Goose Mill Road continues to climb through a quiet neighborhood, ending in a T-junction with Huntington Road. Turn right, then descend to a stop sign at the intersection with West Neck Road and turn left.

After another short descent, signs mark the entrance into the village of Lloyd Harbor and the road climbs back uphill, past a number of lovely, historic homes and a scenic pond at the Fiske Bird Sanctuary. The climb plateaus finally along the grounds of the Immaculate Conception Seminary, and the road becomes Lloyd Harbor Road, just before a steep, curvy descent down to a tranquil marsh, affording views of Long Island Sound on the left, followed by Lloyd Harbor on the right, when the road crosses a flat causeway onto the Lloyd Neck peninsula.

Curve right after the causeway and then turn left, following signs for Caumsett State Park. The park road covers a single steep hill and ends by the

Dairy buildings in Caumsett Park

entrance. Enter the park on Service Drive, past an informational booth and a walled garden on the right.

To the left of the garden, after the info booth, is a dairy complex, followed after a small intersection by equestrian fields and stables on the left. Continue straight onto a quiet, heavily shaded road. Ahead, the road curves left, past the Caumsett Manor, a magnificent home designed by Beaux Arts architect John Russell Pope in the Georgian style. Behind the house is a steep grassy hill with a gorgeous overlook view of an artificial freshwater pond and Long Island Sound. The hill is not suitable for bikes, but perfect for a walk down to the pond and trails that head to the beach.

Service Drive continues on a curving path past the house, through open meadow and fields, before arriving back by the model dairy farm and stables. Turn right to exit the park, retracing the road down to Lloyd Harbor Road, and turn left, riding along the harbor.

The road passes the Henry Lloyd Manor and George Weir Barn on the left, both maintained by the Lloyd Historical Society. The next 2 miles along the harbor serve as nesting and hunting grounds for ospreys, a common sight in the narrow tree line between the road and the water.

When the road curves to the left and heads up another steep climb, it becomes Target Rock Drive. The Target Rock National Wildlife Refuge is just ahead. The refuge consists of more than 80 acres of oak-history forest, rocky beach, vernal ponds, and important wildlife habitats. Admission fees are self-service, payable by cash or check into a secure lock box. The refuge charges a small price for cyclists and pedestrians.

After visiting the refuge, turn around and follow Target Rock Drive back to Lloyd Harbor Road to follow the outbound route back to the start of the ride, at Cold Spring Harbor State Park.

Bike Shops

Bicycle Playground: 256 Main St., Huntington; (631) 683-5522; bicycleplayground.com
Visentin Bike Pro Shop: 51 Pine Hollow Rd., Oyster Bay; (516) 922-2150

MILES AND DIRECTIONS

0.0 Start on Harbor Road at Cold Spring Harbor State Park / NY 25A.

0.2 Continue on Main Street / NY 25A.

0.7 Left onto Goose Hill Road.

1.5 Right onto Huntington Road.

2.0 Left onto West Neck Road.

5.0 Continue onto Lloyd Harbor Road.

6.0 Left onto Caumsett State Park Entrance Road.

6.6 Continue on Service Drive.

9.0 Right onto Caumsett State Park Entrance Road.

9.6 Left onto Lloyd Harbor Road.

11.8 Turn around on Lloyd Harbor Road.

15.4 Continue on West Neck Road.

18.2 Right onto Huntington Road.

18.7 Left onto Goose Hill Road.

19.5 Right onto Main Street / NY 25A.

20.0 Continue on Harbor Road / NY 25A.

20.3 Arrive at finish.

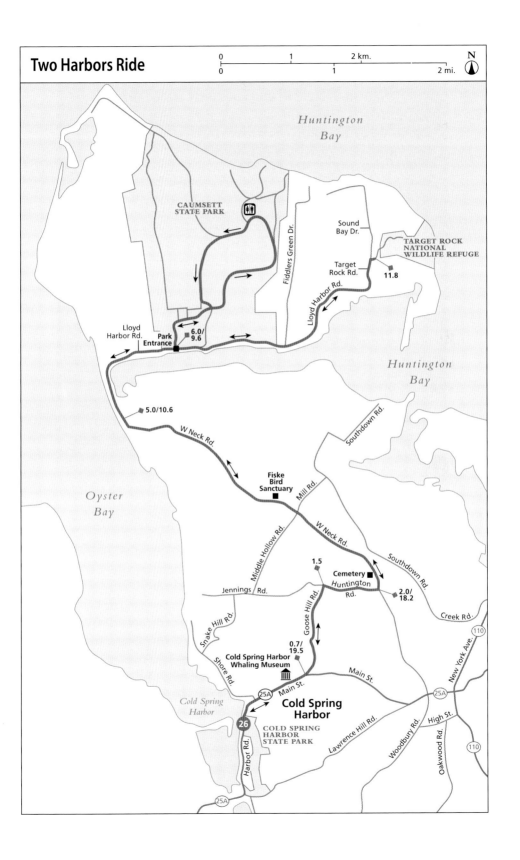

Two Harbors Ride

0   1   2 km.
0   1   2 mi.

N

Huntington Bay

CAUMSETT
STATE PARK

Sound
Bay Dr.

Target
Rock Rd.

TARGET ROCK
NATIONAL
WILDLIFE REFUGE

11.8

Fiddlers Green Dr.

Lloyd Harbor Rd.

Lloyd
Harbor Rd.

Park
Entrance

6.0/
9.6

*Huntington
Bay*

5.0/10.6

W Neck Rd.

Southdown Rd.

*Oyster
Bay*

Fiske
Bird
Sanctuary

Mill Rd.

W Neck Rd.

Middle Hollow Rd.

Southdown Rd.

1.5

Cemetery

2.0/
18.2

Jennings Rd.

Huntington Rd.

Creek Rd.

110

Snake Hill Rd.

Goose Hill Rd.

0.7/
19.5

Cold Spring Harbor
Whaling Museum

Shore Rd

Main St.

Main St.

25A

Cold Spring
Harbor

25A

26

Harbor Rd.

Cold Spring
Harbor

COLD SPRING
HARBOR
STATE PARK

Lawrence Hill Rd.

Woodbury Rd.

High St.

Oakwood Rd.

New York Ave.

110

25A

Marshall Field III and Caumsett State Park

Marshall Field III purchased 1,700 acres in 1921, and hired a team of some of the best designers and architects of his era, among them John Russell Pope, Warren and Wetmore, Marian Coffin, and the Olmstead Brothers, to build his 1,700-acre estate. The work took six years. Educated at Eton and Cambridge, Field was a liberal newspaper publisher, heir to the Marshall Field department store fortune and, despite his aristocratic background, a staunch ally and supporter of Saul Alinsky, the noted community organizer who wrote his most famous work, *Rules for Radicals,* in 1971.

The grand estate included a winter and summer cottage, a garage for Field's fourteen cars, a model dairy farm, gardens, homes for laborers, the manor house, and an equestrian center with a polo field. Field bred horses, including Assignation, the great-great grandfather of Secretariat. Sadly, the manor house would lose some of its Georgian character after it underwent a reduction in size in 1950, six years before Field's death, when the western wing was demolished.

New York State bought the property from his family in 1961 for $4 million, with a goal to maintain the buildings and build a wildlife preserve. The Caumsett Foundation provides more information on the park itself, the history, and tips for visitors, at their website, caumsettfoundation.org.

RIDE INFORMATION

Local Events/Attractions

Target Rock National Wildlife Refuge: This refuge consists of 40 acres on the easternmost tip of Lloyd Neck. Once a garden estate, the property now hosts diverse wildlife including foxes, harbor seals, and over 200 species of birds. The park maintains osprey nesting platforms, a 1.75-mile hiking trail, and an observational post in a blind to photograph wading birds. Admission is by a self-service honor system for motorists, cyclists, and pedestrians. www.fws.gov/refuge/Target_Rock/

Lloyd Harbor Historical Society: This society maintains the Henry Lloyd Manor House, at Caumsett Park, and hosts special events on the grounds of the house and the Weir Barn. The society keeps records on Lloyd Harbor history, including the life of Jupiter Hammon, a slave of the Lloyd family who became the first published African–American poet in Colonial America. lloydharborhistoricalsociety.org.

Cold Spring Harbor Whaling Museum: The whaling museum explores the relationship between humans and whales, both historical and contemporary. Exhibits include artifacts of whaling history, local information, photos and interpretative exhibits geared toward children. cshwhalingmuseum.org.

Restaurants
Sweetie Pies on Main: 181 Main St., Cold Spring; (631) 367-9500; sweetiepiesonmain.com
Gourmet Whaler: 111 Main St., Cold Spring; (631) 659-2977; gourmetwhalerny.com
Cold Spring Plaza Delicatessen: 15 Harbor Rd., Cold Spring; (631) 367-3533
Harbor Mist Restaurant: 105 Harbor Rd., Cold Spring; (631) 659-3888; harbormistrestaurant.com

Restrooms
0.0: Cold Spring Harbor Library
6.1: Caumsett State Park
11.8: Target Rock National Wildlife Refuge

More than a dozen villages and hamlets comprise Huntington, a North Shore town with five separate harbors and miles of beaches on Long Island Sound. Frequently cited as Long Island's cultural capital, Huntington offers a wide range of performing and visual arts attractions, organized by community groups, businesses, and local government. Landmark preservation sites, historical societies, and museums tell the history of the area, dating back to the controversial founding in 1653. English settlers had been living in Lenape lands without any contract or deed for several years before three men from nearby Oyster Bay purchased a deed and gifted it to the settlers. A later expansionary purchase included the Nissequogue River to the east, but the town would lose most of this land in litigation filed by Richard Smythe, founder of Smithtown. The modern boundaries would be established in 1885 in a suit the town won, claiming ownership of Lloyd Neck from Oyster Bay.

Start: The intersection of Main Road, Woodbury Road, and West Neck Road in downtown Huntington.

Length: 21.3 miles

Riding time: 90–105 minutes

Best bike: Road bike

Terrain and trail surface: Asphalt

Traffic and hazards: Downtown Huntington is busy. Use caution and watch the door zone when riding past parked cars. While most of these roads are designated bike routes, not all of them have shoulders, and may be intimidating for novice cyclists. Use caution on angled train tracks.

Things to see: Historic sites and architecture, primarily from the late nineteenth century. Nature preserves, a long harbor view, and scenic ponds throughout.

Fees: None. Parking is free in the municipal lots of Huntington, three of which are located on West Neck Road a block from Main Road, near the start of the ride.

Getting there: Take the Northern State Parkway to exit 37 for Manetto Hill Road toward Plainview/Woodbury. Turn left onto Manetto Hill Road, then right onto Woodbury Road. Follow Woodbury Road, which bears right then turns left, before finally reaching downtown Huntington, where the ride starts at the intersection with Main Road. Free municipal parking lots are on Gerard Street and Nathan Hale Drive, just a block ahead through the intersection with Main Road, off of West Neck Road. Transit users have several options. The Long Island Rail Road stops at Huntington Station, Oyster Bay, and Cold Spring Harbor. The first is less than ideal. From the station, turn right onto the busy and congested New York Avenue for 1.6 miles, then turn left onto Main Road in Huntington. The ride start is 0.2-mile ahead. For a more pleasant option, start in Oyster Bay and turn left from the platform, then right onto Maxwell Avenue to pick up the route on West Main Street. The last option is the Cold Spring Harbor station, just off the route on Woodbury Road, near the 2.8-mile mark. Exit the station and turn left onto Woodbury Road, starting the ride here and adjusting mileage by 2.8.

GPS: N40 51.998' / W73 25.989'

THE RIDE

Downtown Huntington is a trendy and busy commercial district with night-clubs, cocktail bars, upscale boutiques, and independent retail. The Book Revue, three blocks from the ride start on New York Avenue, is especially note-worthy. This family-owned business is the largest independent bookstore on Long Island, and has hosted an incredible range of authors, including come-dians, US Presidents, and literary giants. This ride shares a small overlap with the Two Harbors Ride (CR 26). To combine them into a 40.2-mile ride, follow this route to Cold Spring Harbor, and then pick up the left turn onto Goose Hill Road.

Starting at the intersection of Woodbury Road and Main Road in down-town Huntington, this fairly hilly ride follows designated bike routes in a counterclockwise loop, passing through villages and hamlets. The route turns back through the town of Oyster Bay, then into Cold Spring Harbor, before returning to the ride start in downtown Huntington.

Start southward on Woodbury Road through a dense residential neighborhood, up a gentle ascent, into a sparser, less habited area. Bear left at a fork to continue on Woodbury Road, then right, after a long border with the wooded lot of the Kerber's Farm property.

The road narrows where it passes the Cold Spring Harbor station and then enters the village of Woodbury, a short commercial strip with large parking lots. Outside of the village, turn right onto Syosset Woodbury Road, up a short, steep climb before the road levels out. The road passes through quiet neighborhoods before crossing one major intersection with South Woods Road, and then a set of angled train tracks.

Where the right turning lane opens, curve left, following the road onto Cold Spring Road. The route cuts through Syosset, a built-up suburban stretch. At the fork before a gas station, turn right onto Muttontown Eastwoods Road. The route continues west on this low-volume road, first through a quiet residential neighborhood, then past a country club and into a pretty rural area with split-rail fencing and forested yards.

Cross a four-lane road and continue onto Muttontown Road, on a stretch of road shared with horseback riders from Muttontown Preserve, a preservation property that spans both sides of the road. This road climbs up a slightly steep hill, evening out beside a wooded pond, and then heads downhill to the T-junction with Brookville Road, facing a bird sanctuary.

Turn right and continue descending over patched but serviceable asphalt. Brookville Road bears right after 1 mile, and the route crosses busy NY 25A onto Wolver Hollow Road, over the marked town line into the Village of Upper Brookville. The road ends just after a polo club, in a T-junction with Chicken Valley Road.

Turn right, following the sign for Planting Fields Arboretum onto a moderate climb that peaks in 0.3 mile, before another fast descent. At the next triangle, bear right onto Oyster Bay Road, with a view of Upper Francis Pond to the left.

After one steep climb, the road continues onto aptly named Mill Hill Road for another. These two climbs gain 170 feet of elevation over less than a mile. After the peak, the road descends fast along a curve, into historic Oyster Bay, with a lovely overview of Mill Pond. Continue onto West Main Street, directly ahead, through the charming village.

At the T-junction, turn left onto South Street, then right onto East Main Street, past several shops and the historic First Presbyterian Church, a Gothic-style structure built in 1873.

East Main becomes Cove Road as it curves left and down another descent. Near the 16.0-mile mark, the road passes the Youngs Memorial Cemetery and Theodore Roosevelt Sanctuary, a bird preserve and park.

View of Inner Harbor from Cold Spring Harbor

Turn left at the 17.1-mile mark onto a very steep but mercifully short climb up Moores Hill Road. The road ends in a T-junction with NY 25A at the base of a short, fast descent. Use caution and turn left onto NY 25A, a fast road with no stop for oncoming traffic. The road passes the Cold Spring Harbor Laboratory and then a marshy creek with views of the harbor. Carefully move into the left lane, following signs for East 25A, onto Harbor Road.

Bike Shops

Bicycle Playground: 256 Main St., Huntington; (631) 683-5522; bicycleplayground.com
Visentin Bike Pro Shop: 51 Pine Hollow Rd., Oyster Bay; (516) 922-2150
BicyclePlanet: 340 Robbins Ln., Syosset; (516) 364-4434; thebicycleplanet.com

After a short climb, Harbor Road passes Cold Spring Harbor Park and scenic overlooks of the water, then curves right into the village. The road becomes West Main Street and climbs the last hill as it exits the village. After the crest, the road descends to a signalized intersection ahead. Turn left to continue on Main Road to the finish, a short distance ahead.

MILES AND DIRECTIONS

0.0 Start on Main Road, left onto Woodbury Road.

3.9 Right onto Syosset Woodbury Road.

5.3 Left onto Cold Spring Road.

5.7 Right onto Muttontown Eastwoods Road.

7.2 Continue on Muttontown Road.

8.5 Right onto Brookville Road.

9.7 Cross NY 25A onto Wolver Hollow Road.

11.1 Right onto Chicken Valley Road.

12.4 Right onto Oyster Bay Road.

13.4 Continue on Mill Hill Road.

14.0 Continue on West Main Street.

14.6 Left onto South Street, then right onto East Main Street.

15.7 Continue onto Cove Road.

17.1 Left onto Moores Hill Road.

18.4 Left onto NY 25A.

18.8 Left onto Harbor Road / NY 25A.

19.7 Continue on West Main Street / NY 25A.

21.0 Left to continue on Main Road.

21.3 Arrive at finish.

RIDE INFORMATION

Local Events/Attractions

Planting Fields Arboretum State Historic Park: Like Caumsett State Park, this 409-acre property was once a Gold Coast estate. Coe Hall, a sixty-five-room mansion built in the Tudor-Revival style, is open for tours from spring to fall. The Olmsted Brothers-designed grounds are open year round, and include greenhouses, English gardens, and rolling lawns. plantingfields.org.

Huntington Through Oyster Bay

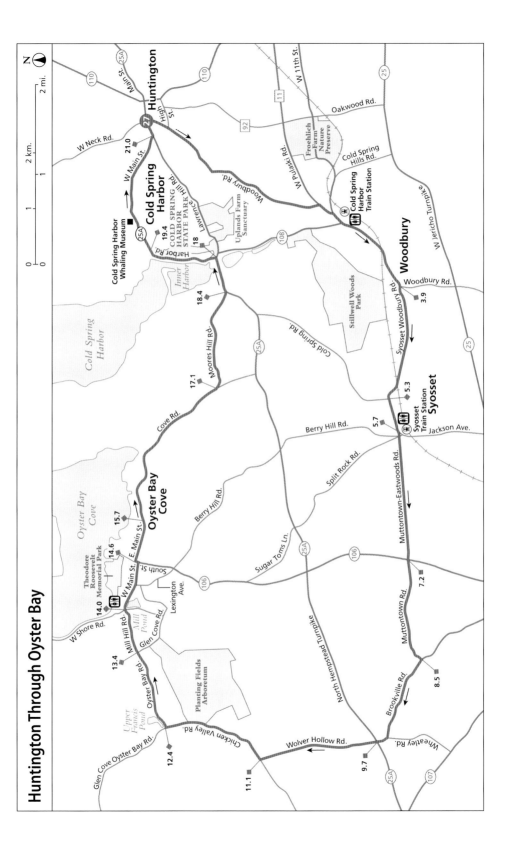

Sagamore Hill National Historic Site: Teddy Roosevelt's former estate is a museum and historical exhibit, situated on 83 acres of nature preserves, in the village of Cove Neck. Just a short detour from this route, about 1.5 miles from the intersection of Cove Road and Cove Neck Road in Oyster Bay Cove, the shingle-style Queen Anne house was Roosevelt's principal residence before and after his terms as president. Park entrance is free, but admission is charged for entrance to Roosevelt's house. nps.gov/sahi/index.htm.

Muttontown Meadows and Nassau Hall: This estate was built in 1903 for Bronson Winthrop by the Beaux-Arts style architectural firm Delano & Aldrich. The property is a historic preservation site with 550 acres of hiking trails winding through the woods around the mansion.

Theodore Roosevelt Memorial Park: Located in Oyster Bay, this park and beach are just off the route by about 1,000 feet, up Larrabee Avenue from West Main Street in Oyster Bay. The park has restrooms and a sandy beach, but no food concessions or other amenities.

Restaurants

Wild Flours Bake Shop: 11 New St., Huntington; (631) 923-1090; wildfloursbakeshop.com

Village Creperie Cafe: 335 New York Ave., Huntington; (631) 423-3057; villagecreperie.com

Woodbury Country Deli: 153 Woodbury Rd., Woodbury; (516) 367-4180

Village Bagels: 114 Jackson Ave., Syosset; (516) 921-9090; villagebagelssyosset.net

Bagel Master: 43 Cold Spring Rd., Syosset; (516) 921-9773; bagelmaster.com

Harborside Delicatessen: 99 South St., Oyster Bay; (516) 922-2950

Cafe Buenos Aires: 23 Wall St., Huntington; (631) 603-3600; cafebuenosaires .net

Restrooms

2.8: Cold Spring Harbor Train Station
19.4: Cold Spring Harbor Library

Oyster Bay Loop

Oyster Bay is the easternmost Nassau County town, comprising some thirty-six villages and hamlets. The 169-square-mile town spans the entire height of the island, bordering Long Island Sound to the north, Suffolk County to the east, and the Atlantic Ocean to the south. The hamlet of Oyster Bay is a scenic community situated around the titular bay, founded in 1667 by Quakers, shell-fish farmers, and sailors. The town would rise to prominence under British occupation during the Revolutionary War. One of the first acts of the occupying army was to arrest local patriot Samuel Townsend. Despite his imprisonment, two of his children, Robert and Sally, managed to serve as undercover agents for General Washington. Their successes include exposing British spy Benedict Arnold, thereby foiling his plan to seize the Continental fort at West Point.

The town faded into obscurity post-war, until area resident Theodore Roosevelt became the President of the United States in 1902. The town became an important aeronautics site during the World Wars, and remains a thriving, balanced community, drawing new residents and visitors alike with a combination of natural beauty, historic preservation, and a healthy job market.

Start: The intersection of Audrey Avenue, Shore Road, and Spring Street, by the Town Hall and a small gazebo.

Length: 20.0 miles

Riding time: About 1 hour 30 minutes

Best bike: Road bike

Terrain and trail surface: Asphalt

Traffic and hazards: Use caution navigating busy downtown Oyster Bay. Bayville Road leaving the beach area of Bayville has a short section with no shoulder and high speeds.

Things to see: Long stretches of unobstructed harbor and Sound views, beautiful back roads through nature preserves, and historic structures throughout Oyster Bay.

Fees: None. Parking is unrestricted in the municipal lot on Shore Avenue, a few hundred feet from the ride start.

Getting there: Take the Northern State Parkway to exit 35 N for NY 106 N/NY 107 N toward Oyster Bay. Turn right, then slightly right onto NY 106 N. Turn left onto Audrey Avenue and continue to the ride start ahead. A free municipal parking lot is available just another 500 feet or so down the road, on Shore Avenue. Transit users can take the Long Island Rail Road to the Oyster Bay stop, and exit the parking lot left onto Shore Avenue to the ride start ahead.

GPS: N40 52.405' / W73 31.951'

THE RIDE

This ride follows scenic waterfront roads, along the eponymous Oyster Bay and the Long Island Sound, visiting beaches and parks on a counterclockwise loop through hamlets and villages on the North Shore.

Starting in the hamlet of Oyster Bay, head east on Audrey Avenue, right onto South Street, then right onto West Main Street, all though a bustling downtown brimming with restaurants and shops. West Main Street passes an Elementary School and then crosses the scenic Mill Pond on a short causeway.

Bear right after the causeway onto West Shore Road and into the village of Mill Neck. This long, narrow road follows the bay for more than 2 miles of scenic waterfront views. Traffic is slow and low in volume, but the sidewalk may still seem tempting. Be aware that it ends suddenly, in a rough patch of dirt and rock, separated from the rest of the route by traffic barriers.

West Shore Road crosses a picturesque drawbridge as it enters the village of Bayville, where the route turns right onto the painted bike lane of West Harbor Drive. The road follows the Oyster Bay National Wildlife Refuge on the right, a long section of marshland and water, and the West Harbor Beach over the next mile.

At the stop sign, turn right onto Bayville Avenue, which becomes Centre Island Road just ahead. The road passes Centre Island Beach and becomes a causeway between Turtle Cove to the south and the Sound to the north, along a quarter-mile stretch of curved sandy beach. The road then enters the tiny Village of Centre Island, an extremely private and exclusive area with only one real public road. If seeking a shorter ride, you can safely turn around here, skipping the Centre Island segment, and save 4.6 miles off the total ride.

Oyster Bay and Northwest Suffolk

Centre Island Beach

Otherwise, simply follow Centre Island Road through quiet, forested neighborhoods, and turn around at the dead end to retrace your steps back to Bayville Avenue.

Continue on Bayville Avenue, past Centre Island Beach, through a dense residential neighborhood. Turn left onto Mountain Avenue, following signs for the Village of Bayville, up a modest climb.

Mountain Avenue curves to the right at the end, onto Creek Road, a tranquil spot along the Mill Neck Creek and the boat launch at Creek Beach. The route follows the road as it curves right again, becoming Perry Avenue, which ends at a T-junction with Bayville Avenue in 0.8 mile. Turn left onto Bayville Avenue, riding in the wide shoulder to the recreation area ahead, along the swimming-prohibited Charles E. Ransom Beach on the right.

After the beach, turn left to continue on Bayville Road, a sometimes-busy four-lane stretch bordering the Mill Neck Preserve. There is no shoulder, but cyclists are a common sight, and drivers should be accommodating. In less than a mile, carefully turn left onto Factory Pond Road, a quieter, narrow road that passes the eponymous pond on the right.

Cyclists ride in the bike lane around Oyster Bay

The route turns left onto Cleft Road at the end of Factory Pond Road, continuing on another scenic causeway bordered by Beaver Lake and the Mill Neck Creek. The road climbs a short, steep hill just after the causeway and the route turns right onto Frost Mill Road, another lovely back road through forests and preserves. Bear left onto Beaver Brook Road where the road forks at Lower Francis Pond and continue until the road ends in a T-junction with Oyster Bay Road.

Bicycle Shops

Visentin Bike Pro Shop: 51 Pine Hollow Rd., Oyster Bay; (516) 922-2150
BicyclePlanet: 340 Robbins Ln., Syosset; (516) 364-4434; thebicycleplanet.com

Turn right, following the Upper Francis Pond, and then left onto Chicken Valley Road, entering the village of Matinecock. Follow the Planting Fields Arboretum signs and turn left onto Planting Fields Road, heading into a gradual but challenging 120-foot climb bordered by Arboretum property to either side. Just after the peak, the road passes the entrance to the park, on the right, and then heads downhill to a sudden stop at Glen Cove Road. Turn

Downtown Oyster Bay

right and continue descending on Glen Cove Road, which levels out and ends at a stop sign, where the route turns left onto Mill River Road.

Follow Mill River Road to its end, and then turn left onto Lexington Avenue, then a quick right onto West Main Street, retracing the route back to a left onto South Street then a left onto Audrey Avenue to arrive at the finish.

MILES AND DIRECTIONS

0.0   Start on Audrey Avenue.

0.1   Right onto South Street then right onto West Main Street.

0.7   Right onto West Shore Road.

2.9   Right onto West Harbor Drive.

3.9   Right onto Bayville Avenue.

4.0   Continue on Centre Island Road.

4.3   **Optional**: Turn around to skip the Centre Island portion, cutting 4.6 miles off the ride.

The First People of Oyster Bay

Oyster Bay was inhabited by succeeding cultures of indigenous people for thousands of years before European contact. The Lenape nation, also known as Delaware Indians, was the dominant force when the Dutch arrived in the sixteenth century. The nation was organized into thirty or so clans, identified with animals, which were tattooed on males when they came of age and left their birth clan to marry, a practice called exogamy. The Lenape were matrilineal: Lineage was traced through mothers, and husbands lived with the birth clan of their wives.

The nation predated other Algonquian-speaking peoples, who revered them as elders. European settlers mistakenly identified the Lenape by their location or tattoos, incorrectly labeling the Lenape of the Oyster Bay area as the Matinecock, and others after the animal of their clan. The arrival of the Dutch heralded the fall of the Lenape, through war with rival tribes, displacement by settlers, and disease.

Their rivals, the Iroquoian-speaking Susquehannock, received sophisticated arms from the Dutch, and used them to defeat the Lenape in Delaware and Maryland. Smallpox spread to even the most remote villages through the practice of exogamy. The nation was left with only three distinct clans by the late seventeenth century, pre-senting a distorted image to European travelers.

The English would displace the Lenape of Oyster Bay following their victory against the Dutch for control of the region. Many of the displaced would join with other Lenape at the mouth of the Delaware River, where Quaker colonists under William Penn had established peace five years prior. However, the sheer number of colonists made life challenging for the Lenape. After Penn's death in 1718, his heirs, John and Thomas, would employ fraud, deception, and threats of vio-lence to drive the remaining Lenape westward.

The majority of Lenape people wound up in Ohio, far from their ancestral homes. Later, they were the first tribal group to sign a treaty with the United States, supporting the Continental Army during the Revolutionary War, and gaining federal recognition. They have almost no presence on Long Island today, except linguistically: Place names, including Manhattan, "island of many hills," come from the Lenape. Members operate the Lenape Center, on Manhattan, preserve the legacy and history of their nation. Learn more on their website, thelenapecenter.com.

Oyster Bay Loop

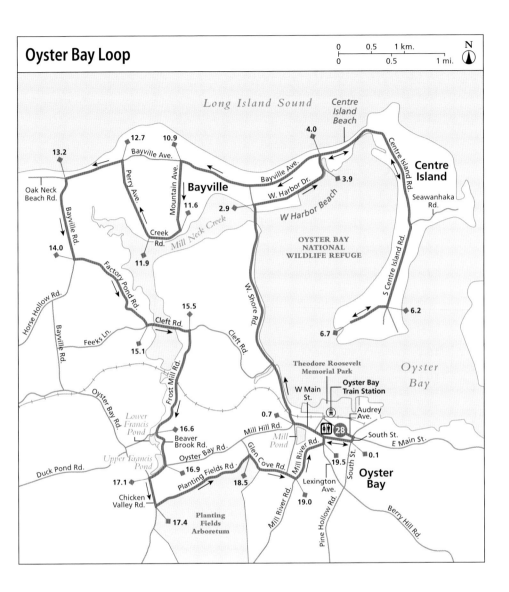

6.2 Right onto South Centre Island Road.

6.7 Turn around.

7.0 Left onto Centre Island Road.

9.3 Continue on Bayville Avenue.

10.9 Left onto Mountain Avenue.

11.6 Right onto Creek Road.

11.9 Right onto Perry Avenue.

12.7 Left onto Bayville Avenue.

13.2 Left onto Bayville Road.

14.0 Left onto Factory Pond Road.

15.1 Left onto Cleft Road.

15.5 Right onto Frost Mill Road.

16.6 Left onto Beaver Brook Road.

16.9 Right onto Oyster Bay Road.

17.1 Left onto Chicken Valley Road.

17.4 Left onto Planting Fields Road.

18.5 Right onto Glen Cove Road.

19.0 Left onto Mill River Road.

19.5 Left onto Lexington Avenue then right onto West Main Street.

19.8 Left onto South Street then left onto Audrey Avenue.

20.0 Arrive at finish.

RIDE INFORMATION

Local Events/Attractions

Planting Fields Arboretum State Historic Park: This 409-acre property was once a Gold Coast estate. Coe Hall, a 65-room mansion built in the Tudor-Revival style, is open for tours from spring to fall. The Olmsted Brothers-designed grounds are open year round and include greenhouses, English gardens, and rolling lawns. Learn more on their website, at plantingfields.org.

Theodore Roosevelt Memorial Park: Located in Oyster Bay, this park and beach are just off the route by about 1,000-feet, up Larrabee Avenue from West Main Street in Oyster Bay. The park has restrooms and a sandy beach, but no food concessions or other amenities. In 1983, the site was used to honor the memory of Roosevelt on what would have been his 125th birthday. The event spawned the Oyster Festival, held every October, to celebrate the history of the region and the bountiful shellfish. theoysterfestival.org.

Oyster Bay Railroad Museum: A community resource, this museum preserves the railroad history of the region, with antique locomotives, miniature displays, and more. http://obrm.org.

Restaurants

Bonanza Stand of Oyster Bay: 25 Shore Ave., Oyster Bay; (516) 922-7796; bonanzastandofoysterbay.com

Sweet Tomato: 91 Audrey Ave., Oyster Bay; (516) 802-5353; mysweettomato.com

Restrooms

0.0: Nearby at Oyster Bay Railroad
3.2: West Harbor Beach
11.8: Creek Beach

Glen Cove Parks

The small city of Glen Cove, one of only two cities in Nassau County, is bordered by Long Island Sound to the north, and in every other direction by the much larger town of Oyster Bay. Despite a relatively small population of some 29,000 residents, the city is home to three important history museums and centers: The North Shore Historical Museum, an exploration of local history dating to the European settlement; the Garvies Point Museum, an archaeological center focused on the indigenous people of Long Island; and the Holocaust Memorial & Tolerance Center of Nassau County, where the history of the Holocaust is taught with an aim toward promoting peace and anti-racism. Glen Cove is currently undergoing an ambitious revitalization of its parks and waterfront, highlighted on this ride.

Start: Sea Cliff Beach, on The Boulevard, a one-way street along Mosquito Cove

Length: 10.3 miles

Riding time: About 45 minutes

Best bike: Road bike

Terrain and trail surface: Asphalt

Traffic and hazards: Glen Cove Avenue can be busy and hectic. Use caution when turning left onto this avenue. If intimidated by traffic, a rider may wish to skip the road by crossing the City Stadium Park instead.

Things to see: Picturesque water views of Hempstead Bay, quiet roads, and several significant historical and cultural centers.

Fees: None. There is a small lot where cars may park for free at the start of the ride. The museums on this route charge admission. Check their websites, listed below, for fees.

Getting there: Take I-495 E to exit 39 toward Glen Cove Road / Hempstead / Glen Cove. Turn left onto Glen Cove Road to NY 107 N / Pratt Boulevard, then turn left onto Glen Cove Avenue. Turn right onto

Shore Road, then left onto Albin Street to Prospect Avenue. Turn right onto Cliff Way to the ride start on The Boulevard. Transit users can take the Long Island Rail Road to the Oyster Bay stop and exit the parking lot left onto Shore Avenue to the ride start ahead. Transit users should take the Long Island Rail Road to Sea Cliff station. Turn right onto Sea Cliff Avenue and follow the road until it ends at Prospect Avenue. Turn right, then left onto Cliff Way. The ride start is just ahead at the start of The Boulevard.

GPS: N40 50.984' / W73 39.136'

THE RIDE

This route links the Sea Cliff Beach, Pratt Park, a newly redeveloped Glen Cove Creek, Morgan Memorial Park, Garvies Point Museum, the Holocaust Memorial, and Welwyn Preserve, on a twisty, sometimes hilly, 10-mile route. The ride achieves a total gain of 555 feet, or it would make for an ideal hybrid ride. The beaches provide scenery, but no access without a town permit during the on-season.

Starting on The Boulevard, follow the boardwalk and harbor vista on the left. The road becomes Shore Road ahead, as it approaches the marina, and then the City Stadium Park. Turn left at the signalized intersection onto Glen Cove Avenue, a major four-lane stretch of road leading into downtown Glen Cove.

If riding a hybrid or nervous about traffic, turn into the City Stadium Park and head north, keeping Glen Cove Avenue to the right, up to Morris Avenue and Park Place to rejoin the route at Charles Street.

Turn left onto Charles Street, riding past Pratt Park. Turn left onto New Street, at the signalized intersection, and then through a small industrial area. At the end of New Street, just ahead, turn left onto Garvies Point Road. This waterfront is undergoing a current revitalization and is projected to have commuter ferry service to Manhattan by early 2017.

Continue past the ferry terminal to a small beach at the end of the road. Turn left into the parking lot and onto the multi-use trail, heading to the mouth of the creek, then turning left and following the off-road trail along the water. The path passes a grounded historic sailing vessel, open to the public, but in a somewhat dilapidated state.

The trail ends at the Ferry Terminal. Turn left, into the parking lot, then exit right onto Garvies Point Road. Retrace the earlier ride through the industrial section and continue straight onto Dickson Street.

Start of Glen Cove ride

Dickson Street is the first climb on the ride. Turn right at the first side street, The Place, and continue climbing to the stop sign. Turn left onto Ellwood Street for another steep stretch, leveling off just before the signalized intersection with Landing Road.

Turn left onto Landing Road and follow the road to Germain Street, just before Morgan Park. Turn left and continue to the T-junction with McLoughlin Street.

Turn right and then left, onto Barry Drive, which ends at the Garvies Point Museum and Preserve in just 0.3 mile. When ready, turn around, and retrace the route back to Landing Road.

Follow Landing Road past the Ellwood Street intersection and turn left onto Crescent Beach Road. This road passes through a quiet neighborhood until reaching the Holocaust Memorial at Welwyn Preserve, at the 6.5-mile mark. Turn right into the preserve and follow the road to the center.

After visiting the center, follow the park road out to the exit, north of the entrance. Turn left onto Crescent Beach Road and retrace the route, turning right onto Landing Road, then left onto Ellwood Street.

Continue straight ahead onto The Place, then right onto Charles Street at the next turn. Ride through the signalized intersection with Herb Hill Road

Boat at the point

and New Street, continuing on Charles Street and bearing right at the fork after the bridge.

Turn right onto Glen Cove Avenue. A possible detour, if interested, is to the North Shore Historical Museum. Turn left instead, then right to stay on Glen Cove Avenue. Turn left onto Bridge Street, then immediately right onto Glen Street, and the Museum is about 500 feet ahead. After visiting, turn around, and turn left onto Glen Cove Avenue to return to the mapped route.

Bike Shops

Road Runners Bicycles: 8 Forest Ave., Glen Cove; (516) 671-8280; roadrunnersbicycles.com

After City Stadium Park, turn right onto Shore Road. The road becomes one-way ahead. Turn left up a short climb onto Albin Street at the 9.6-mile mark and continue onto Prospect Avenue. Turn right onto Cliff Way and descend to The Boulevard and the end of this ride.

MILES AND DIRECTIONS

0.0 Start at The Boulevard.

0.3 Continue on Shore Road.

1.0 Left onto Glen Cove Avenue.

1.4 Left onto Charles Street.

1.6 Left onto New Street.

1.8 Left onto Garvies Point Road.

2.4 Follow trail at end of parking lot through Glen Cove Creek area.

2.9 Exit trail in parking lot, right onto Garvies Point Road.

3.2 Continue onto Dickson Street.

3.4 Right onto The Place.

3.5 Left onto Ellwood Street.

3.8 Left onto Landing Road.

4.4 Left onto Germaine Street.

4.5 Right onto McLoughlin Street, then left onto Barry Drive.

4.8 Turn around on Barry Drive at Garvies Point Museum Preserve.

4.9 Right onto McLoughlin Street.

5.0 Left onto Germaine Street.

5.1 Right onto Landing Road.

5.7 Left onto Crescent Beach Road.

6.5 Right onto Holocaust Memorial and Tolerance Center of Nassau County park road, follow park road around to exit.

7.2 Left onto Crescent Beach Road.

8.1 Right onto Landing Road.

8.2 Left onto Ellwood Street.

8.4 Left onto The Place.

8.5 Right onto Charles Street.

8.8 Right onto Glen Cove Avenue.

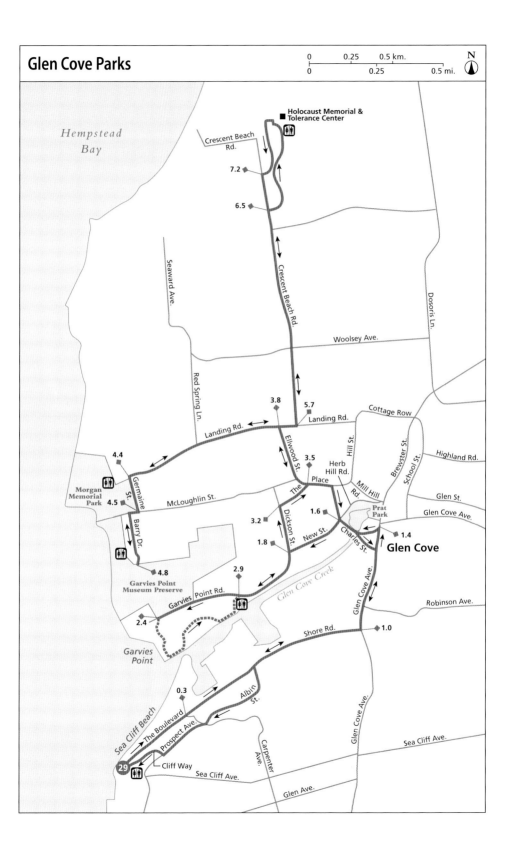

Glen Cove Parks

Hempstead
Bay

Holocaust Memorial &
Tolerance Center

Crescent Beach Rd.

7.2

6.5

Crescent Beach Rd.

Woolsey Ave.

Dosoris Ln.

Seaward Ave.

Red Spring Ln.

Landing Rd.

3.8

5.7

Landing Rd.

Cottage Row

Ellwood St.

3.5

Hill St.

Brewster St.

School St.

Highland Rd.

4.4

Germaine St.

McLoughlin St.

The Place

Herb Hill Rd.

Mill Hill Rd.

Prat Park

Glen St.

Morgan
Memorial
Park

4.5

3.2

Dickson St.

1.6

New St.

Charles St.

1.4

Glen Cove Ave.

Glen Cove

Barry Dr.

1.8

4.8

Garvies Point
Museum Preserve

2.9

Garvies Point Rd.

Glen Cove Creek

Glen Cove Ave.

Robinson Ave.

2.4

Shore Rd.

1.0

Garvies
Point

Sea Cliff Beach

0.3

Albin St.

Glen Cove Ave.

The Boulevard

Prospect Ave.

29

Cliff Way

Sea Cliff Ave.

Carpenter Ave.

Sea Cliff Ave.

Glen Ave.

0   0.25   0.5 km.

0   0.25   0.5 mi.

N

9.1 Right onto Shore Road.

9.5 Left onto Albin Street.

9.7 Right onto Prospect Avenue.

9.9 Cross Carpenter Avenue to continue on Prospect Street.

10.1 Right onto Cliff Way.

10.2 Right onto The Boulevard.

10.3 Arrive at finish.

RIDE INFORMATION

Local Events/Attractions

Garvies Point Museum: This museum focuses on geology and the culture and archaeology of Long Island tribal groups. The park has 5 miles of marked trails on 62 acres of unique, glacial-formed grounds. The Nassau County–operated Museum charges a nominal fee. garviespointmuseum.com.

Holocaust Memorial and Tolerance Center of Nassau County: A permanent exhibit on the Holocaust tells the stories of victims and survivors through archive footage, testimonies written and recorded, and guided interpretations. The museum explores the anti-Semitism that led to the Holocaust, exposing eugenics and racism, and shows the common link between acts of genocide and intolerance. It's in the Welwyn Preserve, former estate of Harold Irving Pratt, and features four blazed trails and an assortment of historical ruins dating to the late nineteenth century. Museum site: hmtcli.org.

North Shore Historical Museum: This museum retells the history of Glen Cove from its 1668 founding as Musquito Cove, through dioramas, archives, and changing exhibitions of photography and other visual arts. The museum is about a half-mile off the mapped route above. northshorehistoricalmuseum.org.

Restaurants

Landing Bakery: 147 Landing Rd., Glen Cove; (516) 676-9299
American Cafe: 5 School St., Glen Cove; (516) 656-0003
Downtown Cafe: 4 School St., Glen Cove; (516) 759-2233;
downtowncafepizza.com

Restrooms

0.0: Sea Cliff Beach
4.8: Garvies Point Museum
6.8: Holocaust Memorial at Welwyn Preserve

Bethpage Bikeway

The hamlet of Bethpage is home to both the most popular bikeway on Long Island and the best tasting drinking water in the state, according to judges at the 2006 New York State Fair. There hasn't been an update from the judges, but local residents claim the taste has declined following the introduction of chlorine in 2010. Not all changes are for the worse, though: During the same period, the Bethpage Bikeway has improved, following an expansion to nearly 13 miles in 2007. The scenic off-road trail is paved and suitable for cyclists of all levels, with multiple access points available along the course.

Start: Trailhead on Woodbury Road in Woodbury

Length: 26.2 miles

Riding time: About 2 hours and 15 minutes

Best bike: Hybrid bike

Terrain and trail surface: Asphalt off-road trail

Traffic and hazards: This route follows a paved off-road trail. Roots may make portions rough for road bikes. Use caution at intersections.

Things to see: Serene forestland in Bethpage, lovely water views throughout the Massapequa Preserve.

Fees: There is no fee to park in Woodbury or to ride the trail, but Bethpage State Park charges a vehicle admission fee if you choose to start the ride there. If starting in Woodbury, drivers can park at a tiny lot on Sunnyside Boulevard, adjacent to the confluence of the two trailheads.

Getting there: Take exit 37 from Northern State Parkway for Manetto Hill Road toward Plainview/Woodbury. Turn left onto Manetto Hill Road, and turn right in a half-mile onto Woodbury Road. The trailhead is on the right. Transit users may wish to start this ride in Massapequa. The Long Island Rail Road station has a bikeway connection to the main route in the easternmost side of the parking lot.

GPS: N40 48.020' / W73 28.982'

THE RIDE

Please note that there are two trailheads on Woodbury Road about 300 feet apart. They connect roughly 500 feet down the trail, so use either, but these directions start at the trailhead next to Manetto Hill Road. This route is fairly easy, mostly downhill on the outbound trip, and with no significant climbs, but total gain will be close to 1,000 feet. Less experienced cyclists may wish to start in the south, by Massapequa Park, or at Bethpage State Park, and exclude the northern section, cutting off the majority of climbing.

Follow the trail along Sunnyside Boulevard, using caution at the crossing over the Northern State Parkway ramps, and then right, following the curvature of the road. Use caution crossing Sunnyside Boulevard ahead, near the 1.0-mile mark, and then turn right to continue on the bikeway past a chain hotel location.

The bikeway turns left and parallels Service Road ahead, then crosses a smaller local road and bears left at a wooded median. Turn right after the median and continue following the bikeway under a series of highway tunnels adjacent to Washington Avenue.

Casual ride on the Bethpage Bikeway

Turn left at the next intersection, crossing Washington Avenue, then left again, to continue following the route. The bikeway turns right ahead, parallel with East Bethpage Road, along a short quiet stretch, before it curves around to Old Country Road and crosses into a beautiful, heavily forested section partially shared with the Long Island Greenbelt Trail.

The route exits this area and crosses Old Bethpage Road, offering a possible detour. Old Bethpage Village Restoration is just about a mile away. To visit the site, it's a series of quick turns in succession through a quiet neighborhood. Turn left onto Old Bethpage Road, left onto Pasture Lane, right onto Simpson Drive, then left onto Prescott Place. Take the next turn, right, onto Adrienne Drive for nearly a quarter-mile, then turn left onto Dahill Road and right onto Melissa Lane. At the intersection with Round Swamp Road, turn left. The historic village is 0.5 mile ahead, on the right.

Back on the mapped route, the bikeway continues across Old Bethpage Road, behind a quiet neighborhood, until an intersection with Haypath Road. Cross the road into Bethpage Park for the longest stretch of quiet riding on the route so far. The easy-to-follow trail winds through the park along the northern border before turning southwest, crossing the park road a few hundred feet from the restrooms and a playground.

The trail continues through the park, exiting by a traffic circle, and crossing two parkway ramps and under turnpike and railroad bridges before entering another narrow span of trees between the parkway and a series of cul-de-sacs.

After crossing an exit ramp in Farmingdale, the bikeway enters the Massapequa Preserve, a forested area with a series of ponds fed by the Massapequa Creek. This is one of the scenic highlights of the ride, particularly after the crossing of Clark Avenue, where the route turns bears right and crosses a large pond on two picturesque bridges.

After the pond, head into the short tunnel under a railroad bridge and then cross Sunrise Highway, continuing southwesterly to the

Bike Shops

Bike Junkie: 272 Broadway, Bethpage; (516) 932-7271; bikejunkie.com
Brickwell Cycling and Multisports: 4 Jackson Ave., Syosset; (516) 588-7841 and 238 Main St., Farmingdale; (516) 586-6914; brickwell.com
The Hub: 80 Smith St., Farmingdale; (631) 406-7251; thehubhq.com
Sunrise Cyclery: 4828 Sunrise Hwy., Massapequa Park; (516) 798-5715; sunrisecyclery.com
The Bicycle Planet: 340 Robbins Ln., Syosset; (516) 364-4434; thebicycleplanet.com
Brands Cycle and Fitness: 1966 Wantagh Ave., Wantagh; (800) 649-3739; brandscycle.com
Williams Cycle: 83 Woodbury Rd., Hicksville; (516) 822-6235

Link to Jones Beach

This ride can link to the Jones Beach ride (CR 31). Exit the bikeway onto Clark Avenue, heading west, for 2.0 miles on neighborhood roads. After the underpass beneath the Seaford–Oyster Bay Expressway, turn left onto West Seamans Neck Road, then a right onto Park Avenue. In one mile, turn left onto Beech Street, cross Sunrise Highway, then left onto Merrick Road to Cedar Creek Park just ahead. Turn right into the park and the Jones Beach path is on the right. This detour is roughly 3.5 miles in one direction.

banks of the Massapequa Lake. The trail ends near the intersection of Ocean Avenue and Merrick Road on a busy, car-centric road not recommended for cyclists. There is a small plaza three blocks to the west with coffee, ATMs, and gas stations, best accessed by walking a bike along the sidewalk.

To return, turn around, and follow the trail back to the start.

MILES AND DIRECTIONS

0.0 Start at the trailhead on Woodbury Road.

0.7 Cross highway exit and entrance ramps.

1.0 Cross Sunnyside Boulevard, continue on bikeway.

2.0 Cross Washington Avenue, left to continue on bikeway.

2.8 Cross Old Country Road, right to continue on bikeway.

3.4 Cross Old Bethpage Road, stay left to continue on bikeway.

4.2 Cross Hay Path Road, stay left to continue on bikeway.

4.4 Left to stay on bikeway.

5.6 Cross park road, continue on bikeway.

6.3 Cross park road, continue on bikeway.

6.9 Cross Plainview Road, continue on bikeway.

7.0 Cross ramp, continue on bikeway.

7.7 Cross ramp, continue on bikeway.

8.5 Cross ramp, continue on bikeway.

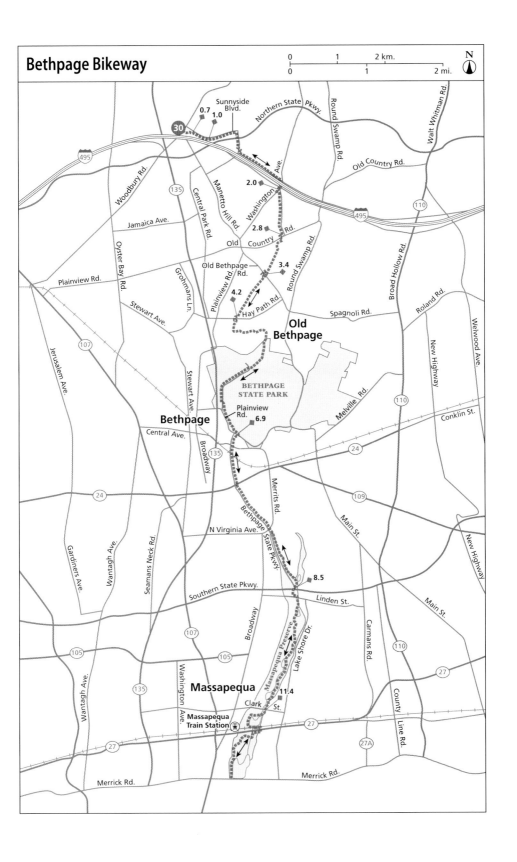

Bethpage Bikeway

0   1   2 km.

0   1   2 mi.

N

0.7   1.0   Sunnyside Blvd.

30

Northern State Pkwy.

Round Swamp Rd.

Walt Whitman Rd.

495

Woodbury Rd.

135

Central Park Rd.

Manetto Hill Rd.

Washington Ave.

Old Country Rd.

110

2.0

495

110

Jamaica Ave.

Old   Country   Rd.

2.8

Oyster Bay Rd.

Plainview Rd.

Grohmans Ln.

Plainview Rd.

Old Bethpage Rd.

3.4

Round Swamp Rd.

Broad Hollow Rd.

Roland Rd.

Welwood Ave.

Stewart Ave.

4.2

Hay Path Rd.

Old Bethpage

Spagnoli Rd.

New Highway

107

Jerusalem Ave.

Stewart Ave.

BETHPAGE STATE PARK

Melville Rd.

110

Conklin St.

Bethpage

Plainview Rd.

6.9

Central Ave.

Broadway

135

24

24

109

Gardiners Ave.

Wantagh Ave.

Seamans Neck Rd.

N Virginia Ave.

Bethpage State Pkwy.

Merrits Rd.

Main St.

New Highway

8.5

Southern State Pkwy.

Linden St.

Main St.

105

107

Broadway

105

Massapequa Preserve

Lake Shore Dr.

Carmans Rd.

110

27

Wantagh Ave.

Washington Ave.

135

Massapequa

11.4

Clark   St.

County Line Rd.

Massapequa Train Station

27

27A

27

Merrick Rd.

Merrick Rd.

9.6　Cross Linden Street, continue on bikeway.

11.4　Cross Clark Street, continue on bikeway.
Optional: Turn right onto Clark Street for alternative directions to the Cedar Creek Park bikeway to Jones Beach (see sidebar).

12.0　Pass through the tunnel under NY 27 and continue on the bikeway.

13.0　Turn around when the bikeway ends at Merrick Road.

14.1　Pass through the tunnel under NY 27 and continue on the bikeway.

14.8　Cross Clark Street, continue on bikeway.

16.5　Cross Linden Street, continue on bikeway.

17.6　Cross ramp, continue on bikeway.

18.5　Cross ramp, continue on bikeway.

19.1　Cross ramp, continue on bikeway.

19.3　Cross Plainview Road, continue on bikeway.

19.8　Cross park road, continue on bikeway.

20.6　Cross park road, continue on bikeway.

21.9　Cross Hay Path Road, stay left to continue on bikeway.

22.7　Cross Old Bethpage Road.

23.3　Cross Old Country Road, right to continue on bikeway.

24.0　Cross Washington Avenue, left to continue on bikeway.

25.1　Cross Sunnyside Boulevard, continue on bikeway.

25.4　Cross highway exit and entrance ramps.

26.2　Arrive at finish.

RIDE INFORMATION

Local Events/Attractions
Old Bethpage Village Restoration: This historic site consists of thirty-six houses, barns, and buildings built between 1765 and 1865. Reenactors bring history to life, providing a glimpse of nineteenth-century Long Island. For events, admission, and more information, visit their website, at obvrnassau.com.

Bethpage State Park: This property contains sports fields, tennis courts, bridle paths, hiking and biking trails, and even a polo field for weekend games, but is best known for its five golf courses. The park charges a vehicle entry fee and additional fees for golf and polo.

Restaurants

Gabby's Gourmet Bagels: 8025 Jericho Turnpike, Woodbury; (516) 496-9000; gabbysgourmet.com

Dugan's Sandwich Shop: 8027 Jericho Turnpike, Woodbury; (516) 921-1182; duganssandwichshop.com

Woodbury Pizzeria & Pasta: 8025 Jericho Turnpike, Woodbury; (516) 921-6910; woodburypizzeria.com

On Parade Diner: 7980 Jericho Turnpike, Woodbury; (516) 364-1870; onparadediner.com

Merritt Bakery: 315 Northwest Dr., Farmingdale; (516) 694-6835; mikethebaker.com

Restrooms

5.6: Bethpage State Park

Hempstead and North Hempstead

Hempstead and North Hempstead were part of the same town before the Revolutionary War, when the two split along partisan lines. The northern residents were quickly occupied by the British, and many prominent citizens jailed for their open support of the rebellion. The two remain separate towns today, and have followed very different patterns of development.

Hempstead is the most populated town in New York, containing more residents than any other community in the state except New York City. This population-dense town is one of the major employers on Long Island, and the majority of it is composed of sprawling, commerciallybooming towns that arenot particularly bike-friendly. Coinciding with the Gilded Age, North Hempstead became part of the Gold Coast, a wealthy slice of the North Shore that served as inspiration for the East Egg and West Egg of F. Scott Fitzgerald's *The Great Gatsby*.

This section starts in the south, in the Hempstead Hamlet of Wantagh, following an off-road path from Cedar Creek Park to Jones Beach State Park. The next ride takes place to the west, in the independent City of Long Beach, a remarkable island city founded by William H. Reynolds, a controversial developer who planned the channel that transformed the peninsula into an island. Next, one of the only places to ride in Hempstead proper is a park named after Dwight D. Eisenhower, a recreational space in the middle of a bustling, sprawling urban environment. The last two rides take place in North Hempstead, the first starting at a scenic port and ending at a Victorian-era village by the sea, while the second explores the real-world inspirations for Gatsby's East and West Egg along the Manhasset Bay.

Jones Beach Bike Path

The Jones Beach Bike Path is a multi-use path extending from Cedar Creek Park in Wantagh to Jones Beach State Park, a beachfront park designed by Robert Moses. This barrier island park is more than 2,400 acres and consists of 6.5 miles of Atlantic Ocean beach, a half-mile bay beach, a boardwalk, bike racks, showers, swimming pools, concessions, a museum, and an outdoor amphitheater. An extension of the trail continues on and ends at Tobay, the Town Beach of Oyster Bay. This beach is beautiful and less busy, thanks to a punitive parking fee for non-residents. Bikes are not allowed in the beach property, but bike racks are installed at the end of the trail. Because the route is so popular and bikes must be locked to access the beach, a hybrid is the recommended bike for this route, unless simply doing an exercise ride at quieter times of day. This ride can be combined with the previous route, Bethpage Bikeway (CR 30), via 3.5-mile connection detailed in that section.

Start: Trailhead in Cedar Creek Park in Wantagh

Length: 17.1 miles

Riding time: About 1 hour

Best bike: Hybrid bike

Terrain and trail surface: Asphalt off-road trail

Traffic and hazards: This route follows a paved, off-road trail. The trail is popular and may be heavily used. On weekends in season, best time to ride is just at dawn.

Things to see: Miles of picturesque water views on a series of islands, through channels and bays. Jones Beach is full of architectural details designed to replicate a cruise ship, such as the funnels that serve as trash bins.

Fees: Cedar Creek Park charges a parking fee between 8 a.m. and 4 p.m. in season. No fee is charged for admission by bike to the park or the two beaches. If starting the ride in Jones Beach, be aware that there are tolls.

THE RIDE

From the trailhead in Cedar Creek Park, this ride travels over a series of barrier islands and bridges to the Art Deco-inspired Jones Beach. The route continues to the entrance to Tobay, then turns around, returning back to the start at Cedar Creek Park.

After entering the park and passing a series of parking fields, the trailhead is to the right. Follow the multi-use path, parallel with Wantagh State Parkway, for a little more than a mile before reaching the first bridge. The wind tends to be very strong here, either as a headwind or tailwind, possibly making this ride a tougher workout than the mostly flat and gentle route suggests.

The first bridge onto Great Island provides the first climb and affords views of Flat Creek and Island Creek along the bridge and Oliver's Island to the right. These barrier islands consist of narrow deposits of sand and sediment, and provide protection to the rest of Long Island against storms. The islands are mostly undeveloped—excepting the infrastructure needed for the road and bikeway—providing unobstructed views of other islands and water.

Bike Shops

Brands Cycle and Fitness: 1966 Wantagh Ave., Wantagh; (800) 649-3739; brandscycle.com
Merrick Bicycles: 1829 Merrick Ave., Merrick; (516) 544-4770; merrickbicycles.com
Bike Junkie: 272 Broadway, Bethpage; (516) 932-7271; bikejunkie .com

The second bridge climbs again and crosses Goose Creek onto Green Island, passing the admission booth for drivers to Jones Beach with views of tidal flats and the South Line Island to the left.

Just ahead is the third and final bridge, the steepest climb of the set, but also the most attractive, with a number of Art Deco-inspired features, including the small towers that mark the drawbridge. This section is very narrow, and signs instruct riders to dismount and walk their bike here, but few do.

Jones Beach Channel

The route curves into the park ahead, crossing the parking lot and heading south, away from the Nikon Theater. At the end of the lot, the route turns left, connecting to the Ocean Parkway Coastal Greenway. The bikeway parallels the Ocean Parkway, with views of the Atlantic to the right and Zachs Bay to the left, for the next 1.2 miles. The route is bordered from here to the beach by the John F. Kennedy Memorial Wildlife property, a nature preserve that is neither suitable nor legal for bicycle riding.

The trail ends at Tobay Beach Park with a few dozen spots to lock bikes. Riders can lock their bike and visit this beach, or turn around, and retrace the route back to the Jones Beach lot, with its much larger assortment of bike racks. When finished, retrace the route from earlier.

MILES AND DIRECTIONS

0.0   Start at the trailhead in Cedar Creek Park.

1.3   Follow bikeway over bridge.

2.4   Follow bikeway over bridge.

31 Jones Beach Bike Path

Jones Beach Water Tower

3.1   Follow bikeway over bridge.

4.4   Cross entrance ramp to Wantagh State Parkway.

4.5   Cross parking lot, follow protected bikeway through lot.

4.8   Right to exit lot, continue on bikeway.

8.5   Exit bikeway at Tobay Beach Park, then Turn around.

12.3   Right to continue on protected bikeway through parking lot.

12.6   Exit lot, continue on bikeway.

12.7   Cross entrance ramp to Wantagh State Parkway.

13.9   Follow bikeway over bridge.

14.6   Follow bikeway over bridge.

15.8   Follow bikeway over bridge.

17.1   Arrive at finish.

Jones Beach Bike Path

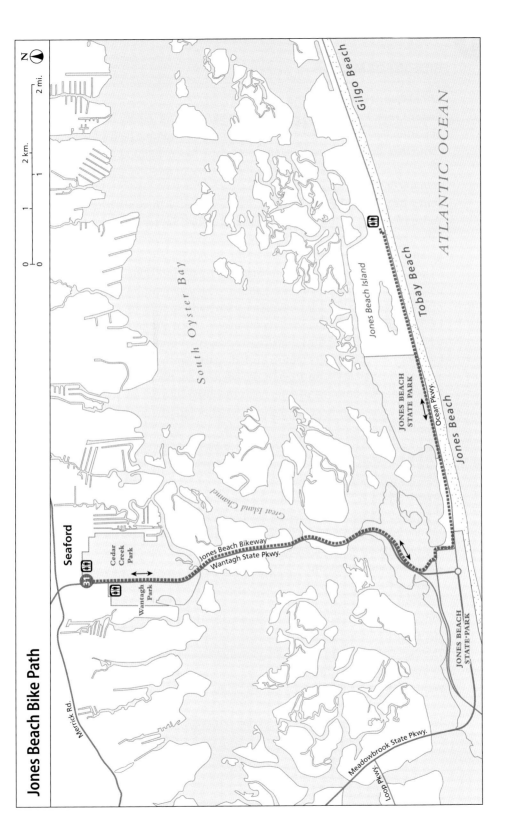

N

2 mi.

2 km.

Merrick Rd.

Seaford

31

Cedar Creek Park

Wantagh Park

Jones Beach Bikeway

Wantagh State Pkwy.

Great Island Channel

South Oyster Bay

JONES BEACH STATE PARK

Jones Beach Island

Ocean Pkwy.

Tobay Beach

Gilgo Beach

Jones Beach

ATLANTIC OCEAN

JONES BEACH STATE PARK

Meadowbrook State Pkwy.

Loop Pkwy.

RIDE INFORMATION

Local Events/Attractions

Cedar Creek Park: This 259-acre county park offers a variety of recreation opportunities, from archery to handball, and an aerodrome field for remote-controlled airplane operation. The park itself has multipurpose trails that are easier and less challenging than the bikeway to Jones Beach, perfect for younger or less experienced cyclists.

Jones Beach State Park: This park was designed with working-class New Yorkers in mind, in the 1920s, by architect Robert Moses. The island was a collection of swamps and brackish water before workers dredged sand to greatly increase the size and scale of the island. The new sand was quickly kicked up by the constant breeze, making further work difficult, until beach grasses and other vegetation were added to prevent erosion. This park is full of amenities, from lifeguard-monitored swimming spots to food concessions to live music theaters, and can become overcrowded quickly on prime beach days. Quieter walking paths stretch east and west, providing opportunities for birders to spot a variety of raptors (including the Northern Harrier Hawk) and shorebirds. Atlantic Ocean access is provided via a series of tunnels under the Ocean Parkway from the parking fields the bike route passes. A local group operates a site with food concessions, weather reports, news, and more, at jonesbeach.org.

The park also contains the Theodore Roosevelt Nature Center. This center includes exhibits of a variety of marine habitats and an environmental board-walk, and charges a modest admission.

Brands Cycle & Fitness Spring Duathlon: Every year in April, local bike shop brands organize an amateur duathlon, consisting of a 2.2-mile run and 11-mile bike ride over multiple laps through Cedar Creek Park. The shop also organizes group rides and maintains a calendar of local biking events on their website, brandscycle.com.

Restaurants

Jones Beach Concessions: Changes annually: Updated list at jonesbeach.org/Restaurants.html.

The Cup Coffeehouse: 3268 Railroad Ave., Wantagh; (516) 826-9533; thecupcoffeehouse.com

Wantagh Bagels: 3056 Merrick Rd., Wantagh; (516) 781-2244; wantaghbagels.com

Town Bagel: 2729 Merrick Rd., Bellmore; (516) 785-8986; townbagel.com

Singleton's Seafood Shack at Tobay: Tobay Beach Access Path; (516) 826-1610; tobaybeachsalsashack.com

East Bay Diner: 3360 Merrick Rd., Seaford; (516) 781-5300

Restrooms

0.0: Cedar Creek Park

4.5: Jones Beach

8.5: Tobay Beach

Long Beach Ride

Long Beach, nicknamed The City by the Sea, is on the westernmost barrier island on the South Shore. The city is bordered by the Atlantic Ocean to the south and Reynolds Channel along the other three compass points. The actual long beach is a 3.5-mile stretch of beautiful ocean beach, with a long, bike-friendly boardwalk. The city has its own bike share program, offering low-cost beach cruiser style bikes perfect for short jaunts on the flat roads and boardwalk. The strange mixture of Mediterranean-style buildings and condominiums is due to the controversial developer of Long Beach, who used restrictive ordinances to shape the character of the area.

Start: East Park Avenue near the intersection with Pacific Boulevard

Length: 6.5 miles

Riding time: About 30 minutes

Best bike: Hybrid bike

Terrain and trail surface: Asphalt roads and a wooden boardwalk

Traffic and hazards: Traffic is mostly slow and easy to navigate. The boardwalk is popular with rollerbladers, dog walkers, runners, and selfie-takers. Use caution and give right of way to pedestrians.

Things to see: Miles of beautiful beach on the Atlantic Ocean. Interesting mix of architecture styles and a number of Mediterranean-style buildings on East and West Broadway.

Fees: Anyone over the age of 13 must have a pass to be on the beaches weekends starting Memorial Day. Passes are required daily from the end of June to the first week of September. There is no fee for the boardwalk. Parking on city streets is free. Check signs for regulations and limitations.

Getting there: Take the Nassau Expressway from the Belt Parkway or I-678S. Continue onto Rockaway Boulevard and turn right to continue on the Nassau Expressway to Atlantic Beach Bridge. Left onto Park Street and continue onto Beech Street for just over 3 miles until a left onto Long Beach Boulevard. Turn right onto East Park Avenue six blocks to the ride start. Mass transit users can take the Long Island Rail Road to the Long Beach station. From the platform, exit right onto the Reverend JJ Evans Boulevard, then right onto West Park Avenue. Take the first left to make a U-turn and follow Park Avenue to the ride start at the intersection with Pacific Boulevard.

GPS: N40 35.330' / W73 38.446'

THE RIDE

If planning to use the SoBi bike share program, use the smartphone application or the website to find a station with an available bike. More information is below in the Ride Information section.

This flat, easy ride visits the quiet neighborhoods along Reynolds Channel before heading south and exploring an area where Mediterranean structures from the early twentieth century are sandwiched between modern homes, apartment complexes, resorts, and retirement communities, before turning onto the boardwalk for a picturesque off-road return to the end of the route.

View of the Atlantic Ocean from Long Beach Boardwalk

Long Beach Boardwalk

Starting on East Park Avenue, turn right onto Pacific Boulevard, then immediately right onto East Chester Street. Turn left on the fourth side street, Curley Street, up a quiet neighborhood at the intersection with East Pine Street. This road crosses the many canals of Long Beach, on charming, rounded bridges with ornamental stonework and decorative metal fencing.

After the stop sign, turn left around a rounded median onto Neptune Boulevard and continue across Park Avenue until the intersection with East Broadway. Turn right and follow the painted bike lane through this neighborhood, a mixture of modest row homes, condominiums, and apartment complexes. At the intersection with New York Avenue, facing a one-way street ahead, turn left, then left again, up to the boardwalk.

The center of the wooden boardwalk, made of darker boards, is designated for bicycles, rollerbladers, and runners. Stay to the right on it and watch for pedestrians over the next 3.5 miles. A number of concessions,

Bike Shops

Local Cycles: 307 West Park Ave., Long Beach; (516) 390-7085
Long Beach Bicycle: 755 East Park Ave., Long Beach; (516) 432-9632; longbeachbicycleny.com

Development of Long Beach

The first inhabitants of Long Beach were the Algonquian-speaking Lenape, incorrectly called Rockaway Indians by early English colonists, who purchased the land for agricultural use and fishing. It wouldn't be a site of year-round habitation until the mid-nineteenth century. In 1880, a builder from Brooklyn partnered with the Long Island Rail Road to lay tracks to the area and bring visitors to his newly constructed hotel. Despite being popular, the hotel and resort failed after winter storms wiped out the train tracks in subsequent years.

The next attempt took place in 1907 by a largely forgotten mover and shaker, William H. Reynolds. Reynolds was a businessman and politician who developed entire neighborhoods in Brooklyn and built Dreamland, the biggest amusement park at the time. Reynolds was a prodigy who created his first successful business at the age of 18, won election as the youngest New York State Senator at 24, and then developed Long Beach at 39. He marched a herd of elephants to the beach from his park on Coney Island, as both a publicity stunt and a practical means to build the boardwalk. The elephants carted lumber while teams of human workers dredged a channel named after Reynolds, and built white stucco buildings with red-clay tile roofs to emulate the Mediterranean Riviera. Until the company went bankrupt in 1918, local ordinances required that all future development follow the same style. Many of the original houses still stand, making for an interesting mixture of architecture, with high-rise condominiums and apartment buildings next to low-slung single-family homes.

The community became a village in 1914 and Reynolds became its first mayor. In addition to the building ordinance, he also passed a discriminatory law mandating that homes could only be occupied by white Anglo-Saxon Protestants. Thankfully, with the bankruptcy of 1918 this restriction was lifted as well. The village would become a city four years later, in 1922, and Reynolds would again be elected mayor. After thousands of dollars went missing from city coffers during this tenure, Reynolds was indicted for grand larceny and fraud and sentenced to 10 years in prison. This coincided with Prohibition enforcement against the city, which gained a corrupt, seedy reputation.

Despite allegations of corruption, overt racism, and his other personal flaws, Reynolds was so beloved by the citizens of Long Beach that they stopped the clock in town hall on the day he was indicted. The town clock was started a year later when he was released on appeal. Reynolds would move on from Long Beach and continue to be a popular yet controversial figure until his death, at 63, following months of ill health from heart disease.

restrooms, water fountains, and several bike repair stands with pumps and tools dot the way.

At the end of the boardwalk, exit onto Neptune Boulevard, then right onto Shore Road. Shore Road passes the Pacific Playground and then the route turns left onto Pacific Boulevard then right onto East Broadway. Follow East Broadway to the end, and turn left, onto Maple Boulevard, to East Park Avenue.

Turn left and finish the ride just ahead.

MILES AND DIRECTIONS

0.0 Start on East Park Avenue, right onto Pacific Boulevard, right onto East Chester Street.

0.1 Left onto Curley Street.

0.3 Left onto East Pine Street.

0.8 Left onto Neptune Boulevard.

1.3 Right onto East Broadway.

3.4 Left onto New York Avenue, left onto the Boardwalk.

5.6 Left onto Neptune Boulevard, right onto Shore Road.

5.9 Left onto Pacific Boulevard.

6.0 Right onto East Broadway.

6.1 Left onto Maple Boulevard.

6.4 Left onto East Park Avenue.

6.5 Arrive at finish.

RIDE INFORMATION

Local Events/Attractions

SoBi Long Beach Bicycle Share: SoBi Long Beach offers heavy, smooth-riding beach cruisers, with adjustable seats and solar-powered displays to keep track of cost, distance, and time. Bike repair stands are all along the boardwalk in case of problems. Visit their website, at sobilongbeach.com, to learn more or to download a smartphone application.

Long Beach Ride

N

| 0 | 0.25 | 0.5 km. |
| 0 | 0.25 | 0.5 mi. |

Reynolds Channel

Broad Channel

Reynolds Channel

ATLANTIC OCEAN

Long Beach

Long Beach Train Station

Austin Blvd.

Long Beach Blvd.

Park Pl.

Rev. J. Evans Blvd.

Shore Rd.

Long Beach

Boardwalk (off road)

Streets (top section):
Regent Dr.
Greenway Rd.
Fairway Rd.
Blackheath Rd.
Richmond Rd.
Maple Blvd.
Pacific Blvd.
Roosevelt Blvd.
E Broadway
Neptune Blvd.
Franklin Blvd.
Lincoln Blvd.
Monroe Blvd.
Riverside Blvd.
Edwards Blvd.
National Blvd.
Magnolia Blvd.
Laurelton Blvd.
Washington Blvd.
Lindell Blvd.
Grand Blvd.
New York Ave.

Curley St.
Farrell St.
Dalton St.
E Bay St.
E State St.
E Harrison St.
E Pine St.
E Fulton St.
E Hudson St.
E Market St.
E Chester St.
E Park Ave.

W Park Ave.
W Beech St.
Ocean View Ave.
W Bay Dr.
W Fulton St.
W Hudson St.
W Market St.
W Chester St.
W Park Ave.
Lafayette Blvd.
W Pine St.
W Walnut St.
W Olive St.
W Beech St.
W Penn St.
W Broadway

Mile markers:
6.4
6.1
5.9
6.0
0.3
0.1
0.8
1.3
?
?
3.4

32

Long Beach Beach: The beach hosts running races, biathlons, a free summer concert series, and several fairs and festivals. Recreational access to the beach requires a pass, sold either online or on premises. Long Island Rail Road users can obtain a discounted pass when they purchase their ticket by opting for the Getaway Package. For more on the beach, including upcoming events and regulations, visit the City of Long Beach site, at longbeachny.gov, and select Parks & Recreation from the sidebar menu.

Restaurants

Long Beach Bagel Cafe: 757 East Park Ave., Long Beach; (516) 432-2582; libagelcafe.com

Gentle Brew Coffee Boardwalk: 1 National Blvd., Long Beach; (516) 605-2370; gentlebrewcoffee.com

Shoregasboard (Concessions): 1 Riverside Blvd., Long Beach

Restrooms

3.4–5.6: At regular intervals on Boardwalk

5.8: Pacific Playground

Eisenhower Park

Once an exclusive country club, 930-acre Eisenhower Park is one of the largest public spaces in the New York metropolitan area, even larger than Central Park. Nassau County seized the land during the Depression to cover the taxes owed by the Salisbury Country Club. The current name stems from the 1969 rededication as a memorial to Dwight D. Eisenhower, adding a prominent statue of the 34th President. Today, the park is brimming with recreational activities, including tennis courts, ice-skating rinks, athletic fields, an aquatic center, basketball courts, a fitness trail, and three 18-hole golf courses and one miniature course. Other attractions include the memorials, a lovely rose garden, and a fine-dining restaurant.

Start: Trailhead near park entrance

Length: 2.3 miles

Riding time: About 15 minutes

Best bike: Hybrid bike

Terrain and trail surface: Asphalt multi-use trail

Traffic and hazards: The path is offroad and is primarily used by joggers and other fitness seekers. Give priority to pedestrians and be attentive. If continuing on the Park Boulevard, watch for traffic. This park road is mostly safe, but cars sometimes speed through, using it as a cut-through to skip the busy turnpikes around the park.

Things to see: A number of memorials and monuments, dedicated to veterans, firefighters, Dwight D. Eisenhower, and the victims of 9/11. Other sights include Salisbury Lake, a small pond with fountains, and the rose garden near the water.

Fees: Parking fees vary by season, charged on weekends from Memorial Day to Labor Day. Attractions like the golf course, batting cages, and aquatic center all have additional fees and require a Nassau County Leisure Pass.

THE RIDE

This very short ride is an oasis in what is otherwise a busy, car-centric area with few opportunities for cyclists. It lends itself to repeating laps and can be easily extended with the park road to make for a longer ride if the road isn't intimidating.

Starting at the pedestrian entrance on Hempstead Turnpike, turn right onto the Fitness Trail, at the restrooms, then immediately take a left toward the tennis courts, turning left to continue following the trail before reaching the courts.

Follow the trail straight and across Parking Field 4, turn right, then turn left, passing another restroom and following the trail between two picnic areas. Bear left toward Parking Field 5, then turn left, following the edge of the lot and then curving away toward another picnic site.

Make a hairpin right to continue following the path around a softball and football field, down to Parking Field 6A. Turn right to follow the trail along the next parking lot, Field 6, down to the Salisbury Lake and the Harry Chapin Lakeside Theatre.

Follow the trail counterclockwise, around the lake, past the Veterans Memorial and the Nassau County 9/11 Memorial, turning right to get back onto the trail, past the Rose Garden. The path veers around Field 6 again and then makes a hairpin turn right through a playground and picnic area heading toward the skating rink. Follow the trail past the rink and around the athletic field, past Parking Field 1 and the bocce courts, back to the start of the ride.

Eisenhower Park Pond

To expand the ride for an optional 4.1 miles, continue along the trail as before, but bypass the turn, leaving the tennis courts on the left. Follow the path to Parking Field 2, and then the lot to Park Boulevard. Turn right and then make a U-turn to continue on Park Boulevard in the opposite direction, along the golf courses on the right. Follow the park road to the exit and turn right onto the bike path along Merrick Road. Follow the bike path until it ends, and make a U-turn, retracing the bike path back to Park Boulevard and continue on the bike path until it ends at Hempstead Turnpike. Make another U-turn and head back to the park entrance, then turn right and rejoin the fitness trail ahead. Follow the fitness trail around the

Bike Shops

East Meadow Bikes: 349 Merrick Ave., East Meadow; (516) 481-1880
Hempstead Village Bike Shop: 48 Main St., Hempstead; (516) 485-0661
Cannondale Sports: 233 Glen Cove Rd., Carle Place; (516) 279-1245; cannondalesportsstore.com
Eastern Mountain Sports: 204 Glen Cove Rd., Carle Place; (516) 747-7360; ems.com
Merrick Bicycles: 1829 Merrick Ave., Merrick; (516) 544-4770; merrickbicycles.com

athletic fields, in a circular clockwise route, back to the start of the ride near the pedestrian entrance.

MILES AND DIRECTIONS

0.0 Start at the park entrance, right, then left, between tennis courts and field.

0.3 Cross a small parking lot and continue on the trail.

0.5 Follow trail left, then hard right to continue around football field.

0.8 Right across park drive into parking lot.

1.0 Right around pond.

1.4 Cross park drive and left.

1.5 Right then right past Rose Garden.

1.8 Enter parking lot, continue on trail.

1.9 Exit parking lot, continue on trail.

2.0 Left then right, following field to entrance.

2.3 Arrive at finish.
Optional: Follow the footpath past the tennis courts.

2.4 Exit the path into the parking lot and ride toward the exit.

2.6 Turn right onto Park Boulevard, then use the cut through to make a U-turn onto the other lane and follow Park Boulevard away from the intersection with Hempstead Turnpike.

4.3 Turn right onto the bike path along Merrick Road.

4.9 Turn around at the end of the bike path.

5.9 Turn around at the end of the bike path.

6.0 Turn right into the park to the bike path ahead.

6.1 Turn right onto the bike path.

6.4 Arrive at finish.

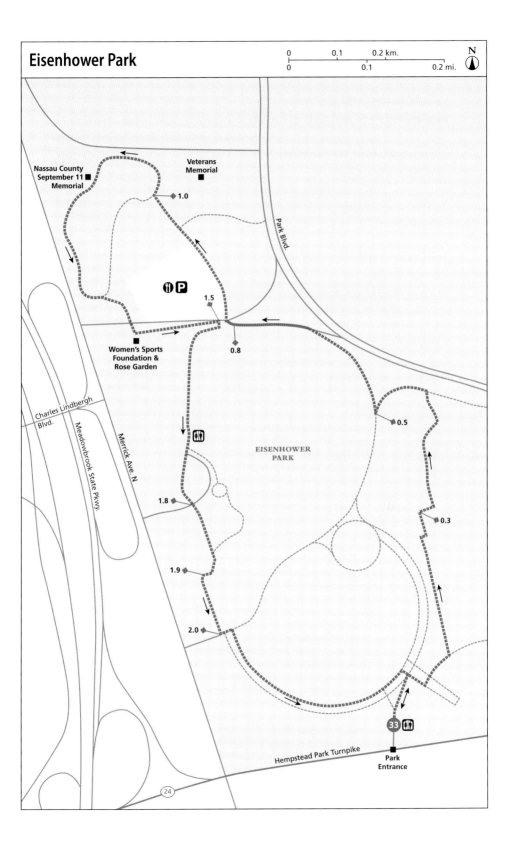

Eisenhower Park

0 0.1 0.2 km.
0 0.1 0.2 mi.

N

Nassau County
September 11
Memorial ■

Veterans
Memorial ■

◆ 1.0

◆ 1.5

← 0.8

Women's Sports
Foundation &
Rose Garden

Park Blvd.

◆ 0.5

EISENHOWER
PARK

Charles Lindbergh
Blvd.

Meadowbrook State Pkwy.

Merrick Ave. N

◆ 1.8

◆ 0.3

◆ 1.9

◆ 2.0

33

Park
Entrance

Hempstead Park Turnpike

24

RIDE INFORMATION

Local Events/Attractions

Eisenhower Park and Nassau County Events: The park holds a number of concerts and free events, all of which are listed on the Nassau County events calendar, available on the Nassau County website at nassaucountyny.gov/calendar.aspx.

Restaurants

Colony Diner: 2019 Hempstead Bethpage Turnpike, East Meadow; (516) 794-5159

The Greene Turtle: 1740 Hempstead Turnpike, East Meadow; (516) 280-7251; thegreeneturtle.com

Fairway Market Westbury: 1258 Corporate Dr., Westbury; (516) 247-6850; fairwaymarket.com

Restrooms

Restrooms are spread widely throughout the park.

Port Washington to Sea Cliff

Port Washington to Sea Cliff

The villages of Port Washington and Sea Cliff are separated by Hempstead Harbor, a tranquil bay on the North Shore of Long Island. The two villages are alike: Both are picturesque, small, full of parks, and rich in history. The larger of the two is Port Washington, 5 square miles, to the 1 square mile of Sea Cliff. Despite being small, Sea Cliff is home to sixteen parks and dozens of late nineteenth-century structures, from which it derives its slogan, "A Victorian Village by the Sea." The two villages are connected by a third, Roslyn, immediately recognizable by a distinctive clock tower built at the end of the nineteenth century.

Start: Town Dock at Sunset Park in Port Washington

Length: 19.2 miles

Riding time: About 1 hour 30 minutes

Best bike: Road bike

Terrain and trail surface: Asphalt

Traffic and hazards: Make sure to follow the sign for the marginal road on the route back on West Shore Road to avoid a short stretch of shoulder-less road in a high-speed corner. The Village of Roslyn is extremely popular with tourists and very busy. Use caution when navigating the short ride through the downtown.

Things to see: Picturesque water views of tranquil bays and harbors, Victorian-era homes.

Fees: None. Parking is free at the Town Dock. Metered parking is available nearby in the town municipal lot.

Getting there: Take exit 36 toward Port Washington / Searingtown Road from I-495E/LI Expressway. Merge onto Nassau Boulevard / South Service Road, then left onto Searingtown Road. Turn left onto Main Street to the ride start at Town Dock. Transit users can take the Long

Island Rail Road to either the Port Washington or Sea Cliff stops and pick up the ride either at the start or at the turn around point in Sea Cliff. From Port Washington station, turn left onto Main Street to the ride start. From Sea Cliff station, exit the station right onto Sea Cliff Avenue to the loop in the village district.

GPS: N40 49.919' / W73 42.104'

THE RIDE

This ride starts in Port Washington and travels through downtown to a long stretch of road along Hempstead Harbor before passing through the northernmost portion of the village of Roslyn en route to a long ride up the eastern bank of the harbor into Sea Cliff.

Historic village of Sea Cliff

The route passes several historic landmarks in Sea Cliff and the scenic overlook at Veteran's Memorial Park before turning around and retracing to Port Washington. Feel free to start in either village on this simple out-and-back route.

From Town Dock, head up Main Street, into downtown Port Washington, up a short, steep climb. The road levels out as it passes the train station and ends in a T-junction with Port Washington Boulevard. Turn left then right onto Beacon Hill Road, into a steeper, taller climb on a quiet road with a wide shoulder.

On the downhill, the route passes a signalized intersection and continues ahead on West Shore Road, on a fast, curving descent with a small road shoulder. Unfortunately, light industrial-use facilities obscure the water views along most of this road, which is otherwise perfect for road cyclists, being mostly flat, straight, and bordered by trees and fields.

Bear left after passing under the NY 25A bridge, onto Old Northern Boulevard, then left at the iconic clock tower. This is the charming village of Roslyn, an incredibly cute town center that could have been a filming location for the *Gilmore Girls,* full of tourist shops and casual dining.

At the signalized intersection, turn left to continue on Old Northern Boulevard, 0.1 mile to the fork. Bear left onto Bryan Avenue, heading uphill and out of town on a well-shouldered road through forested preserve lands. On the left, the route passes Cedarmere Park, once the home of William Cullen Bryant. To the right are the forested preserves around Clayton Estate and the Nassau County Museum of Art, accessible from NY 25.

At the next intersection, turn left onto Glenwood Road before the rustic sign for the village of Roslyn Harbor. The road passes a country club and a distinctive brick wall before heading downhill to the T-junction with Scudders Lane. Turn left and follow the road, which becomes Shore Road just ahead.

A mixture of industrial sites and water views make up this 0.8-mile stretch, which becomes Prospect Avenue after passing a beach on the left. The rest of the road is much prettier, with unobstructed views of the water beyond a tree-lined sidewalk path.

Prospect Avenue curves uphill after the water view for a challenging climb up to Veterans Memorial Park at the intersection with Sea Cliff Avenue. The best vista is just within the park, about a dozenyards forward. Turn right onto Sea Cliff Avenue, noting the lovely Victorian-era homes on the left of Sea Cliff, then bear right to continue. The Village Hall and Library are on the left, in a former church. The library has a wealth of historic information on the village.

Turn left onto Roslyn Avenue at the next intersection, then left again onto 10th Ave. The former Parish House for the church houses the Sea Cliff

Victorian-Era home in Sea Cliff

Bike Shops

Port Washington Bicycles: 20 Soundview Marketplace, Port Washington; (516) 883-8243; portbicycles.com
Brickwell Cycling and Multisports: 1463 Northern Blvd., Manhasset; (516) 439-5553; brickwell.com
Road Runners Bicycles: 8 Forest Ave., Glen Cove; (516) 671-8280; roadrunnersbicycles.com

Village Museum, on the left, before the route passes the other side of the Village Hall and Library. Bear left onto Summit Avenue and continue onto Sea Cliff Avenue, then left onto Prospect Avenue, down the long hill from before.

The route continues along familiar territory, back into Roslyn, then up West Shore Road. On the big climb up West Shore Road, near the curve, make sure to bear right at the "Marginal Road, Keep Right" sign. This is a side street paralleling a short stretch of West Shore Road with no shoulder and high speeds on a tight curve. It exits just after the curve, where the route turns right onto West Shore Road and continues up Beacon Hill Road to Main Street, to arrive at the finish in about a mile.

Bridges at William Cullen Bryant Preserve

MILES AND DIRECTIONS

0.0 Start at the Town Dock, proceed on Main Street.

0.9 Left onto Port Washington Boulevard (NY 101), then right onto Beacon Hill Road.

1.7 Continue on West Shore Road.

5.0 Continue on Old Northern Boulevard.

5.2 Left to continue on Old Northern Boulevard.

5.4 Left to continue on Old Northern Boulevard.

5.5 Bear left onto Bryant Avenue.

6.6 Left onto Glenwood Road.

7.1 Left onto Scudders Lane.

7.3 Right onto Shore Road.

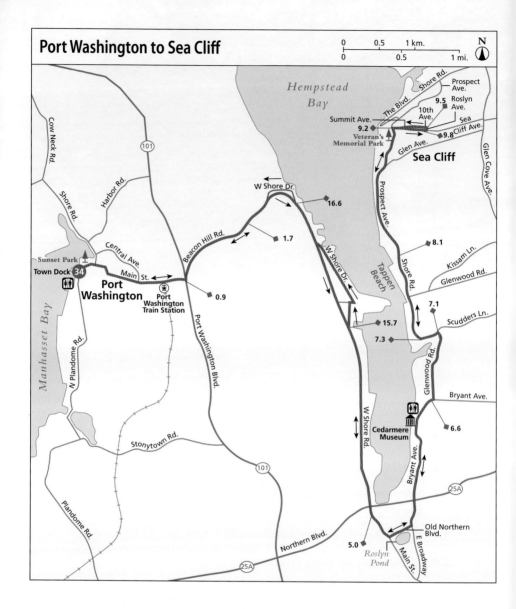

Port Washington to Sea Cliff

8.1 Continue on Prospect Avenue.

9.2 Right on Sea Cliff Avenue.

9.5 Left onto Roslyn Avenue, then left onto 10th Avenue.

9.7 Left onto Summit Avenue.

9.8 Continue on Sea Cliff Avenue, then left onto Prospect Avenue.

10.9 Continue on Shore Road.

11.7 Left onto Scudders Lane.

11.9 Right onto Glenwood Road.

12.5 Right onto Bryant Avenue.

13.5 Continue on Old Northern Boulevard.

13.7 Right to continue on Old Northern Boulevard.

13.8 Right to continue on Old Northern Boulevard.

14.0 Continue on West Shore Road.

15.7 Right onto first West Shore Drive for Bar Beach detour.

16.6 Right onto second West Shore Drive.

16.9 Keep right for marginal road.

17.3 Exit marginal road, right onto West Shore Road.

17.4 Continue onto Beacon Hill Road.

18.2 Left onto NY 101, then right onto Main Street.

19.2 Arrive at finish.

RIDE INFORMATION

Local Events/Attractions

Cedarmere Museum: William Cullen Bryant lived at this scenic spot over the harbor until his death in 1878. The property passed through his daughter to her nephew, who restored much of the home after a fire in 1902. After his nephew's death, the house passed through other family members before it was bequeathed to Nassau County. The home is still undergoing renovation, with plans to reopen as a historic house museum. The grounds are open for sightseeing and hiking. friendsofcedarmere.org.

Nassau County Museum of Art: This suburban museum is ranked among the nation's largest and most important ones. The museum hosts original exhibitions on a rotating basis in the three-story Georgian mansion, a private estate during the late nineteenth-century Gold Coast period. The permanent collection includes one of the largest sculpture gardens open to the public on the East Coast and hundreds of works by European and American artists. Some of the artists represented include Rodin, Braque, Vuillard, Bonnard, Lichtenstein, and Rauschenberg. Learn more on their website, at nassaumuseum.org.

Sea Cliff Village Museum: Located in the old parish hall, this community museum keeps the village history through photos, documents, costumes, and town records. Learn about current exhibits and more on their website, at seacliffmuseum.com.

Restaurants

Dolphin Bookshop & Cafe: 299 Main St., Port Washington; (516) 767-2650; thedolphinbookshop.com

Ayhans Mediterranean Marketplace & Cafe: 293 Main St., Port Washington; (516) 767-1400; ayhansmarketplace.com

Coffeed: 5 Irma Ave., Port Washington; (516) 883-2721; coffeednyc.com

Port Cafe: 900 Port Washington Blvd., Port Washington; (516) 767-1813; portcafeli.com

Delicacies Gourmet: 1354 Old Northern Blvd., Roslyn; (516) 484-7338; delicaciesdeli.com

B. Browns Kitchen: 64 Roslyn Ave., Sea Cliff; (516) 609-2939

Restrooms

0.0: Town Dock

9.3: Sea Cliff Village Hall

Manhasset Bay Peninsulas Loop

Manhasset Bay separates Cow Neck and Great Neck, two large peninsulas containing more than a dozen North Hempstead villages and hamlets. On the eastern border of Queens, and well served by the Long Island Rail Road, villages range from tourist sites to bedroom communities. The area is wealthy, but not to the same degree it was during the 1920s' Gold Coast era, when F. Scott Fitzgerald lived in a modest Great Neck home. The house, and Fitzgerald, possessed more than superficial similarities to the home and character of Nick, fictional narrator of The Great Gatsby. *The nearby village of Kings Point served as a model for nouveau riche West Egg, where Gatsby's mansion was located, and the more traditional East Egg of Daisy and Tom came from Sands Point, across the bay.*

Start: The intersection of Plandome Road and Bayview Avenue in downtown Manhasset

Length: 25.5 miles

Riding time: 105–120 minutes

Best bike: Road bike

Terrain and trail surface: Asphalt

Traffic and hazards: The town centers can be busy and congested. Use caution and ride safely out of the door zone.

Things to see: Scenic water views, historic homes, mansions in a variety of architectural styles, and the vista from Steppingstone Park.

Fees: Parking is in high demand. There may be a fee to park in municipal lots, including the Long Island Rail Road lot near the start of this ride. Follow posted signs and purchase parking vouchers from the muni-meters as needed.

Getting there: Take exit 33 toward Community Drive / Lakeville Road from I-495 E. Merge onto South Service Road, then left onto Community Drive. Turn right onto Northern Boulevard E/25A, then left onto

Plandome Road. The ride start is a half-mile ahead at the intersection with Bay Avenue. Transit users can take the Long Island Rail Road to the Manhasset stop, and exit the parking lot left onto Plandome Road to the start of the ride, just ahead.

GPS: N40 47.879' / W73 41.990'

THE RIDE

This ride is the second hilliest in the book, with a total elevation gain of 1,409 feet. None of the individual climbs are particularly challenging, with the total gain spread over a dozen or so efforts on the route. The hardest

Manhasset Bay

section is near the end after a pretty section of Sands Point, where a rolling stretch of road climbs to a peak of 187 feet over 2.0 miles.

Starting in downtown Manhasset, follow Bayview Avenue for a fast descent down a narrow road. When the water comes into view, bear left to continue on Bayview Avenue in a wide shoulder along the Manhasset Bay.

The shoulder narrows and disappears as the road passes under a railroad bridge. Turn right onto East Shore Road, around the southern tip of the bay, then right again to stay on East Shore at the signalized intersection. Turn right and continue up East Shore Road, which narrows into a lower-volume road just ahead.

East Shore Road widens again and gains a small shoulder as it approaches a lovely bay vista, sometimes obscured by foliage, until the road curves left up a short, steep hill. Turn right at the intersection to continue on East Shore Road.

The road curves and winds along into Kings Point, through a quiet neighborhood of large, impressive homes bordered by traditional iron or split-rail fences. At the stop sign before a tiny circular median, continue slightly right onto Wildwood Road. This even quieter road heads up a slight hill and then over a small, lovely creek before curving right and past a narrow tree-lined median to the next stop sign.

Turn right onto Cherry Lane, then continue straight onto Split Rock Drive after passing the North Shore Hebrew Academy on the right. This road and the next, Kings Point Road, are classic West Egg, featuring a mix of modest suburban homes and towering mansions on small plots. Turn left at the stop onto Kings Point and continue into the village center. Leisure riders may wish to make a quick detour after approaching the Kings Point Park property by turning right, onto Stepping Stone Lane, to a scenic vista at Steppingstone Park just a block ahead. The view of the bay is a regional highlight and worth the short detour. From here, continue on Stepping Stone Lane, past the US Merchant Marine Academy and an athletic field, and then turn left, onto Steamboat Road, then right, onto Kings Point Road to continue.

Bear left at the next fork onto West Shore Road. This quiet road gains a shoulder near the end when it crosses a bridge over picturesque Udalls Millpond into Saddle Rock. Continue after the bridge onto Bayview Avenue, past a municipal park on the left, onto a busier, faster road with a wide median and shoulder.

After 1.3 miles, turn left onto Cuttermill Road, just before a congested section of Great Neck. Cuttermill passes apartment complexes and hotels, built along the railroad, before ending in the charming downtown section of Great Neck. Turn left, onto Middle Neck Road, then right, onto Grace Avenue, past a municipal park and into a more residential neighborhood. Bear left at the fork to stay on Grace Avenue. After a fast downhill, the road ends at an intersection with East Shore Road. Turn right and retrace the route from earlier, left to continue on East Shore Road, then left onto Bayview Avenue, then bear right to continue on Bayview toward downtown Manhasset.

Just before the ride start, turn left onto Locust Place. Turn right at the end onto Colonial Parkway, then left at the traffic signal onto Plandome Road through a busy block. The road opens up immediately, making for a pleasant mile of road riding.

At a stop sign before a small road triangle, turn left, to continue on Plandome Road along the banks of picturesque Leeds Pond. Plandome Road curves right, affording a scenic view of the bay on the left and the pond on the right, just before the entrance to the Science Museum of Long Island.

The route follows Plandome to a stop sign and continues ahead onto Main Road in Port Washington, passing wharves and piers before scenic Sunset Park. Turn left ahead, just after the Dolphin Bookshop, onto Shore Road, entering the village of Baxter Estates. Shore Road follows the bay through a busy stretch. After the Mill Pond, riders may wish to use the marked crosswalk to access the multi-use waterfront path across the street. At the end of the path, it's two more blocks of built-up roads, and the route crosses at the intersection onto quiet Sands Point Road.

The road enters the village of Sands Point, past historically significant estates and tranquil wetlands. Turn left at the end, onto Middle Neck Road, and follow the road up through a small loop of impressive architecture, including a gothic tower, after the road turns left onto Lighthouse Road.

Lighthouse Road affords a quiet view of the bay and curves back to Middle Neck Road, where the route turns right. Middle Neck Road passes preserves and country clubs until entering a car-centric commercial strip in Port Washington. The road climbs past Nassau Knolls Cemetery and peaks around 180 feet before heading into a fast descent to a signalized intersection. Turn right, onto quiet, forested Stonytown Road. At Leeds Pond, the route continues up a slight hill, and then continues straight onto Plandome Road. Follow Plandome Road for the next 1.2 miles to finish this ride.

Bike Shops

Port Washington Bicycles: 20 Soundview Marketplace, Port Washington; (516) 883-8243; portbicycles.com
Brickwell Cycling and Multisports: 1463 Northern Blvd., Manhasset; (516) 439-5553; and 3 Northern Blvd., Great Neck; (516) 482-1193; brickwell.com
Peak Bicycle Pro Shop: 42-42 235th St., Douglaston; (718) 225-5119; peakmtnbike.com

0.0 Begin on Bayview Avenue by intersection with Plandome Road.

0.8 Right onto East Shore Road.

0.9 Right to continue on East Shore Road.

2.3 Right to continue on East Shore Road.

4.0 Continue on Wildwood Road.

4.5 Right onto Cherry Lane.

4.6 Continue onto Split Rock Drive.

5.4 Left onto Kings Point Road.

6.7 Left onto West Shore Road.

7.7 Continue on Bayview Avenue.

9.0 Left onto Cuttermill Road.

9.6 Left onto Middle Neck Road.

9.7 Right onto Grace Avenue.

10.3 Bear left to continue on Grace Avenue.

10.8 Left onto East Shore Road.

10.9 Left onto Bayview Avenue.

11.3 Right to continue on Bayview Avenue.

11.6 Left onto Locust Street.

11.8 Right onto Colonial Parkway, then left onto Plandome Road.

12.9 Left to continue on Plandome Road.

14.6 Left onto Shore Road.

15.5 Continue on Sands Point Road.

16.9 Left onto Cedar Knoll Drive.

17.1 Left onto Middle Neck Road.

17.5 Left onto Lighthouse Road.

18.0 Right onto Middle Neck Road.

22.9 Right onto Stonytown Road.

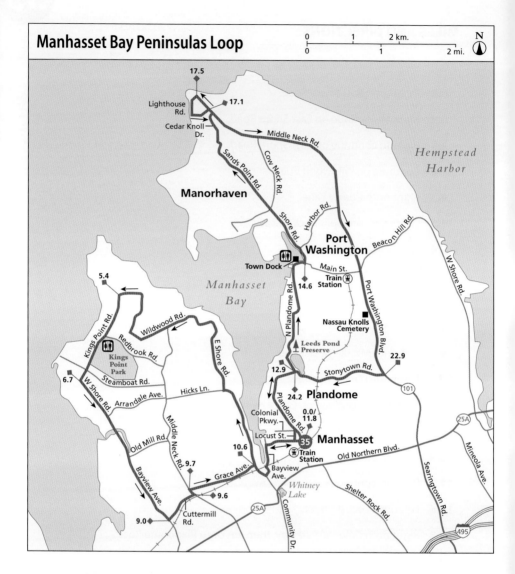

Manhasset Bay Peninsulas Loop

24.2 Continue on Plandome Road.

25.4 Arrive at finish.

RIDE INFORMATION

Local Events/Attractions

Cow Neck Peninsula Historical Society: This society manages two historic house museums and provides donation-supported tours to the public, in addition to a robust educational program. cowneck.org.

Stepping Stones Lighthouse: A lovely Victorian-era lighthouse in Sands Points, visible from Steppingstone Park, this property has suffered from neglect. Efforts are underway to save and restore the property, which is visited by boat tours from Sands Point. steppingstoneslight.com.

Restaurants

Bagel Time: 93 Manorhaven Blvd., Port Washington; (516) 767-3822

St. Honore Pastry Shop: 993 Port Washington Blvd., Port Washington; (516) 767-2555; sainthonorepastry.com

Douglas & James Ice Cream Makers: 405 Main St., Port Washington; (516) 708-1706

Louie's Manhasset: 339 Plandome Rd., Manhasset; (516) 627-0022; louiesmanhassetrestaurant.com

Let There Be Bagels: 475 Port Washington Blvd., Port Washington; (516) 944-8822; lettherebebagels.com

Tropical Smoothie Cafe: 11 Old Shore Rd., Port Washington; (516) 441-5150; tropicalsmoothiecafe.com

Restrooms

6.4: Kings Point Park or Steppingstone Park

14.5: Port Washington Town Dock

New York City: Queens and Brooklyn

Long Island is frequently used as a reference to Nassau and Suffolk counties, but the island includes the boroughs of Queens and Brooklyn. The two aren't commonly thought of as part of Long Island, nor are they regarded as bike-friendly, but popular opinion is wrong in both cases. Brooklyn has the first bike path in America, built in the 1890s, and the city is experiencing a renaissance of cycling infrastructure.

The three rides in Queens highlight Fort Totten, Cunningham Park, and Jamaica Bay, respectively. The first of these takes place on the Cross Island Parkway bike path, and visits Fort Totten, a Civil War-era fort with buildings built under the supervision of Robert E. Lee when he was still just a US military engineer. The second ride covers Cunningham Park, a 358-acre park with pristine nature preserves and a major mountain-bike trail system. The third and final ride loops around Jamaica Bay, a wildlife refuge situated on more than 9,000 acres near JFK Airport and surrounded by a greenway and bike lanes. The two rides in Brooklyn highlight a north-to-south network of bike lanes and shared trails, from Greenpoint to Coney Island, and the western half of the Shore Park Greenway, a Robert Moses-designed bike path with stunning views of the Verrazano–Narrows bridge and water. A second segment of the Shore Park Greenway, along the Belt Parkway, was omitted from the guide, but could serve as a connection between the Brooklyn rides and Jamaica Bay, a small portion of which is in Brooklyn.

Fort Totten

Fort Totten was built in 1862 and intended to defend the East River in tandem with Fort Schuyler, an earlier fort built in the Bronx at the mouth of the river and named after Revolutionary War hero Philip Schuyler, father-in-law of Alexander Hamilton. The two forts would be superseded by gun emplacements along the Long Island Sound. Today, Fort Totten is owned by the City of New York and operated as a park, offering historic tours, which has a quiet road perfect for cycling and running, and a small museum at the visitor center. The New York Police and Fire departments use part of the park for training exercises.

Start: Trailhead of Little Bay Park Greenway on Utopia Parkway

Length: 8.1 miles

Riding time: 30–45 minutes

Best bike: Hybrid

Terrain and trail surface: Asphalt off-road trails and a limited access park road

Traffic and hazards: Most of this ride takes place on an off-road trail. Fort Totten is a park with a limited access road, only open to authorized personnel.

Things to see: Miles of scenic bay views and stunning angles of the Throgs Neck Bridge.

Fees: None. There is free parking at the trailhead, and Fort Totten charges no admission.

Getting there: Take I-678E to exit 33 toward I-295 / Bell Blvd. / Clearview Expressway. Turn right onto the Cross Island Parkway, then right onto Utopia Parkway. The trailhead is just ahead, at a small parking lot by the water. Transit users can take the Long Island Rail Road to Bayside station; turn right onto Bell Boulevard, then left onto 43rd Ave. Turn right onto 223rd St. at the end, then walk your bicycle on the sidewalk on Northern Boulevard to the trailhead just ahead.

GPS: N40 47.343' / W73 47.633'

THE RIDE

This route follows popular greenways in an out-and-back ride, from Little Bay Park into historical Fort Totten, then onto the Cross Island Parkway Trail by way of Joe Michael's Mile. The route hugs Little Neck Bay and passes Crocheron Park en route to Alley Pond before returning on the same route to the start.

The greenways are pancake flat and Fort Totten is very mild. This would be a perfect ride for bringing children or completely inexperienced cyclists along, with a combination of safety, ease, and scenery.

Starting off Utopia Parkway, follow the trail past the dog park and run, under the highway ramp from I-295 above. The trail curves along a scenic water view with views of Throgs Neck Bridge, the Bronx, and part of Kings

View of Little Bay near ride start

Point on the right. Follow the trail around the parking area and turn left, onto Totten Avenue, into the former military base.

At the fork, turn right, continuing along Totten Avenue to the intersection past the historic church and beside the Officers Club, a Late Gothic Revival castle. Most of the historic buildings are dilapidated but are still attractive and make for interesting sightseeing. Turn all the way to the left, nearly a U-turn, onto Murray Avenue, and ride up the narrow street to the intersection with Abbott Road. Cross Abbott onto North Loop and continue, around the base-ball field, until the left turn onto Ordnance Road.

The route passes bathrooms on the right and the visitor center on the left before turning right, by the water, onto Shore Road. Left is a short path to the Battery at Willets Point, which may only be accessible via the visitor center depending on season and current staffing.

The Castle at Fort Totten

The route continues along Shore Road with lovely water views by a low-stone wall before curving to the right, passing through FDNY training facilities. Turn right at the end of the road, before the fenced-off Army area, on the Sgt. Charles M. Beer Road. This road passes the Fort Totten green and then approaches the intersection with Totten and Murray Avenue from earlier. Bear left onto Totten Avenue and follow the road past the Little Bay park, following signs for Joe Michael's Mile, a dedicated mile-long portion of the Cross Island Parkway trail.

Bike Shops

Roberts Bicycles: 33-13 Francis Lewis Blvd., Flushing; (718) 353-5432; robertsbicycles.net
Peak Bicycle Pro Shop: 42-42 235th St., Douglaston; (718) 225-5119; peakmtnbike.com

Turn left onto the trail, a wide, very comfortable bikeway, separated from the Parkway by steel girders. After a mile, the trail enters the parking lot for the Bayside Marina. Travel past the parked cars and continue on the trail ahead. In a half-mile, a footpath bridge connects the trail with the Crocheron Park, across the Parkway.

The trail continues for nearly another mile before ending at Northern Boulevard (NY 25A). To visit Alley Pond and the environmental center at the park, carefully use the crosswalk to cross, and then walk your bicycle on the sidewalk a short distance to the center.

To return, turn around and retrace the path until Fort Totten Avenue. Turn right onto the avenue, then left onto the next section of trail, and follow the finish at Utopia Parkway.

MILES AND DIRECTIONS

0.0 Start at the trailhead for the Little Bay Park Greenway off Utopia Parkway, into Little Bay Park.

0.7 Exit bikeway, left onto Totten Avenue.

0.8 Left onto Bayside Street.

0.9 Right onto Abbott Road.

1.0 Left onto North Loop.

1.1 Right onto Ordnance Road.

1.3 Right onto Shore Road.

1.7 Continue on Sgt. Charles M. Beer Avenue.

1.8 Right to continue on Sgt. Charles M. Beer Avenue.

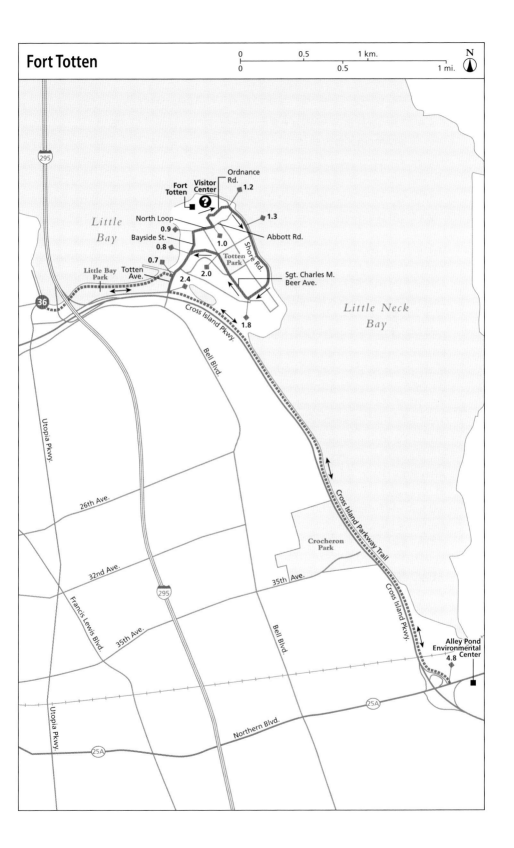

Fort Totten

0		0.5		1 km.
0		0.5		1 mi.

N

295

Little Bay

Fort Totten ■

Visitor Center ❓

Ordnance Rd.
■ 1.2

North Loop
0.9
Bayside St. ■
0.8
0.7 ■

Totten Ave.

Little Bay Park

2.4

2.0

1.0

Totten Park

Shore Rd.

■ 1.3

Abbott Rd.

Sgt. Charles M.
Beer Ave.

■ 1.8

36

Little Neck Bay

Cross Island Pkwy.

Bell Blvd.

Utopia Pkwy.

26th Ave.

32nd Ave.

295

Francis Lewis Blvd.

35th Ave.

35th Ave.

Bell Blvd.

35th Ave.

Crocheron Park

Cross Island Parkway Trail

Cross Island Pkwy.

Alley Pond
Environmental
Center
4.8 ■
■

25A

Northern Blvd.

25A

Utopia Pkwy.

25A

2.0 Left onto Totten Avenue.

2.4 Left onto Joe Michael's Mile / Cross Island Parkway Trail.

4.8 Turn around at Northern Boulevard / NY 25A near Alley Pond Environmental Center.

7.3 Right onto Totten Avenue.

7.4 Left onto Cross Island Parkway Trail.

8.1 Arrive at finish.

RIDE INFORMATION

Local Events/Attractions

Fort Totten: The park is home to dozens of historic structures, migratory waterfowl, and an athletic complex with an outdoor pool and sports fields. The visitor center operates a small museum that contains Civil War artifacts and provides historical information on the fort and battery behind it. Admission is free. The Bayside Historical Society operates a headquarters near the park entrance, in the Officers Club, a late Gothic revival-style building called "the Castle."

The Castle was designed under the supervision of a young Robert E. Lee, in his role as a military engineer, before he'd become General Lee and fight in the Civil War. Check their website, at baysidehistorical.org, for information on visiting, current events, and more.

Alley Pond Park: This 654-acre park is on part of a terminal moraine, a deposit of rocks and sediments, left by a glacier at the end of its journey. The park has salt and freshwater habitats (making it an important wildlife habitat) and extensive forests and meadowlands. One of the natural highlights of the park is The Queens Giant, a 133.8-foot Tulip Poplar tree that is the largest tree in New York City. The Alley Pond Environmental Center offers guided tours and a variety of educational programs. alleypond.com.

Restaurants

Utopia Bagels: 1909 Utopia Pkwy., Flushing; (718) 352-2586
Ponticello Bay Bridge Pizzeria: 20818 Cross Island Pkwy., Bayside; (718) 352-6606

Restrooms

0.5: Little Bay Park
1.1: Fort Totten Visitor Center
4.0: Over bridge in Crocheron Park

Cunningham Park

Cunningham Park is remarkable, both for the quality of its mountain bike trails and for its location in northwest Queens. This was the first park to gain mountain bike trails in New York City, in 2007, through a partnership between the GreenApple Corps, NYC Parks, and CLIMB, the Concerned Long Island Mountain Bicyclists. The 358-acre park was established in the 1920s and is split into two sections. The southern section is designated a Forever Wild Preserve, and contains a pristine landscape that may never be developed. The northern section, formerly agricultural fields and farms, has been developed for mountain biking, hiking, and sports. The property is well maintained and has clear, consistent signage detailing what to expect—although signage could be better in the northwest corner of the park.

Start: The trailhead at 67th Ave. and 210th St.

Length: 6.2 miles

Riding time: 45–75 minutes

Best bike: Mountain bike

Terrain and trail surface: Single track, hard-packed dirt

Traffic and hazards: This ride takes place in a car-free park. Use caution around joggers and runners. Watch out for poison ivy, which provides important wildlife habitats and may encroach on particularly narrow parts of the trail. The Black Diamonds are actually quite challenging, and suitable only for experienced mountain bicyclists.

Things to see: Peaceful trails through a public forest. Passerines are the most common bird species, notably including red-winged blackbirds and yellow warblers, and a number of migratory birds on annual trips north and south.

Fees: None. Cunningham Park is free both for parking and admission.

Getting there: Take exit 27S from I-495 onto Clearview Expressway South. Take first exit for 73rd Ave. and then turn left onto 73rd Ave. Turn left onto 210th Street. Trailhead is on the left at 67th Ave. Transit users will take the New York City subway F Train to Jamaica/179th St. Ride east on Hillside Avenue, then left onto 188th St. right on 73rd Ave. then left onto 210th St. Trailhead on the left across from 67th Ave.

GPS: N40 44.534' / W73 45.910'

THE RIDE

This park is suitable for riders of all levels. The Green Blaze Trail is two separate loops, roughly 2.0 miles long, of wide, flowing trail, connected by a white-blazed trail crossing the Clearview Expressway below. The Blue Blaze trails are named trails featuring twisty turns, very short climbs, rocks and logs, and rollercoaster-like up-and-down sections. The Black Diamond portions are truly challenging, and should be approached with caution. All of the named portions can be bypassed by staying on the Green Blaze Trail. The mapped route includes all features for a 6.2-mile ride with very little elevation gain.

Starting at the trailhead, head left on the Green Blaze Trail, until a right turn onto Teepee, a blue-blazed side trail of switchbacks and small logs, easy to roll over. After a few short hills, Teepee ends and the route turns right, back onto the Green Blaze Trail, for a short distance until Thrilla.

Turn left onto Thrilla, one of the less challenging Black Diamonds, a quick up-and-down trail featuring bailouts and bypasses for the log balances and jumps throughout. This is a fast, flowing technical ride, but the second half is even faster, separated by the Green Blaze Trail near the 1.2-mile mark. Cross-over into a zippy section of climbs and jumps, then free-ride to the Green Blaze Trail ahead.

A short, 40-foot climb leads to IMBA, another blue-blazed trail. Roll over the large log at the start and head into a curvy, twisty section of berms that crosses the Green Blaze Trail several times. The last cross enters Iguana, a fairly easy ride of long straightaways and very few challenges. At the end, turn left onto the Green Blaze Trail and follow it through the park to the west, over a white-blazed trail that crosses the Clearview Expressway on a bridge.

The western half of the park is more challenging, with tighter turns and more rock features in general. These Black Diamonds are generally tougher than the Thrilla section from before.

Rider at Cunningham Park

Follow the Green Blaze Trail to Green Apple, a blue-blazed trail on the left. Switchbacks and rock gardens make up the majority of challenges, but a few steep little hills will challenge single-speed riders. The Black Diamond loop, to the left, has more challenging rock gardens and some large logs to roll over. At the end, turn left, back onto Green Apple, for an easier, fairly fast ride to the Green Blaze Trail.

Turn left and then right onto Viper, a Black Diamond trail with some very technical log piles and short but very steep climbing features. Viper crosses the Green Blaze Trail and

Bike Shops

718 Cyclery: 254 3rd Ave., Brooklyn; (347) 457 5760; 718c.com (not local but hosts races at park)
Bellitte Bicycles: 169-20 Jamaica Ave., Jamaica; (718) 739-3795; bellbikes.com
Roberts Bicycles: 33-13 Francis Lewis Blvd., Flushing; (718) 353-5432; robertsbicycles.net
Bike Shop At The St. Albans Mini Mall: 188-19 Linden Blvd., St. Albans; (718) 527-3672; bikeshopatminimall .com
Tulip Bike: 76 S Tyson Ave., Floral Park; (516) 775-7728; tulipbike.com
Kissena Bicycle Center: 4570 Kissena Blvd., Flushing; (718) 358-0986

enters a less challenging blue-blazed section of fast, flowing riding, in a clock-wise loop back.

Bear left onto the Green Blaze Trail and roll around to Ringer, an easy-to-miss Black Diamond on the left. Like most of these trails, it starts with a log-over, then some steep climbs and large fallen trees in a heavily rooted section. The trail curves downhill over a truly challenging log and then goes up a steep rock climb before more log-overs and quick switchbacks. Cross the Green Blaze Trail to continue into a free-ride section, then right onto the Green Blaze Trail.

Turn left to continue on the Green Blaze Trail, heading east, back over the white-blazed bridge. Follow the Green Blaze Trail to the trailhead to finish the ride.

MILES AND DIRECTIONS

0.0   Start at the trailhead near 210 th St. turn left on Green Blaze Trail.

0.1   Right onto Teepee (Blue Blaze).

0.7   Right onto Green Blaze trail.

1.0   Left onto Thrilla (Black Diamond).

1.2   Cross Green Blaze trail to continue on Thrilla (Black Diamond).

1.5   Left onto Green Blaze Trail.

1.6   Left onto IMBA (Blue Blaze).

2.0   Cross Green Blaze Trail onto Iguana (Blue Blaze).

2.4   Right onto Green Blaze Trail.

2.6   Right onto Green Blaze Trail.

2.8   Cross over I-295 on the pedestrian bridge.

3.0   Left onto Green Apple (Blue Blaze).

3.3   Left onto unnamed Black Diamond Loop.

3.4   Left to continue on Green Apple (Blue Blaze).

4.2   Left onto Green Blaze Trail.

4.3   Right onto Viper (Black Diamond).

4.7   Cross Green Blaze Trail to continue on Viper (Blue Blaze).

Cunningham Park

4.9 Left onto Green Blaze Trail.

5.0 Left onto Ringer (Black Diamond).

5.4 Cross Green Blaze Trail to continue on Ringer (Black Diamond).

5.6 Right onto Green Blaze Trail, then left to continue.

5.7 Cross over I-295 on the pedestrian bridge.

6.2 Arrive at finish.

RIDE INFORMATION

Local Events/Attractions

Concerned Long Island Mountain Bicyclists (CLIMB): This nonprofit organization maintains trails and organizes mountain bike events all over Long Island. Check their website to learn about local events Cunningham Park, at climbonline.org. Local riders use the CLIMB forums to coordinate group rides, too, which may be of interest to visitors. A Brooklyn-based bicycle shop, 718 Cyclery, has hosted several popular races at Cunningham Park, detailed on their website, at 718c.com.

Restaurants

Lulu's Bakery: 18526 Union Turnpike, Fresh Meadows; (718) 454-4300; lulusbakeryshop.com

Fresh Meadows Pizzeria & Restaurant: 195-09 69th Ave., Fresh Meadows; (718) 217-2700; fmpizzeria.com

Qdoba Mexican Eats: 61-40 188th St., Fresh Meadows; (718) 454-9400; qdobali.com

Restrooms

0.7: Restroom at baseball field

Jamaica Bay Loop

Jamaica Bay is part of the Gateway National Recreation Area, a major urban wildlife refuge on 9,155 acres of salt marsh, upland field and woods, fresh and brackish ponds, and a massive bay full of small islands. The park is home to hundreds of bird species, rare coastal flora, over sixty butterfly species, and nearly fifty species of fish. The bay is located at the confluence of several estuaries, contributing to the ecological richness and diversity of the area.

Start: Canarsie Pier in Brooklyn on Jamaica Bay

Length: 21.2 miles

Riding time: About 1 hour 30 minutes

Best bike: Hybrid bike

Terrain and trail surface: Off-road paved trail, some on-road sections of asphalt

Traffic and hazards: Most of the route takes place off-road on a greenway with the occasional stretch of cracked or broken asphalt. The on-road portion through Broad Channel can be congested, so use caution, especially when making the broad left turn onto East 21st Rd. to the next section of trail. The painted bike lane on the Cross Bay Bridge may feel unsafe considering the speed of traffic. If nervous, walk bikes on the sidewalk along the bridge.

Things to see: Beautiful wetlands, marshes, and bay views all along an off-road bikeway. Several scenic vistas from bridges on the course. Atlantic Ocean views from Jacob Riis beach.

Fees: Parking is free at Canarsie Pier. There are no fees to access any section of the route. Parking fees apply at the other fields along the route if starting from Jamaica Bay or Jacob Riis beach.

Getting there: Take exit 13 from the Belt Parkway / Shore Parkway, into a traffic circle. Exit the traffic circle into the park. Transit users should probably take the A train to Broad Channel station and turn right onto Noel Road to the Cross Bay Boulevard and start the ride from there. A bike path connects with the Coney Island Boardwalk.

GPS: N40 37.748' / W73 53.069'

THE RIDE

This is a fairly flat ride on mostly car-free bikeways through a beautiful section of Brooklyn and Queens, near the JFK airport. Starting at Canarsie Pier, the trailhead is just before the entrance, extending left and right. Facing the park entrance and sign, turn left, heading northeast, to begin the ride.

This portion of the trail runs parallel to the Shore Parkway, separated by a wide grassy median and highway railings on the left. The trail makes three scenic bridge crossings in a row, leaving Brooklyn into Queens on the final crossing, overlooking the Old Mill Creek on the right. The trail currently ends abruptly at 84th St. but is undergoing work to extend it to the Cross Bay Boulevard. If the trail continues, follow it until its end and then turn right, heading toward 91st St. which has an on-road bike lane, and rejoin the mapped route.

From the current end, turn right onto 84th St. then left onto 157th St. through a residential portion of Howard Beach. Turn right onto 91st St., which has a painted bike lane, and follow the road until it ends at the intersection with 165th Ave. Turn left and then right onto the Cross Bay Boulevard bike lane, a painted lane that continues up and over the Joseph P. Addabbo Memorial Bridge ahead.

The bridge offers a scenic vista of Jamaica Bay below, but the painted lane may not feel safe for all riders, especially on the descent to the island with the thundering roar of the automobiles behind. If you're uncertain, take the sidewalk before the bridge, dismounting to walk your bike along the narrow path.

At the end of the bridge, the bike lane continues, but so too does the off-road bikeway. Carefully cross the entrance to a parking lot onto the bikeway and continue. The route passes the Jamaica Bay Wildlife Refuge, on the right, before continuing on into the Queens neighborhood of Broad Channel.

The bikeway ends at a built-up area and diverts to the on-road painted bike lane. Businesses here frequently obstruct the lane with large trucks and containers. Watch the door zone and continue into the commercial downtown district.

Toward the end, and the five-lane toll plaza, cautiously turn left from the end of the bike lane onto East 21st Road to Van Brunt Road. At the end, turn right onto the bikeway, which follows the boulevard to Rockaway Beach. The bikeway ends below at Beach Channel Drive. This route may have better bike access in the future but, currently, cyclists detour or ride the wrong-way down 92nd St. In the interest of safety, and to access a longer route along the boardwalk, turn left, following Beach Channel Drive for 0.8 mile to Beach 73rd Street.

Turn right, and follow Beach 73rd St. to a small traffic circle. Following the signs, turn right into the circle and follow it around to the boardwalk access on the other side. This is a beautiful 2.5-mile stretch along Rockaway Beach. Pedestrians have priority, so be considerate and watch out, preferably riding toward the center of the boardwalk.

At the end, the route curves right onto sharrow-painted 126th St. Turn left onto Newport Avenue in 0.3 mile. Follow Newport Avenue to the end, then turn left onto Beach 147th St. to busier Rockaway Beach Boulevard. Turn right and follow the boulevard into the traffic circle, exiting onto the parallel lane of the boulevard, then onto the sidewalk and right, onto the Jacob Riis

Jamaica Bay view from Floyd Bennett Field

Promenade. The route follows this path to the right turn ahead, onto a mile-long portion of the Jacob Riis Boardwalk. The boardwalk passes the beach park and some kiosks, then curves right and goes through the Riis Park food court, offering a wide diversity of casual eats.

At the end, turn right onto Beach 169th St. and follow it to the end at a confusing intersection. Carefully cross the road and turn right to continue on the off-road bikeway, up to the Marine Parkway Bridge. Cyclists are required to dismount and walk, due to the narrow width, but the extra time is worth it for the spectacular views. At the end, follow the route as it crosses Flatbush Avenue and then turns left to continue along the Floyd Bennett Field property.

The bikeway continues, curving to the right, until the finish, in roughly 4.1 miles.

> ## Bike Shops
>
> **Bellitte Bicycles:** 169-20 Jamaica Ave., Jamaica; (718) 739-3795; bellbikes.com
> **Larry's Cycle Shop:** 1854 Flatbush Ave., Brooklyn; (718) 377-3600; larryscycleshop.com
> **Brooklyn Vintage Bicycles:** 51 Fane Ct., Brooklyn; (347) 733-2079; bkvbicycle.flavors.me
> **Sheepshead Bay Bicycles:** 113 Noel Ave., Brooklyn; (917) 273-0673
> **Ride Bikes Pro Gear:** 4176 Bedford Ave., Brooklyn; (718) 552-0738; ridebikeprogear.com

MILES AND DIRECTIONS

0.0 Start on Jamaica Bay Greenway at Canarsie Pier.

3.0 Right onto 84th Street.

3.1 Left onto 157th Avenue.

3.4 Right onto 91st Street.

4.3 Left onto 165th Avenue.

4.4 Right onto Cross Bay Boulevard.

5.3 Continue on Cross Bay Boulevard Greenway.

7.0 Continue on Cross Bay Boulevard.

8.2 Left onto East 21st Road.

9.0 Right onto Beach 92nd Street then left onto Beach Channel Drive.

9.8 Right onto Beach 73rd Street.

10.1 Enter traffic circle, 2nd exit toward and onto boardwalk.

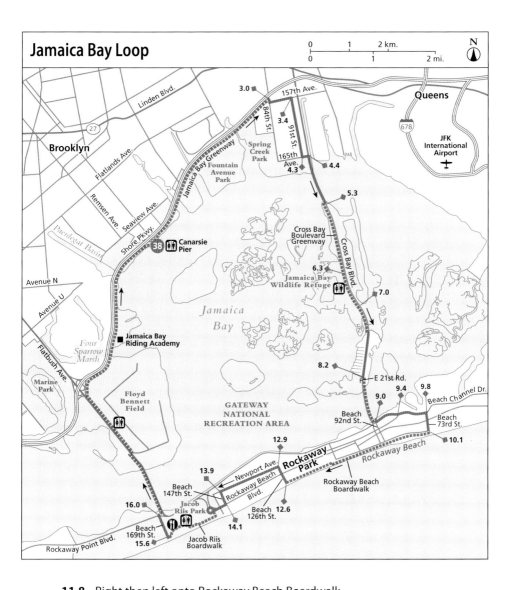

Jamaica Bay Loop

0	1 2 km.
0	1 2 mi.

N

Linden Blvd.

3.0

157th Ave.

Queens

84th St.

3.4

91st St.

678

JFK International Airport

Brooklyn

27

Flatlands Ave.

Jamaica Bay Greenway

Spring Creek Park

Fountain Avenue Park

165th Ave.
4.3

4.4

Remsen Ave.

Seaview Ave.

5.3

Cross Bay Boulevard Greenway

Pacrdegat Basin

Shore Pkwy.

38 Canarsie Pier

Cross Bay Blvd.

Avenue N

6.3

Jamaica Bay Wildlife Refuge

7.0

Avenue U

Jamaica Bay

Flatbush Ave.

Four Sparrow Marsh

Jamaica Bay Riding Academy

8.2

Marine Park

E 21st Rd.

9.4

9.8

Floyd Bennett Field

9.0

Beach Channel Dr.

GATEWAY NATIONAL RECREATION AREA

Beach 92nd St.

Beach 73rd St.

12.9

10.1

Rockaway Park

Rockaway Beach

13.9

Newport Ave.

Rockaway Beach Blvd.

Rockaway Beach Boardwalk

Beach 147th St.

16.0

Jacob Riis Park

Beach 126th St.

12.6

14.1

Beach 169th St.

15.6

Jacob Riis Boardwalk

Rockaway Point Blvd.

11.8   Right then left onto Rockaway Beach Boardwalk.

12.6   Right onto Beach 126th St.

12.9   Left onto Newport Avenue.

13.9   Left onto Beach 147th St.

14.1   Right onto Rockaway Beach Boulevard.

14.5   Enter traffic circle, complete loop, exit right onto Jacob Riis Boardwalk.

14.6 Right to continue on Jacob Riis Boardwalk.

15.6 Right onto Beach 169th St.

15.9 Left then cross Rockaway Point Boulevard onto Beach Channel Drive Greenway over bridge.

17.1 Right across Flatbush Avenue then left to continue on greenway.

21.2 Arrive at finish.

RIDE INFORMATION

Local Events/Attractions

Jamaica Bay: This wildlife refuge features extensive walking trails and a visitor center, open every day except major holidays. The visitor center offers free maps and checklists in addition to a series of field guides and ecology books. A number of outside groups hold events and maintain information on the area. The Brooklyn Bird Club hosts regular birding walks via their website at brooklynbirdclub.org. Look for the upcoming documentary, *Saving Jamaica Bay*, to learn more about the dangers facing this unique natural preserve on the website savingjamaicabay.com.

Floyd Bennett Field: This park used to be an airport. Now, it is a camping and hiking site, boat launch, horseback riding academy, and golf course. A large sports and recreation center offers athletic fields and indoor exercise, including child-friendly play zones, and R/C enthusiasts use the old airstrips to fly their planes.

Restaurants

Riis Park Beach Bazaar: 16702 Rockaway Beach Blvd., Queens; riisparkbeachbazaar.com
All American Deli Market: 925 Cross Bay Blvd., Broad Channel; (718) 945-5400; aachannelmarket.com
All American Bagel & Barista II: 2010 Cross Bay Blvd., Broad Channel; (718) 945-2233
Rippers: 8601 Shore Front Pkwy., Rockaway Beach
Tacoway Beach: 302 Beach 87th St., Queens; tacowaybeach.com

Restrooms

0.0: Canarsie Pier
6.9: Jamaica Bay Wildlife Refuge
10.4: Rockaway Beach
14.8: Jacob Riis Beach

Brooklyn North to South

Greenpoint is the northernmost neighborhood in Brooklyn. It's bordered by Newtown Creek both north and east, the East River to the west, and Williamsburg to the south. The neighborhood is home to several historical landmarks, primarily churches and apartment buildings, and is prized for having small town charm in the middle of the city. The area has experienced a recent development boom, raising fears that the largely working-class, multi-generational neighborhood, once defined by its Polish-American community, might lose its character and become the next Williamsburg. A similar fate seems to await Coney Island, on the southern end of Brooklyn. The former island, now a peninsula, comes to life in Neil Simon's semi-autobiographical Brighton Beach Memoirs, *set in the titular Coney Island neighborhood once known for a large population of working-class Jewish families. In the 1990s, neglected areas entered a context-sensitive revitalization, but recent rezoning has allowed developers to bulldoze most of the iconic early-1900s structures in favor of retail chains, hotels, and large housing developments.*

Start: Newtown Creek Nature Walk, at the northern end of Manhattan Avenue

Length: 30.6 miles

Riding time: About 2 hours 15 minutes

Best bike: Road bike

Terrain and trail surface: Off-road paved trail, painted on-road bike lanes, and asphalt roads.

Traffic and hazards: The Ocean Parkway path has numerous crossings. Watch for cars and come to a full stop. Use caution when navigating the parked cars in the bike lanes and sharrows on Flushing and Vanderbilt Avenues.

Things to see: Prospect Park, Prospect Park Lake, Coney Island, iconic Brooklyn businesses and landscapes.

Fees: None. Parking is free at Newtown Creek Nature Walk.

Getting there: From the north, take the Pulaski Bridge to McGuinness Boulevard. Turn right onto Freeman Street, then right onto Manhattan Avenue to the start. From the south, take I-278E to McGuinness Boulevard. Turn left onto Freeman Street, then right onto Manhattan Avenue to the start. Transit users can take the G line to Greenpoint Avenue Station and head north on Manhattan Avenue to the ride start.

GPS: N40 44.341' / W73 57.301'

THE RIDE

This ride follows several miles of New York City Road to link together bikeways, park trails, and boardwalk across the entire vertical axis of Brooklyn, from Greenpoint through Williamsburg to Prospect Park, and then along the Ocean Parkway bike path to Coney Island. The ride follows the boardwalk, then turns around, and returns.

Striking statues overlook the Newtown Creek Park

From the Newtown Creek Park follow Manhattan Avenue south, turning right onto Commercial Street just out of the parking lot. Turn left at the Greenpoint Playground, onto Franklin Street, and follow the sharrow markings through a fairly dense area that shifts easily through areas that feel commercial, industrial, or residential. Bear right at a fork to stay on Franklin Street, which gains a painted bike lane as it approaches the Bushwick Inlet on the right, and then turn right onto Kent Avenue, where the bike lane is two-way and buffered by a parking zone. Kent Avenue enters trendy Williamsburg along the East Shore, passing waterfront industry, chic boutiques, and upscale eateries.

After nearly 3 miles, the route approaches a built-up area with a highway overpass along the Brooklyn Naval Yard. Turn right and follow the bike lane onto Williamsburg Street West, then right again, onto Flushing Avenue. The lane becomes just an on-road painted lane here, but traffic is low in volume.

Turn left onto Vanderbilt Avenue, marked with sharrows here, and follow the road (which has a painted bike lane ahead) for 1.6 miles to Prospect Park. Turn right onto Plaza Street West, in the bike lane, and follow the road as it circles the Grand Army Plaza and Bailey Fountain. After the intersection with Prospect Park West, turn left onto West Drive, into the park, past the plinths that mark the entrance.

Ocean Parkway bike lane

Follow West Drive, counterclockwise, down to and around Prospect Park Lake. At the bottom, turn right, onto South Lake Drive, toward Machate Circle, and follow the bike lane around the circle and onto the greenway beside Ocean Parkway.

The greenway ends at Church Avenue, where the route turns right and then left, onto a contra-flow green-painted bike lane down Ocean Parkway. This nearly 3-mile multi-use path is shared with pedestrians, dog walkers, and runners. On Saturdays, in particular, this is a popular path for the many Jewish residents who observe Shabbat and travel on foot. Be considerate and share the path safely with pedestrians. It is hard to achieve any great speed on this path, as it has numerous crossings. Watch for traffic and come to a stop between sections.

Follow the path until reaching Sea Breeze Avenue, and turn left, across Surf Avenue. Watch for oncoming traffic, and head up to and turn right onto the boardwalk ahead.

The boardwalk is primarily for pedestrians, but cyclists are permitted from 5 to 10 a.m. on the angled boards in the center. Restrooms and concessions are all along the boardwalk, which passes historic and contemporary

Coney Island Boardwalk

New York City: Queens and Brooklyn

attractions, from amusement parks with bumper cars and roller coasters to the New York Aquarium.

Continue on the boardwalk to the western end, near W 37th St., then turn around and follow it to the opposite, eastern, end. After traversing the entire boardwalk, ride back to the entry point and exit onto Ocean Parkway. Follow the opposite side of Ocean Parkway on the return, and after Machate Circle turn right onto East Drive. Follow East Drive out of the park and turn right onto the bike lane, to Plaza Street East and around to Vanderbilt Avenue. The return is unchanged until near the end, where Commercial Street becomes one-way. Turn right onto Box Street, then left onto Manhattan Avenue, to arrive at the finish.

Bike Shops

Silk Road Cycles: 76 Franklin St., Brooklyn; (718) 389-2222; silkroadcycles.net
Greenpoint Bikes: 1078 Manhattan Ave., Brooklyn; (718) 389-3818
Ride Brooklyn: 468 Bergen St., Brooklyn; (347) 599-1340; ridebrooklynny.com
Ride Bikes Pro Gear: 4176 Bedford Ave., Brooklyn; (718) 552-0738; ridebikeprogear.com
718 Cyclery: 254 3rd Ave., Brooklyn; (347) 457 5760; 718c.com

MILES AND DIRECTIONS

0.0 Start at the Newtown Creek Nature Walk, proceed on Manhattan Avenue, right onto Ash Street, then right onto Commercial Street.

0.2 Left onto Franklin Street.

1.1 Right onto Kent Avenue.

3.0 Continue on Williamsburg Street West.

3.2 Right onto Flushing Avenue.

3.6 Left onto Vanderbilt Avenue.

5.2 Right onto bike lane around western side of Prospect Park.

6.3 Left onto West Drive.

6.8 Right onto West Lake Drive.

7.3 Right onto Prospect Park Circle Entrance, right onto South Lake Drive.

7.4 Left onto Ocean Parkway bike lane around traffic circle, right to continue on bike lane.

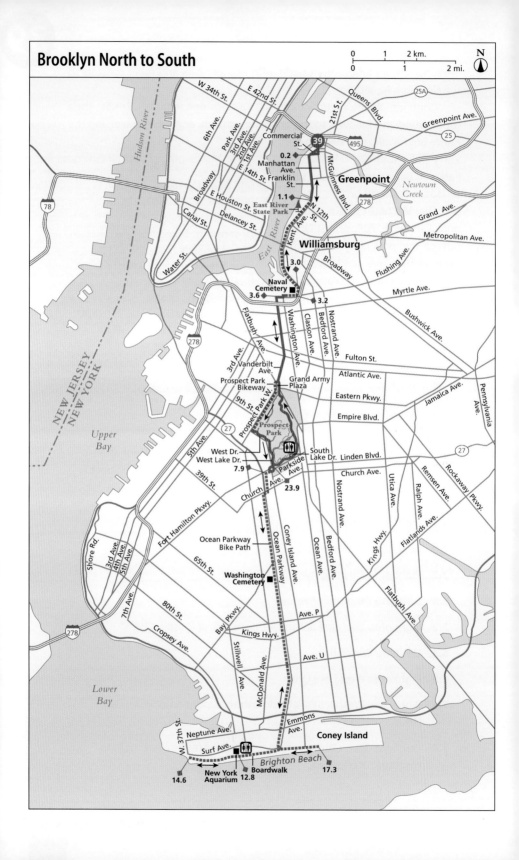

Brooklyn North to South

0   1   2 km.

0   1   2 mi.

N

Hudson River

W. 34th St.

E 42nd St.

S 21st St.

Queens Blvd.

25A

Greenpoint Ave.

25

6th Ave.

Park Ave.

3rd Ave.

2nd Ave.

1st Ave.

Broadway

E 14th St.

Commercial St.

39

0.2

McGuinness Blvd.

495

Greenpoint

Newtown Creek

Manhattan Ave.

Franklin St.

E Houston St.

Delancey St.

Water St.

Canal St.

78

NEW JERSEY
NEW YORK

Upper Bay

East River State Park

1.1

Kent Ave.

N 12th St.

278

Grand Ave.

Metropolitan Ave.

Williamsburg

3.0

Broadway

Flushing Ave.

East River

278

Naval Cemetery

3.6

3.2

Washington Ave.

Classon Ave.

Bedford Ave.

Nostrand Ave.

Myrtle Ave.

Bushwick Ave.

Flatbush Ave.

3rd Ave.

Vanderbilt Ave.

Prospect Park Bikeway

9th St.

Prospect Park W.

Fulton St.

Atlantic Ave.

Grand Army Plaza

Eastern Pkwy.

Jamaica Ave.

Pennsylvania Ave.

27

Empire Blvd.

Prospect Park

5th Ave.

39th St.

West Dr.
West Lake Dr.

7.9

27

South Lake Dr.

Parkside Ave.

23.9

Linden Blvd.

Church Ave.

Nostrand Ave.

Bedford Ave.

Utica Ave.

Ralph Ave.

Remsen Ave.

Rockaway Pkwy.

27

Church Ave.

Kings Hwy.

Flatlands Ave.

Shore Rd.

3rd Ave.

4th Ave.

5th Ave.

Fort Hamilton Pkwy.

Ocean Parkway Bike Path

65th St.

7th Ave.

80th St.

Cropsey Ave.

Bay Pkwy.

Stillwell Ave.

McDonald Ave.

Washington Cemetery

Coney Island Ave.

Ocean Parkway

Ocean Ave.

Ave. P

Kings Hwy.

Ave. U

Flatbush Ave.

278

Lower Bay

W. 37th St.

Neptune Ave.

Surf Ave.

Emmons Ave.

Coney Island

Brighton Beach

17.3

New York Aquarium

Boardwalk

14.6

12.8

7.9 Right onto Church Avenue then left onto Ocean Parkway Bike Path.

12.7 Cross Surf Avenue.

12.8 Right, then right onto Boardwalk.

14.6 Turn around at western end of Boardwalk.

17.3 Turn around at eastern end of Boardwalk.

17.9 Right off boardwalk to Surf Avenue.

18.0 Cross Surf Avenue, turn right onto Ocean Parkway Bike Path.

22.7 Right onto Church Avenue.

22.8 Left onto Ocean Parkway bike lane.

23.2 Right and through traffic circle to Prospect Park.

23.3 Right onto South Lake Drive.

25.2 Right onto Grand Army Plaza.

25.3 Continue on Vanderbilt Avenue.

27.0 Right onto Flushing Avenue.

27.4 Left onto Williamsburg Street West.

27.6 Continue on Kent Avenue.

29.5 Continue on Franklin Street.

30.3 Right onto Commercial Street.

30.5 Continue on Manhattan Avenue.

30.6 Arrive at finish.

RIDE INFORMATION

Local Events/Attractions

Coney Island: Although the boardwalk only allows bicycling between 5 and 10 a.m., it's still a lovely place to walk a bike, and cyclists with a lock will have many entertainment options. Live theater, minor league baseball, roller derby, and amusement parks line the boardwalk. A website with a full list of rides, attractions, food, and events is maintained by the Alliance for Coney Island, a nonprofit dedicated to improving and revitalizing the park, at coneyislandfunguide.com.

Restaurants

Eagle Trading Company: 258 Franklin St., Brooklyn; (718) 576-3217

Bakeri: 105 Freeman St., Brooklyn; (718) 349-1542; bakeribrooklyn.com

Brooklyn Roasting Company: 200 Flushing Ave., Brooklyn; (718) 858-5500; brooklynroasting.com

Doña Zita Mexican Restaurant: 1221 Bowery St., Brooklyn; (347) 492-6160; donazita.com

Nathan's Famous: 1310 Surf Ave., Brooklyn; (718)946-2202; nathansfamous .com

Totonno Pizzeria Napolitano: 1524 Neptune Ave., Brooklyn; (718) 372-8606; totonnosconeyisland.com

Restrooms

0.0: Newtown Creek Nature Walk

5.3: Prospect Park

12.9: Coney Island Boardwalk

Shore Park Greenway

The Shore Park Greenway Trail was built and designed by city planner Robert Moses, the New Haven native who planned much of New York City and Long Island from the 1920s to the 1960s. At the time, Brooklyn was crisscrossed by more than 30 miles of biking paths, many of which would deteriorate and fade away. The last decade has seen a huge investment in biking in New York City, including a massive rehabilitation of this greenway in 2007. The trail today is a beautiful, nearly 5-mile long cycling route along the bay, with a gorgeous view of the Verrazano-Narrows Bridge.

Start: The trailhead near Owl's Head Park

Length: 8.4 miles

Riding time: 30–45 minutes

Best bike: Hybrid bike

Terrain and trail surface: Off-road paved trail

Traffic and hazards: This is a heavily used off-road trail. Watch for pedestrians, dogs, and other users.

Things to see: Views of the Verrazano-Narrows Bridge, water views of the Narrows, small parks along the path. Peregrine falcons are often visible flying along the Verrazano-Narrows Bridge. From the trail, the Statue of Liberty, the new World Trade Center, Fort Wadsworth, and Fort Hamilton can all be spotted.

Fees: None. Street parking is available near the ride start. If spots are occupied, park at the other end, in the large lot near the intersection of Bay and Shore parkways.

Getting there: Take exit 1 from the Belt Parkway toward 65–67th streets. Merge onto Shore Road Drive, then exit toward 2nd Ave. / Ridge Boulevard, and turn right. Turn right onto 67th St. then left onto Colonial Road, then right onto 68th St. The park is just ahead. Transit users can take the R train to the Bay Ridge Avenue Station on 4th Ave. Subway riders can take the R train to the Bay Ridge Avenue Station. Exit the station and turn left onto 4th Ave. then left onto 68th St. Cross 3rd Ave. to continue on 68th St. which has a bike lane, from here to the park, about four blocks.

GPS: N40 38.331' / W74 02.165'

THE RIDE

Starting at the end of 68th Street, take the bike path to Bay Ridge Avenue and turn right, under the Parkway overpass. Ahead is the 69th St. Pier, with a larger-than-life sized memorial for the dead of 9/11. Turn left onto the trail and follow this flat, easy bikeway for a scenic ride along the water. Pedestrians have a separate path, to the right, but often will use the bicycle path as well. Stay alert, and watch for crossover.

The path has benches at regular intervals, but very few other amenities. At the 0.6-mile mark, a pedestrian bridge above provides access to Shore Park, which has comfort stations and water fountains.

Around the 2.0-mile mark, a small parking lot from the Belt Parkway accesses the park. Just ahead is another pedestrian bridge, this one to the John Paul Jones Park, named for the Revolutionary War hero known as the father of the Navy. This park has a comfort station, spray shower, and water fountains.

View from the Parkway

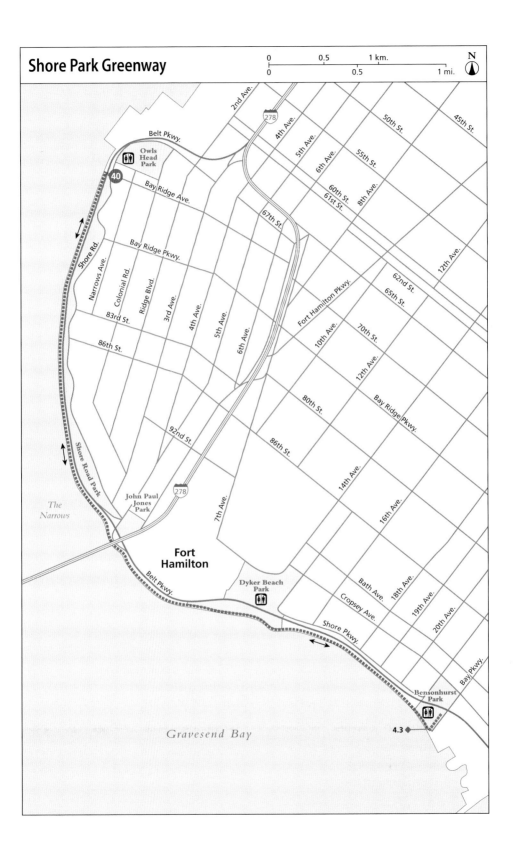

Shore Park Greenway

0   0.5   1 km.
0   0.5   1 mi.

N

Belt Pkwy.

2nd Ave.

278

4th Ave.

5th Ave.

50th St.

45th St.

6th Ave.

55th St.

8th Ave.

Owls
Head
Park

Bay Ridge Ave.

60th St.
61st St.

40

67th St.

Shore Rd.

Narrows Ave.

Bay Ridge Pkwy.

62nd St.

12th Ave.

Colonial Rd.

Ridge Blvd

3rd Ave.

4th Ave.

5th Ave.

Fort Hamilton Pkwy.

65th St.

83rd St.

10th Ave.

70th St.

6th Ave.

12th Ave.

86th St.

80th St.

Bay Ridge Pkwy.

86th St.

14th Ave.

Shore Road Park

92nd St.

16th Ave.

278

The
Narrows

John Paul
Jones
Park

7th Ave.

**Fort
Hamilton**

Belt Pkwy.

Dyker Beach
Park

Bath Ave.

18th Ave.

Cropsey Ave.

19th Ave.

Shore Pkwy.

20th Ave.

Bay Pkwy.

Bensonhurst
Park

4.3

Gravesend Bay

The Verrazano-Narrows Bridge towers overhead at nearly 700 feet. This double-deck suspension bridge is the longest spanning bridge in the Americas, at 4,260-feet long, and was the last major project by Robert Moses.

Continuing on, the bikeway passes another parking area, and then a pedestrian bridge providing access to the Bath Beach Park, at the 3.1-mile mark. This park is in the neighborhood of Bath Beach, historically significant as an early African-American settlement for people who'd been newly released from enslavement. The park has bathrooms and water.

The route ends in another mile or so at a series of big box stores and a major parking lot, adjacent to Bensonhurst Park. This area isn't particularly bike-friendly, and food options here are primarily fast-food, but a few places exist up Bay Parkway for a stop. When ready, turn around, and retrace your route back to the trailhead to finish this ride.

Bike Shops

Bay Ridge Bicycle World: 8916 3rd Ave., Brooklyn; (718) 238-1118; bayridgebikes.com
Verrazano Bicycle Shop Inc: 7308 5th Ave., Brooklyn; (718) 680-6521; verrazanocycles.com

MILES AND DIRECTIONS

0.0   Start at trailhead off Bay Ridge Avenue, near Owl's Head Park.

4.3   Turn around after Bensonhurst Park, at shopping plaza parking lot.

8.6   Arrive at finish.

RIDE INFORMATION

Local Events/Attractions
Narrows Botanical Garden: Diverse plants flourish in this 4.5-acre park along the Shore Parkway. Exhibits include a native plant sanctuary, lily pond, zen garden, and both an old and modern rose garden. narrowsbg.org.

Restaurants
Arepas Crepes Colombian Cuisine: 241 Bay Ridge Ave., Brooklyn; (718) 836-0006
Gourmet Fit: 6819 3rd Ave., Brooklyn; (347) 662-6821; gourmetfit.net
Casa Pepe: 114 Bay Ridge Ave., Brooklyn; (718) 833-8865
Piccolo's Pizzeria: 8774 Bay Pkwy., Brooklyn; (347) 587-5777; piccolospizzeriabrooklyn.com

Restrooms
0.0: Owl's Head Park
4.1: Bensonhurst Park

Bibliography

This is a very incomplete list of additional resources and places to find out more about the places these rides visit.

Books

Mowrer, Lilian. *The Indomitable John Scott: Citizen of Long Island, 1632–1704*. Long Island, NY: Farrar, Straus and Cudahy, 1960.

Dickerson, Charles P. *A History of the Sayville Community, Including Bayport, Bohemia, West Sayville, Oakdale, and Fire Island*. Bayport, NY: Ariel Graphics, Postal Instant Press,1975.

Hammond, John E. *Images of America: Oyster Bay*. Charleston, SC: Arcadia, 2009.

Websites

BradleyHarris, Smithtown Historian http://smithtownhistorical.org/heres-to-the-bull-and-richard-smythe

Long Island Wine Country: Industry site for region.
http://www.liwines.com

Discover Long Island: Tourism information and more.
http://www.discoverlongisland.com

Biking Resources

Bike New York, http://www.bike.nyc

CLIMB, Concerned Long Island Mountain Bicyclists, http://climbonline.org

Five Borough Bicycle Club, http://www.5bbc.org

Huntington Bike Club, http://huntingtonbikeclub.com

League of American Bicyclists, http://www.bikeleague.org

Long Island Bicycle Club, http://www.bicyclelongisland.org/libc

Massapequa Park Bicycle Club, http://massparkbikeclub.org

Nassau-Suffolk Bicycle Coalition, http://bicyclelongisland.org

New York Bicycling Coalition, http://nybc.net

Suffolk Bicycle Riders Association, http://www.sbraweb.org

Triangle Cyclists, http://www.trianglecyclists.com

Ride Index

About the Author

David Streever is a writer and cyclist, originally from the shores of the Connecticut River. He started out recreationally riding in his hilly hometown of East Haddam, and became a dedicated road cyclist and advocate with the help of his New Haven community. David is a professional writer who covered the 2015 UCI bike race in Richmond. In addition to cycling, he writes essays on a range of topics. This is his second guidebook for Falcon.

He and his wife live in Richmond, Virginia, in a rambling home in the historic Fan district.